D0535511

Gioacchino Rossini

By the same author

Music

THE WORLD OF MUSICAL INSTRUMENTS

BENJAMIN BRITTEN

THE TENDER TYRANT – NADIA BOULANGER

VIVALDI

THE LIFE OF BEETHOVEN

BEETHOVEN AND HIS WORLD

MOZART AND HIS WORLD

MUSIC: ITS STORY IN THE WEST

PAGANINI

GEORGE GERSHWIN

TCHAIKOVSKY

History

MEDIEVAL PILGRIMS

VOYAGES OF DISCOVERY

ELIZABETH I

THEIR FINEST HOUR

ROBERT DUDLEY, EARL OF LEICESTER

DAVID GARRICK

Gioacchino Rossini
The Reluctant Hero

ALAN KENDALL

LONDON
VICTOR GOLLANCZ LTD
1992

First published in Great Britain 1992
by Victor Gollancz Ltd
14 Henrietta Street, London WC2E 8QJ

A CIP catalogue record is available from the
British Library.

ISBN 0-575-05178-7

Photoset by Rowland Phototypesetting Ltd
Bury St Edmunds, Suffolk
Printed in Great Britain by Butler & Tanner Ltd
Frome, Somerset

For Michael Stapleton,
in whose company I have spent
many happy hours in the opera house.

Contents

List of Illustrations

ILLUSTRATIONS WITHIN THE TEXT

Introduction

Over the centuries, very few composers have enjoyed unassailable reputations. Tastes change, styles change, new generations of performers, conductors and musicologists appear, so that it is almost inevitable that successive generations should adjust their response to, and appreciation of, composers and their music. It is basically a healthy process, and in this respect Rossini has been no exception. But he has suffered more harshly than most from changing tastes and attitudes. Until relatively recently he was known to the majority of opera-lovers as the composer of one superb comic opera and certain overtures to other operas that were, for the most part, rarely performed.

What is perhaps more puzzling in Rossini's case is not only that his reputation should have shifted so dramatically, but also that within his own lifetime opinions about him were so sharply divided. It was Beethoven who advised him to go on writing 'more Barbers', and posterity has largely fallen into line. This view tends to go hand-in-hand with the perception of Rossini as a jolly gourmet after whom a method of preparing steak was named *tournedos Rossini*. And yet one cannot overlook the fact that many of his contemporaries thought of him as a serious composer, in fact one of the greatest composers of the day. Nor was this simply blind adoration; in some cases it was a reluctant acceptance of a reality that ran directly counter to their personal tastes and opinions. They saw that his music had the ability to appeal to all sorts and conditions, from the most refined to the most popular. In time his music could be seen to support liberal, even revolutionary sentiments, as it could also be identified with the Romantic movement, especially in its literary manifestation. At the same time, however, there was a vociferous body of opinion that condemned Rossini for being an opportunist, for taking whatever advantage he might achieve in the interests of popularity and financial gain. There is some justification for this latter point of view, especially when one looks at the self-borrowings, and the *pasticcios* of his operas which, if not actually encouraged by the composer, were tacitly permitted.

Rossini began his career at a time when Italian opera was all but dead. Previously, throughout the eighteenth century, Italy had been providing musical directors and opera-composers for the courts and theatres of Europe from St Petersburg to Lisbon, and from Vienna to London, but it had done so from what was still a living regenerative tradition. By the end of the century, however, those opera-composers who had vision and ambition, and might have regenerated Italian opera on its own soil, had migrated to Paris. Writers of music history, then, may accord to Rossini the role of having kept Italian serious opera alive on its own territory, which in itself was no mean achievement. Such a conservative view would doubtless have surprised some of his admirers, let alone those contemporaries for whom he was too advanced.

Equally, however, music history may also say that Rossini failed to go far enough, that his role was not simply to keep native Italian opera alive, but to take it forward into a new stage of its development. After all, he had the necessary technical skill. Indeed, when compared with his contemporaries on that count, he outshone both Bellini and Donizetti, and his old friend Meyerbeer. In some people's opinion he ought to have followed Beethoven's advice and stuck to comic opera, but such an opinion has often been formed through sheer inability to see or hear Rossini's serious operas. His first important *opera seria*, *Tancredi*, was written for Venice in 1813, but two years later Rossini moved to Naples, where he began to show a dramatic vision which, allied to his musical talent, produced some excellent opera, if not entire operatic masterpieces. And yet he failed to take the initiative, to seize the potential, either because of some deep flaw in his artistic personality or because he did indeed see the way ahead and simply declined to follow it. He decided to leave that to the others.

Initially, however, it seemed that Rossini was pursuing the same course as many of his predecessors. Having conquered Italy, he, too, became an internationally famous composer. Preceded by his operas, he took Europe by storm. He, too, settled in Paris. There, however, the parallels stop, for with *Guillaume Tell* in 1829 he suddenly abandoned the operatic stage and from then until his death in 1868 composed only two major works, the *Stabat Mater* and the *Petite Messe solennelle*.

Here is the first enigma of the Rossini phenomenon. Why was it that a man who had composed almost forty operas in twenty years and led opera towards a new phase of its evolution virtually single-handed, should turn his back on such an enormous achievement, apparently overnight? The second enigma arises directly from the first. How did Rossini's reputation remain so bright despite those long years of creative darkness, with virtually nothing to sustain it apart from intermittent performances of a relatively few works?

It was a reputation which infuriated several of the musical *cognoscenti*, who dismissed him as the exponent – if not, indeed, the progenitor – of everything that was wrong with opera in particular, and with a good many aspects of music besides. It is, of course, a viewpoint which is still encountered today, and one must admit that there is an element in Rossini's music which to some seems too light, carefree and even inconsequential. This was also an element inherent in his personality, which, again, infuriated some of his contemporaries – especially those who had reason to be jealous of his reputation. He loved a joke, and he had an acerbic tongue at times. His detractors saw this as evidence of self-satisfaction, vanity or conceit, and stories were often attributed to him totally without justification; it was rare for him to take the trouble to deny them if they came back to him.

To Wagner, for example, in the conversation that took place in 1860, reported by Edmond Michotte, Rossini more or less dismissed his entire operatic output with the words 'J'avais de la facilité, et beaucoup d'instinct' ('I had facility, and a lot of instinct').[1] How many other composers, one wonders, among the Romantics and post-Romantics, would have even dreamed of uttering such a statement? Wagner must scarcely have believed his ears even though Rossini's words may well have confirmed what he himself believed.

Or, again, Rossini constantly referred to himself as a pianist 'of the fourth class', when he was patently a highly accomplished keyboard-player and a wonderful accompanist, as one might expect of one so sensitive to singers and voices. Of course he did not help matters by referring on one occasion to Verdi as a pianist of the fifth class, but there was a reason for this.[2] Verdi was refused admission to the Milan Conservatoire because his pianistic ability was regarded as inadequate. One sees more clearly, however, why it was that two such giants of nineteenth-century opera, Wagner and Verdi, should have been infuriated by Rossini the man and Rossini the monument. He stood as a huge question mark poised over the entire concept of the great Romantic composer as creative artist. There was nothing mystical or sacred in the role of the composer for Rossini, and his whole attitude towards his career might well be summed up in the statement already quoted: 'I had facility, and a lot of instinct.' Indeed, it required a certain amount of courage to declare something which ran totally counter to current musical aesthetics.

It was, however, as a result of such statements that Rossini's stock began to sink, so that even as his monument was being dedicated in the Church of Santa Croce in Florence in 1902 his reputation was in great part destroyed, especially outside Italy. Interestingly, it was another of his expatriate fellow-countrymen, though of a much later generation, Ferruccio Busoni, who in 1920 – most unusually for his time – put Rossini along with Cherubini and Mendelssohn as the most significant successors to Mozart. It was also Busoni, incidentally, who in 1914 gave what may well have been the earliest Liszt recitals in Paris since the composer's death. The more usual attitude to Rossini, certainly outside Italy, is epitomised by a biography of 1934 which opens with the words: 'To the best of my belief there is no demand whatever for a life of Rossini in English.'[3] The long-overdue reappraisal of Rossini is now happily well under way, though it still has a long way to go. Let us hope that it continues to progress.

CHAPTER ONE

The Genius Takes Wing

Gioacchino Antonio Rossini was born on 29 February 1792 in Pesaro on the Adriatic coast of Italy. In those days Pesaro was, as Stendhal described it in the opening chapter of his *Vie de Rossini*, 'a delightful little town in the Papal States on the shores of the Gulf of Venice . . . a port with a busy life of its own. It rises up from wooded hills, and the woods reach down to the very edge of the sea.'[1] Unfortunately the subsequent exploitation of the sandy stretches of the Adriatic coast of Italy has made its impact on Pesaro, as it has on similar towns and cities, such as Rimini, and given rise to a succession of resorts stretching northwards to Milano Marittima, but if one turns one's back on the sea it is possible to ignore the more insistent encroachments of the twentieth century. In Pesaro, certainly, it is possible to recapture the intimate scale of the place in earlier days, as one walks along the narrow streets of the old town and stands outside the birthplace. Gioacchino (this is the common spelling of the name, though he used Gioachino) was destined to be the only child of his parents, Giuseppe Rossini and Anna Guidarini, and the fact that he was born within six months of their marriage suggests that there was at the very least an element of constraint involved. Nevertheless, there is no evidence that they were unhappy in matrimony, and there was no lack of affection for their son when he was born. For his part, the composer remained devoted to his parents all their lives.

It is possible that Giuseppe Rossini was a descendant of a once noble family, but by the time he was born in 1758 in Lugo, a small town near Ravenna, that branch of the family was neither wealthy nor particularly artistically inclined. In 1864, a year which saw many Rossini celebrations, Lugo sent Gioacchino a patent of local nobility, and he maintained a house there for many years. His father undoubtedly had some musical ability, however, for he played the trumpet and horn, and during the Carnival (winter) opera season of 1788–9 played in the orchestra at the Teatro del Sole in Pesaro. As he became acquainted with the musical life of that town, Giuseppe Rossini decided that he would like to become part of it, and on 14 March 1789 wrote to the town council to ask that, if and when a post of town trumpeter (there were two) fell vacant, he might be considered for it. In that letter, incidentally, he described himself as the town trumpeter of Lugo, and referred to his engagement in Pesaro during the preceding opera season. His request was granted in a vote which went twenty-one to four in his favour, and his *sopravvivenza*, or right of succession, was to run for one year. His letter of thanks is dated 25 March 1789.

In the mean time, however, he had to live, and the conditions in Lugo apparently did not provide the same opportunities as Pesaro. He consequently kept up his contacts there, and in particular with one of the town trumpeters, Luigi Ricci. In short, he agreed to pay Ricci an annuity of twenty scudi (Ricci had asked for twenty-four) if the latter would vacate his post in Giuseppe Rossini's favour. This still did not provide an answer to his immediate financial problems, however, so he joined the garrison band in Ferrara on a temporary basis. In January 1790, Ricci wrote from Pesaro to tell Giuseppe to be there early in Lent to complete their arrangement. However, the garrison commander in Ferrara refused to release Giuseppe, who was insubordinate in return and was consequently thrown into prison. He managed to make a sufficient apology to gain his freedom, however, and make his way to Pesaro. Ricci was still waiting to cede his post, but was nevertheless holding out for the extra four scudi for his annuity. This prompted Giuseppe Rossini to approach the town council – for, apart from anything else, his year's *sopravvivenza* was running out. More seriously, what Ricci had been proposing was illegal, for the post, being a public appointment, was not his to dispose of. When the facts were put before the council he was dismissed, and Giuseppe Rossini was appointed in his place – at least, for one year in the first instance. With fitting realism, no doubt, the council stipulated that Giuseppe was not to pay anything to Ricci, since the whole of the salary was necessary to maintain the Pesaro town trumpeter in appropriate style. In practice, however, it was barely adequate, and it was fully expected that he would earn additional fees for playing in churches and at festivities where music was incorporated as part of the proceedings, such as banquets, engagement celebrations and weddings.

The entire episode is interesting for its indications as to the character of Giuseppe Rossini, and the qualities that he might have handed on to his son. The one which most seems to have impressed his contemporaries and the inhabitants of his adopted town was his liveliness, for he was given the nickname of 'Vivazza' in Pesaro. There is also, it must be said, something of his son's own opera plots in the serio-comic events that finally resulted in his gaining his municipal appointment. It says a good deal, too, about the status of musicians towards the end of the eighteenth century, and the ways in which it was possible to earn a living, and one may contrast his financial position with the comfortable situation in which his son found himself towards the end of his life.

Now that he was to live permanently in the town, Giuseppe took lodgings in Via del Fallo, in a house where the Guidarini family also lived. Domenico Guidarini was a baker, and his wife Lucia Romagnoli came originally from Urbino. They had a son and three daughters, the second of whom (Annunziata) seems later to have been denounced to the police as being a prostitute. Whether this apparent lightness of morals was a family characteristic or not is difficult to say, though Annunziata's eldest sister, Anna (born in 1771), seems to have shared something of her reputation for flirtatiousness. On the one hand, the *denuncia* was, and is, a fairly common Italian method of dealing with neighbours whom one wants to harm or teach a lesson. On the other hand, it may simply have been an over-zealous police force, for every now and then it was thought necessary to increase vigilance where morals were concerned in the Papal States.

At the time that Giuseppe Rossini took up residence under the same roof, Anna Guidarini was a seamstress, though she had a pleasing soprano voice which she was later able to put to good use. Although she did not have any musical training, she had – according to her son – a good ear and a very good memory. At all events she was attracted to the vivacious musician who lived in the house, and during the summer of 1791 it became clear that she was pregnant. On 26 September that year they married in Pesaro cathedral, Anna then being nineteen and her husband thirty-two.

Their first home consisted of two (later four) rooms in a house in Via del Duomo, subsequently renamed Via Rossini, and it was in one of them that the composer was born. He was baptised in the cathedral the same day. His godparents were Conte Paolo Macchirelli and Catterina Semproni-Giovanelli, who, like Anna's mother, came from Urbino. This demonstration of association with members of the aristocracy was the cause for a certain amount of speculation, fuelled no doubt by the reputation of Anna's sister and her own flirtatious nature, but there was no hard and fast division between classes in Pesaro at this time; and the Urbino connection, Anna's own disposition and good looks, and her husband's personality and position in the community all helped in their endeavours to find as distinguished a set of godparents as they could for their son. At the same time, it must be said that the connection did not last into Rossini's maturity. From now on, Giuseppe's role in the affairs of Pesaro was to become even more prominent as the town became involved in the events which were shaking Italy, and indeed the whole of Europe, in the wake of the French Revolution.

The house in Pesaro in which the composer was born.

Pesaro was part of the Papal States, which at this time ran across central Italy from Rome and a region to the south, and then northwards up the eastern side of the peninsula as far as the River Po. The territory was held and ruled by the popes as secular sovereigns, and it was not surprising that Pesaro, in common with many towns and cities that endured an unenlightened and at times heavily repressive papal domination, began to yearn for the freedom which had been announced by the French Revolution. French troops arrived in the north of Italy in 1792. Late in the year 1793, the citizens of Pesaro complained to Pope Pius VI (1717–99, Pope from 1775) that one of the local magistrates was a liar who 'drank the blood of the poor'. Relief was eventually at hand in the shape of Napoleon, who assumed command in Italy in 1796 and set up the Cispadane Republic in the north, to be incorporated the following year into the Cisalpine Republic as he increased his hold over Italy. French troops entered Pesaro on 5 February 1797. A statue of Urban VIII (Pope 1623–44) which stood in the Piazza San Ubaldo was removed, and it was said that Giuseppe Rossini put a sign on his door which read: 'Home of Citizen Vivazza, a true republican'. He also led an orchestra for one of the 'Tree of Liberty' ceremonies so favoured in the first flush of republicanism wherever people deemed themselves to have been liberated, which is probably why, when the papal forces regained control of Pesaro, Giuseppe was voted out of office on 13 December 1797 – only by nineteen votes to fifteen – by the town council. His period of disgrace was short-lived, however, for later that same month the papal troops were driven out, the papal governor arrested, and the people elected to join the Cisalpine Republic. Giuseppe was voted back into office.

In those heady days in the spring of 1798, the tide of enthusiasm engulfed even the six-year-old son of Giuseppe Rossini. Two entries in the records of the Cisalpine authorities dated 6 and 14 April respectively record payments to the 'civil guard Giovacchino Rossini – 30 [bajocchi]', and the same sum to him as '*Listaro* of the band'. There is some doubt as to what the function of the *listaro* was. From the meaning of cognate words in Italian, he may have kept the register or list of performers, or he may have played a triangle, made from a strip (*lista*) of bent metal.

More to the point, in view of their son's future development, the following month Giuseppe and Anna Rossini began a somewhat intermittent career as travelling musicians when they went south to

Jesi to take part in a performance of Vicente Martin y Soler's opera *La capricciosa corretta*, which had had its first hearing in St Petersburg in 1789. Giuseppe played in the band whilst his wife sang on stage – no mean feat in what had been papal territory, where women were forbidden to appear in public theatres (in theory, at least) on stage. Rather like the control of public morality in general, however, the authorities waxed and waned in their application of the law. In the earlier part of the century, Vivaldi had been allowed to mount his operas in Ferrara with his protégée Anna Girò starring one season, and then suddenly found that a ban was placed by the papal legate the following season – or, rather, that the existing ban was now suddenly to be enforced. This prejudice against women, however, greatly contributed to the rise of the *castrati*, men who had undergone castration in order to preserve a treble voice. In their heyday the *castrati* enjoyed the sort of adulation enjoyed by some opera stars today.

The Rossinis were back in Pesaro in mid-June, however, for the *gazzetta di Pesaro* reported that when the ratification of the treaty between the Cisalpine and French republics was celebrated on 17 June 1798 local people were awakened that day by the trumpet call of 'the excellent patriot Rossini, known by the nickname of Citizen Vivazza'.

We have two indications from the composer himself – though dating from a much later period – about his mother's inability as a singer. The first was when he told Ferdinand Hiller in 1855 that his mother had a beautiful voice 'which she used out of necessity'.[2] He went on to say that she was by no means unintelligent, but that she was unable to read a note of music and sang entirely by ear. Then to Edmond Michotte he said that she sang all the time, even if she was simply doing housework.[3] Her extraordinary memory enabled her to learn roles easily, and he maintained that her beautiful voice was expressive by nature, graceful and charming – as, indeed, was her appearance. In the autumn of 1798 the Rossinis were in Bologna for operatic engagements (though it may only have been Giuseppe who was actually performing), and during the Carnival season of 1798–9 they were in Ferrara. It was then back to Bologna for the Lent season of 1799, but Anna was unable to sing until after Easter because of throat trouble. Once she was well again, however, she stayed with the company there until the middle of September.

Sometimes the absences from Pesaro were relatively short; but, whatever the intervals, the young Rossini had to be looked after. This task seems to have fallen to his maternal grandmother, Lucia Guidarini, as well as to one of his mother's sisters. He attended school at least some of the time, though on occasion he was punished by being sent, so the story went, to blow the bellows in a blacksmith's forge, and that when that had no effect he was said to have been sent to Bologna to live in the house of a pork butcher for a time. Later in life Rossini jokingly speculated that he might have become a butcher rather than a composer, had things been different. It seems certain that he was a spirited youngster, for when he was seventy-three one of his childhood friends from Pesaro, Francesco Genari, wrote to thank him for an autographed photograph and in so doing referred to the scar he still bore on his neck where Rossini had thrown a stone at him. In those days, apparently, Rossini was quite a handful, and was adept at raiding church sacristies for the contents of the cruets used at Mass.

In Pesaro, Rossini had lessons in reading and writing, basic grammar and calligraphy, and in Bologna reading and writing, arithmetic and Latin. It is true to say that spelling was never Rossini's forte, and it was at best erratic throughout his life. Nor can his handwriting be described as calligraphy by any stretch of the imagination. However, in view of the composer's subsequent musical development, it was significant that he encountered his first keyboard teacher in Bologna: Giuseppe Prinetti, a native of Novara. In the account that Rossini gave to Ferdinand Hiller already referred to, there is some colourful detail about Prinetti which ought, perhaps, to be regarded with a certain amount of reservation. He seems to have been a *buffo* character straight out of one of Rossini's operas. According to the composer, Prinetti scraped a living by distilling brandy and giving keyboard lessons. He did not own a bed, but slept upright, wrapped in his cloak, under the arcades of Bologna. He became a familiar figure to the nightwatchmen of the city, who left him in peace. Rossini maintained that his instruction was to play scales with the thumb and index finger.

It was in Bologna that Giuseppe Rossini was arrested in 1800, for the papal troops and their Austrian and Russian allies had regained the initiative during 1799. He was taken, via Imola, Forlì, Cesena, Rimini and Cattolica, back to Pesaro, where he was imprisoned for a time. When the French were victorious at the battle of Marengo on 14 June 1800, Pesaro came once more within the Cisalpine Republic and Giuseppe Rossini was freed. For the Carnival opera season that year he and the local commander were given the use of the Teatro del Sole for the performance of two *opere buffe*. During the period of his arrest and detention, Anna Rossini continued singing, and appeared at Jesi once more. She evidently became well liked as a singer there, for when she sang at the Teatro Concordia during the following Carnival season a collection of verses in her honour was published.

It was at Trieste in 1802, however, that she probably reached the peak of her popularity. She had been engaged as *seconda donna* for the spring season at the Teatro Grande, or Comunale, for performances of Sebastiano Nasolini's *La morte di Semiramide* and a new opera by Giuseppe Farinelli. The leading lady was Giuseppina Grassini, already of international repute, but Nasolini was dissatisfied with the soprano engaged for the lesser part of Azema, and persuaded the impresario to engage Anna Rossini – La Guidarini – instead. Her husband and ten-year-old son accompanied her to Trieste. A certain amount of competition – fuelled, if not indeed entirely stimulated, by *aficionados* of the opera – grew up between the two stars, and Anna Guidarini, possibly copying Grassini, responded to a burst of whistling by fainting on stage. Rossini, standing by his father in the wings, is said to have rushed on stage to comfort his mother. Whatever else the Trieste incident may have demonstrated, it made the composer's parents consider his future.

Rossini, with typically laconic humour, told Alexis-Jacob Azevedo that, had it not been for the French invasion of Italy, he would have been either an apothecary or an oil merchant.[4] Be that as it may, he had a fine soprano voice, and was able to earn fees for singing in churches. His barber uncle even suggested that he might preserve his voice by joining the ranks of the *castrati*, then still enjoying something of a sunset splendour, but Anna Guidarini would have none of it.

In the event, matters to some extent resolved themselves when Giuseppe Rossini took his wife and son back to his home town of Lugo in 1802. Here the boy came under the influence of a priest, Giovanni Sassoli, who later acted as his agent in the town, supervising the care of the house that he eventually inherited and which he refused to sell, although he never lived in it again. Of rather more importance to his education were two brothers, both priests: Giuseppe and Luigi Malerbi. In their *palazzo* Rossini sang and played the cembalo, and delved into their collection of music, which included a good deal of Haydn and Mozart, and at the same time was exposed to the witty, even acerbic, conversation of Luigi Malerbi. No doubt Rossini's love of good food, too, was inculcated at this early stage, since the Malerbi family was rich and the brothers lived in some style. All this was in marked contrast to the somewhat picaresque life he had experienced when he accompanied his parents to his mother's operatic engagements, but both streams of influence were invaluable in the formation of the composer's development and the eventual discovery of his own talent and direction in the future. In a very practical way, Giuseppe Malerbi encouraged Rossini to write his own music. Giuseppe Rossini also taught him to play the horn, an instrument for which he was to write some notable passages in his mature works.

Two examples from 1804 show how Rossini's experience was gained. He appeared with his mother in a costumed concert at Imola on 22 April, and that summer composed six *sonate a quattro* for two violins, cello and double bass for Agostino Triossi, a landowner and merchant who had a country house at Conventello, near Ravenna, where the sonatas were played through by Triossi himself on the double bass, his cousins the Morini brothers on first violin and cello, and Rossini himself on second violin. Many years later he wrote a note on the autograph manuscript of these sonatas, in which he described them as appalling, claiming that he had not at that time had any lessons in thorough bass, which was perhaps not true.[5]

The string sonatas enjoyed considerable popularity after five of them were published in an arrangement for string quartet in Milan in 1825–6. The missing one (the third in the series) was the first publication of the *Quaderni Rossiniani* in 1954. The editor, Alfredo Bonaccorsi, expressed the opinion that the arrangements for string quartet were probably not the work of Rossini himself, since he had written so specifically for the double bass in the original versions, and would have been reluctant to change the sound for that of a cello. Moreover, Bonaccorsi pointed out that it was significant that the third sonata had been omitted, since it includes a set of variations for double bass which would lose their point when played on any other instrument.

In time the freshness and grace of these early works has appealed to many generations of listeners. They combine an easy lyricism with an epigrammatic humour; they have pace and a directness of expression. One feels that the composer is in control of the medium, takes delight in the tonal contrasts available to him in the choice of instruments, and exploits them to the full.

The fruitful and agreeable interval in Lugo turned out to be all too brief. During the course of 1804 it became clear that Anna Rossini's voice, which had never been properly trained, was beginning to show signs of strain, in addition to which she now contracted a throat infection. One must bear in mind that then, as now, it was usual for professional singers to have several years of training, not only for the purely basic vocal production, but also so as to learn the extensive range and variety of embellishment that singers were automatically expected to introduce into the music, knowing what was appropriate in any given situation. The *castrati* in particular excelled in this area, but it was a major factor which contributed to their eventual downfall. Rossini himself came to deplore the liberties taken by singers with his music, and so wrote down the embellishments he desired and insisted that they be observed.

As Anna Rossini's contribution to the family income decreased, it fell to her son to make good the loss whenever possible, and for both father and son it was clear that there would be more opportunity for them to work in a larger city which supported several churches and theatres, and for this reason they decided to base themselves in Bologna. Their calculations cannot have been solely commercial, however, for what was also true was that Bologna, with its long and distinguished musical tradition, offered the young composer the chance of a much higher standard of instruction than anything Lugo, or for that matter Pesaro, had to offer.

Bologna drew musicians to it – as, indeed, it had drawn the Rossinis – and in 1805 Rossini met a family of musicians, the Mombellis, who were to give a modest, if significant, stimulus to the launching of his career as an operatic composer. We hear of him singing on stage in the autumn of that year 1805, in the role of Adolfo, son of Camilla, in Ferdinando Paër's opera of that name (1799) at the Teatro del Corso in Bologna. This was a very popular work, and in order to facilitate as many performances as possible two *prime donne* – Anna Cittadini and Chiara Leon – were engaged to alternate in the part. It was noted by certain observers that Adolfo ran to his mother's arms with markedly more enthusiasm on the nights that the former star was playing, since Cittadini was physically much better endowed than Leon.

Rossini is said to have taken singing lessons at this time with the tenor Matteo Babini (1754–1816), a native of Bologna who, after a career that had taken him to Berlin, St Petersburg, Vienna, Lisbon, Madrid, London and Paris, where he had sung duets with Queen Marie-Antoinette, had more or less retired to Bologna at this time. Azevedo recounted that when Rossini first arrived in Paris in 1823 he amazed Cherubini by singing an aria from his London opera of 1786, *Giulio Sabino*, that Babini had taught him. It was on the strength of his singing that Rossini was elected to the prestigious Accademia Filarmonica of Bologna on 24 June 1806 by acclamation, and so was excused any contribution. His age, too, was a contributory factor. In theory members should not be under twenty years of age; and so, until then, Rossini would have no voting rights in the academy. Mozart, it will be recalled, was admitted at the same age – fourteen – in October 1770. Rossini once said of him that he was 'the admiration of my youth, the desperation of my mature years, and the consolation of my old age'.

It was Padre Giovanni Battista Martini (1706–84) who had introduced Mozart to the Accademia, and indeed it was he who had consolidated the reputation of Bologna as one of the most important centres of the musical world in the eighteenth century. A Franciscan monk, he was appointed *maestro di cappella* at the church of San Francesco in Bologna in 1725, and he spent the rest of his life in the city, teaching and writing. He published his book on counterpoint in 1744–5, and at the time of his death was working on the fourth volume of his *Storia della musica*. Burney maintained that he had a library of 18,000 books, a small part of which is now in the library of the Liceo Musicale in Bologna.[6]

Rossini had begun studying privately in Bologna with one of Martini's pupils, Padre Angelo Tesei, and his lessons included singing, figured bass and keyboard accompaniment. This paved the way for his acceptance into the Liceo Musicale of Bologna in April 1806, where he studied singing with Lorenzo Gibelli, cello with Vincenzo Cavedagna and keyboard with Gian Callisto Cavazzoni Zanotti. His first class in counterpoint, on 20 May 1806, was with the Director of the Liceo himself, Padre Stanislao Mattei, the pupil and successor of Martini. On 8 August, Rossini took part in a vocal and instrumental concert given by the students, in which he sang a duet composed by Andrea Nencini, one of the students, with another pupil, Dorinda Caranti, who later became an opera singer. After this Rossini's voice began to break and settled down to the light baritone of subsequent years.

It is possible that from 1806 dates an overture in D – commissioned by Agostino Triossi once more, and known as 'al conventello', the first theme of which Rossini used later in the overture to *Il signor Bruschino* (1813) – and five duets for two horns. The fact that the horn was his father's instrument must surely account for the composition of the latter group. Also surviving among these early works is an overture *obbligato a contrabasso* in D, which is rather difficult to date with precision, but was almost certainly written between 1807 and 1810. The title is somewhat deceptive, for the double bass part is not as important as might be expected from the title; but there are, on the other hand, some interesting uses of orchestral colour which indicate the composer's future development in that direction.

At the same time, Rossini was earning money as a *répétiteur* and continuo-player, so that hand-in-hand with his purely academic studies went a very practical increase in his existing knowledge of the workings of the opera house and the ways of singers. For a performance of *L'amor marinaro* by Joseph Weigl (1766–1846) in 1806 he was billed as '*Maestro al cembalo* sig. Giovacchino Rossini Accademico Filarmonico de Bologna', and in the following year he played in Pier Alessandro Guglielmi's *La serva astuta* in Faenza. In the course of 1809, in what had now become his home town, he played in operas by Cimarosa, Paër and Sarti. Rossini did not, therefore, embrace the career of opera-composer in any idealistic or romantic way, but in full awareness of its limitations and less admirable aspects.

There were times when he was unable to contain himself as he was subjected to the more unbridled and harmonically impossible cadenzas delivered by some of the singers. One such was Adelaide Carpano, who had been engaged by a rich Venetian, Marchese F. Cavalli (who was no doubt her lover, too) for a season of opera in Senigallia. After the first occasion Rossini took her on one side and explained to her precisely why her cadenza was impossible. She appeared to accept his explanation – though she may not have understood it, of course – but at the very next performance she again produced a ridiculous cadenza, to the point where Rossini burst out laughing, and so did members of the audience. Naturally the singer complained to her protector, who summoned the young man and threatened dire punishments until Rossini explained to him, too, the nature of the problem. The impresario became more sympathetic, and eventually told Rossini that he was to come and see him when he was ready to compose an opera. That promise was kept with *La cambiale di matrimonio* during the winter of 1810, and Adelaide Carpano went on to create the role of Zaida in *Il turco in Italia* in 1814.

It was back in Bologna, however, that Rossini first heard the soprano of Spanish origin who was to play such an important part in his life and career. Isabella Colbran arrived in the city in early April 1807, having been elected to membership of the Accademia Filarmonica the previous November. She was twenty-two years old. On 11 April she sang at the Accademia Polimniaca, and eight days later at the Accademia Filarmonica itself. She then left for Milan three days later, where she made her début at La Scala in Nicolini's *Coriolano*. According to the accounts in the Bologna newspapers, we may well appreciate the effect that she had on those who saw and heard her, for she was both vocally and physically striking in her younger days. Stendhal gave added emphasis to her appearance, on stage at least. When she sang in Naples, he described her thus:

> It was beauty in the most regal tradition – noble features which on stage radiated majesty; an eye like that of a Circassian maid, flashing fire, and on top of everything, a genuine and profound feeling for the tragic. Off stage she had about as much dignity as the average milliner's assistant, but as soon as she was on stage, with a royal diadem on her head, she automatically drew respect.[7]

Unfortunately one cannot claim that it was Rossini's initial experience of Isabella Colbran that inspired him to compose his first opera, though an amorous involvement may well have been one of the elements in its genesis. The circumstances, however, are of a rather more prosaic nature, though in view of what has already been said about Rossini's early experiences in the opera house that should come as no surprise.

Furthermore, it is difficult to date the composition of Rossini's first opera, if only because it did not have its first performance, on 18 May 1812, until some time after it was written. That date establishes a *terminus ad quem*, but it is almost impossible to know when Rossini began it, or how long it took, since he said that he composed it piecemeal, as the various sections of text (it was hardly a question of a libretto) were given to him. It came about in the following way.

As we saw earlier, in about 1805 Rossini had made the acquaintance of the tenor Domenico Mombelli (1751–1835). Mombelli's first wife, Luisa Laschi (1760–90), was Mozart's first Countess Almaviva in *Le nozze di Figaro* (1 May 1786), and also sang Zerlina in the Vienna revival of *Don Giovanni* in May 1788. She last sang in Vienna in September that year, and died in 1790, possibly in childbirth. Mombelli then married Vincenza Viganò, a niece of Boccherini and sister of the choreographer Salvatore Viganò, who created Beethoven's *Die Geschöpfe des Prometheus* ballet. Two daughters of this second marriage, Ester and Marianna, were competent singers, and the family formed itself into a touring opera group, which came to Bologna in 1805. Vincenza provided the libretto for what became Rossini's first opera, but not before the latter had convinced Mombelli of his musical ability.

Rossini told the story to Ferdinand Hiller, and the fact that the composer was recalling an incident that had happened at least fifty years earlier, it must be borne in mind, indicates caution, but briefly the thirteen- or fourteen-year-old Rossini had been asked by a patroness (and possibly more than that, despite the boy's tender age) to obtain for her a copy of an aria by Portogallo that was in the Mombelli family repertoire at this time.[8] At first Rossini asked the copyist to provide him with the aria in question, and when he was refused asked Mombelli himself, who also declined. Such arias were often jealously guarded, and certain singers had their *arie di baule*, or suitcase arias, written for them by a favourite composer and then took them around as part of their baggage, to be introduced into an opera when the singer thought fit and was able to impose his or her will.[9]

Undeterred by his rebuff, Rossini then declared that he would go to the opera and listen to the aria again and then write it out from memory. His revered Mozart, it will be recalled, had performed a similar feat when hearing the Allegri *Miserere*, long guarded as the exclusive possession of the Sistine Chapel.[10] In fact there are basically only two sections in that setting of the *Miserere*, repeated several times, so it is not quite such an amazing feat as might at first appear. Not surprisingly, when Rossini fulfilled his promise, and showed the result to Mombelli, the latter initially thought that the copyist had capitulated, but when Rossini convinced him of his ability the two became friends. It was then that Rossini was offered the individual items piecemeal – duets, quartets, ariettas – that eventually became his first opera (though not the first to be staged), *Demetrio e Polibio*.

There is some ear-catching writing for solo woodwind in the overture, but in general it is not well put together, and when Diabelli published it in a piano reduction in Vienna in the 1820s he made some 'improvements' to it, including 'tidying up the second subject group and writing a more formally correct recapitulation', as Philip Gossett has put it.[11]

The Demetrio and Polibio of the opera's title are kings of Syria and Parthia respectively. Polibio is portrayed as much the more generous of the two kings, seen both in the role of actual father to his daughter Lisinga and as adoptive father to her lover Siveno, Demetrio's son, who has left his father's court and come to live in Parthia. Demetrio now arrives in Parthia in disguise, demands that Siveno return to Syria and, when he refuses to do so, carries off Lisinga, which provokes Polibio to seize Siveno. This inspires the quartet 'Donami ormai Siveno', which is one of the most memorable parts of the opera musically, and certainly the most dramatic and humanly alive. Its opening movement has some affecting chromaticism in Lisinga's part, and it is to her that Rossini also gives, still as part of the quartet, a melodically beguiling *andante*, 'Padre, qual gioia prova'. It was this quartet which Stendhal placed among Rossini's greatest achievements and maintained that, if he had composed nothing else, Mozart and Cimarosa would have recognised him as their equal as an artist. Stendhal particularly praised Rossini's lightness of touch, which he said he had never encountered in Mozart. From the purely musical point of view, however, the best moment in the opera is the duet for the lovers, 'Questo cor ti giura amore'. Rossini was to use the tune later on several occasions. Nevertheless, the piecemeal way in which the work was written is evident in the lack of any very consistent indications of character or dramatically convincing motivation. To say as much is to apply criteria of a subsequent period of operatic development. In his early operas Rossini was very much in the tradition of eighteenth-century opera as practised by Handel and Vivaldi, and those who followed them, as late as Mozart who, only a year before Rossini was born, had written a full-blown *opera seria* with *La clemenza di Tito*.

In general, different types of opera were still fairly clearly defined at this time, and it was unusual for composers to deviate from the well-trodden paths. Although comic or *buffo* characters had appeared in seventeenth-century operas by Monteverdi and Cavalli, for example, the standard Italian opera of the eighteenth century, whether written by Handel in London, or Vivaldi in Venice, or the young Mozart for Milan, was the *opera seria*, an internationally recognised convention. It was 'serious' in that it dwelt on the nobler sentiments of love and duty, even though the plots (when not incomprehensible at their worst) involved changes of identity, deliberate deception and disguised lovers – indeed, elements which were still very much in evidence in the operas current in Rossini's youth and in his own early works.

The standard musical components of the *opera seria* were recitative, which was only very lightly accompanied, and therefore known as *secco* or 'dry', and which carried the plot forward, and aria, which permitted the singers to show off their voices and express sentiments – in that order of priority. The number of arias allocated to each singer was strictly regulated according to the relative importance of the singers – *prima*, *seconda donna*, and so on. There were virtually no ensembles, no chorus, and no *buffo* elements. Orchestral forces were minimal, as were the accompaniments, too, much of the time. Even the arias themselves were constructed on a fixed pattern, known as *da capo*, or 'from the beginning', since the singer sang two contrasting sections, then went back to the beginning and repeated the first section, but this time with copious embellishment. One of the arguments advanced for the adherence to existing form was that, with such a huge demand for operas, composers had to write quickly, in a way that made production in different theatres easier for all concerned. Similarly, the divide between *opera seria* and *opera buffa*, whatever alternative nomenclature might be used, was a very sharply defined one, which suited almost everyone in the business, audience included, so there was little incentive for change or experiment.

It was to be one of Rossini's greatest achievements that he eventually managed to break the moulds, mingle the elements, and breathe new life into moribund tradition. Here, it must be said, the *buffa* tradition had much more to offer him by way of inspiration – as, indeed, it had had for Mozart.

Rossini was not, however, immediately inspired to launch himself into opera after this first attempt with *Demetrio e Polibio*, and much of the music of this period is what one might expect from one who was basically a student steeped in church music and with little chance of having his opera performed. There is a good deal of liturgical music, most of it for male voices, since women were forbidden to

Facsimile of one of the composer's early works, a gradual for two tenors and bass with instrumental accompaniment.

sing in church choirs – a matter Rossini was to take up with no less an authority than Pope Pius IX in later life. There is also the 'Bologna' *sinfonia* in D and a cantata *Il pianto d'Armonia sulla morte d'Orfeo* for tenor and chorus. The text is by Abbate Girolamo Ruggia, and the work was given by fellow-students on 11 August 1808 as part of the prize-giving ceremony. Despite the fact that the manuscript of this work bears corrections by Padre Mattei, Rossini received a medal for counterpoint on this occasion. The *sinfonia* was heard for the first time, also in Bologna, at the Accademia Polimniaca on 23 December 1808. It is scored for flute, two oboes, two clarinets in C, bassoon, two horns in D, two trumpets in D, timpani and strings. As the writer in *Il redattore* noted: 'The concert began with a *sinfonia* specially composed by Signor Rossini, a member of the Accademia Filarmonica, a young man of whom a great deal is expected. It turned out to be unbelievably harmonious. It is a completely new sort of work, and the composer reaped unanimous applause.' Rossini used the second theme later in his opera *L'inganno felice* (1812).

With such encouragement it is not surprising that the work was repeated at the next annual prize-giving, which in 1809 was held on 25 August; but now Rossini had another work to offer: *Sinfonia a più istrumenti obbligati concertata* in E flat, which was to serve as overture (adapted appropriately) to two subsequent operas, *La cambiale di matrimonio* (1810) and *Adelaide di Borgogna* (1817). Another composition of this year is the set of variations for obbligato instruments – two violins, viola, cello and B-flat clarinet – and orchestra in F. The work has virtually no development, and the variations are simply embellishments of the theme for each of the obbligato instruments in turn. This was, however, a process that Rossini went through like any other student, since the variation technique offers the possibility of extended composition without much structural sophistication. A set of variations in C for clarinet and orchestra dates from the same year; and Rossini's next two purely instrumental and orchestral works were likewise cast in variation form.

If nothing else, these student pieces indicate Rossini's concern with instrumental timbres and ranges, so useful in his later development of orchestral colour; but they also induce a certain degree of speculation as to what Rossini might have written had he not been so steeped in opera. Of course, Italy had no tradition of symphonic music – and, indeed, precious little purely orchestral music at all during the nineteenth century. To have developed along those lines,

Rossini would have had to leave Italy and go to Austria or Germany – an idea which does not seem to have occurred to him for a moment. Unfortunately, at the same time the standard of teaching and general musicianship at the Liceo Musicale in Bologna was going into decline, and Rossini was to devote a great deal of energy in future years to trying to arrest that decline.

Rossini still continued to play in the pit for opera – at the Teatro Comunale in Bologna during 1809, for example, when he may well have heard Isabella Colbran sing in Cimarosa's *Artemisia* and Nicolini's *Traiano in Dacia*, with the tenor Nicola Tacchinardi, and the last of the great *castrati*, Giovanni Battista Velluti (1781–1861). The effect of this voice, and those of the *castrati* in general, was something which Rossini never forgot, as he told Michotte: 'The purity, the wonderful flexibility of those voices and, above all, their deeply penetrating quality – all that moved and intrigued me more than I can say. I should add that I myself wrote a role for one of them, one of the last, but not of the least – Velluti. That was in my opera *Aureliano in Palmira* (1813).' Such a fascination well explains why Rossini later found himself dissatisfied with the majority of voices that he heard in Paris.

In addition to playing in theatre orchestras, Rossini performed at the keyboard at the Accademia dei Concordi in Bologna on 1 April and 28 May 1810; and his interest in vocal writing is seen in the *cavatina* for tenor and orchestra, 'Dolci aurette che spirate', which he composed this year. Apart from the earlier song 'Se il vuol la molinara', this is the first published vocal piece by Rossini.

In August 1810 two old friends of Rossini's parents arrived in Bologna. They were Giovanni Morandi, composer and conductor (1777–1856), and his wife Rosa, née Morolli (1782–1824), who were *en route* for Venice where they were to appear in a season of *farse* at the Teatro San Moisè under the direction of Marchese Cavalli. After their arrival in Venice, the company began to have problems with the repertoire. The Morandis recalled that Rossini was looking for an opportunity to write to commission and, as we saw earlier, Cavalli had already made the composer's acquaintance at Senigallia as a cembalo-player and forthright critic of one of his singers.

La cambiale di matrimonio, the play which formed the basis for the libretto he was presented with, had already been set in a somewhat similar version by a pupil of Paisiello, Carlo Coccia (1782–1873), for Rome in 1807. The story is an early example of poking fun at the

North American (in this case Canadian) in Europe. Slook comes to buy a wife from an English merchant, Tobias Mill, who is happy to oblige with his daughter Fanny (the role created by Rosa Morolli), despite the fact that she already has a lover, Edoardo Milfort. The plot turns around the efforts of the lovers, assisted by their servants Norton and Clarina, to outwit Slook, though in the event he is generous at heart and makes Fanny over to Edoardo as part of a deed of gift.

For the overture Rossini revised the E-flat overture that he had written in Bologna the year before (1809), but if the overture was not brand-new there was nevertheless a freshness in the music of the opera as a whole which captivated the Venetians and assured the success of Rossini's first foray into the world of commercial opera in Italy. It was given at least twelve times between 3 November and 1 December that year (1810), and he was paid forty scudi, or two hundred lire, for his pains.

Unfortunately, we have no record of Rossini's initial reaction to the magical city, and the theatre in which his opera was heard no longer exists. There is, however, a wall tablet on a building in the Calle del Teatro at San Moisè which bears the inscription: 'On this site, where the Teatro San Moisè once stood, the genius of Gioachino Rossini, then eighteen years old, joyfully took wing towards immortal glory on 3 November 1810, with the presentation of his first opera, *La cambiale di matrimonio*. The Municipality.'

The independent state of Venice had come to an ignominious end in 1797, and had then been handed over by Napoleon to Austria under the terms of the Treaty of Campo Formio. He took it back, however, after the battle of Austerlitz in 1805, and incorporated it into the Italian kingdom he had created. That arrangement only lasted for ten years, however, for the Congress of Vienna in 1815 returned it to Austria, and it remained an Austrian possession until 1866, apart from seventeen heroic months in 1848–9 when the Venetians under Daniele Manin revolted and declared their own republic.

If Venice had lost its independence, it nevertheless found a perfectly acceptable role, as far as the Venetians themselves were concerned, as one of the obligatory resorts for those visiting Italy, and one of the most celebrated and romantic of them all. To a large extent, of course, this was merely a continuation of the role it had played throughout the previous century, but the Age of Romanticism saw it in a somewhat different light. For Rossini, Venice was to be an especially welcoming city, and from *La cambiale di matrimonio* of 1810 to *Semiramide* of 1823 provided him with a series of commissions. It was, after all, the city in which the first public opera houses were opened, and where a succession of composers, starting with Monteverdi, had delighted audiences from generation to generation. Sadly Venice no longer had any composer of its own of note. The sands of time had run out faster there than they were doing in Bologna, but the Venetian audiences were happy to welcome the man who became known as the Swan of Pesaro, and who was at least Italian.

CHAPTER TWO

Failures and Successes

After the heady success of Venice, Rossini's return to Bologna must have seemed rather an anticlimax, though in his capacity as coach and keyboard-player to the Accademia dei Concordi he was praised for his part in a performance of Haydn's *Die Jahreszeiten* which the society gave in the following year (1811). As the reporter in Bologna's *Il redattore del reno* put it: 'Signor Gioacchino Rossini, *maestro al cembalo*, not to mention Signor Giuseppe Boschetti, first violin and leader of the orchestra, earned especial praise for the unfailing energy and exactness in directing the choruses, the players, the singers, and in the difficult co-ordination of so many parts and so many instruments.'

It is interesting that Rossini himself was regarded as a 'Germanic' composer in some quarters – and, indeed, during the early rehearsals of his opera in Venice the singers had complained of what was, in their opinion, heavy orchestration and uncomfortable vocal lines. In fact Rossini was persevering with his vocal writing, independently of opera, and this year wrote a cantata, *La morte di Didone*, for soprano, chorus and orchestra, for Ester Mombelli. It was not heard until 1818, however, when she sang it at the Teatro San Benedetto in Venice on 2 May that year.

It was possibly as a result of his success with *Die Jahreszeiten*, still fresh in people's minds in Bologna, but also because of his ever increasing reputation in the world of music theatre, that Rossini was engaged as keyboard-player and composer for a season that was opening that autumn at the Teatro del Corso. The first two operas were Portogallo's *L'oro non compra amore* and Pavesi's *Ser Marcantonio* (the libretto of which was reworked for Donizetti as *Don Pasquale*), and it was Rossini's lot to write an opera to a libretto by the Florentine Gaetano Gasparri entitled *L'equivoco stravagante*, which had its first night on 26 October 1811.

The title means primarily 'The ridiculous misunderstanding', but there is also a strong implication of a secondary meaning that does not translate succinctly into English, and requires a periphrasis such as 'The eccentric person of dubious sex', for reasons which will soon become apparent. The story tells of the love of Ermanno for Ernestina, the daughter of a newly rich farmer, Gamberotto. Ernestina is fond of literature, and Ermanno acts as her tutor, so that although his love for her remains clandestine they nevertheless are able to be in each other's company a good deal. However, both Ernestina and her father are taken in by the young Buralicchio, who is rich, though stupid to boot. In an attempt to get rid of Buralicchio, Ermanno, assisted by two cunning servants, tells his rival that Ernestina is not only a boy, but also a *castrato* (hence the title of the opera) and a deserter from the Army. Ernestina is eventually arrested, thus enabling Ermanno to reveal the truth and exchange his role of tutor for that of husband.

Unfortunately the work was a fiasco, though it is not clear why. In all probability it was the libretto, with its reference to desertion from the Army, that caused the opera to fall foul of the police authorities, as much as the sexual ambivalence implied by the title, as has been suggested by some commentators. Travesty roles had long been forced on opera-composers, especially in the Papal States, because of the ban on women appearing on stage in public, so that there was nothing scandalous from that point of view, though censorship has ever been a somewhat arbitrary practice, and the papal deputies and governors were no exception. From a musical point of view, however, the opera did not deserve such a fate, and some of it was used later by Rossini. No overture has survived.

One very positive feature of the experience was that Rossini worked with Marietta (Maria) Marcolini, who created the role of Ernestina in his opera, and the association was to encourage the development of Rossini's operatic talent. She was, after all, the most important *prima donna* he had met before Colbran. They evidently got on very well together, and there can be little doubt that they were attracted to each other over and above their purely professional relationship. Stendhal certainly maintained as much. Rossini seems to have been attractive to, and attracted by, women in his younger days, and must have had considerable charm. Unfortunately it is also clear by this time, since he was far from inactive sexually, he had contracted gonorrhoea. As a medical report expressed it in later years, he 'abused Venus from his earliest youth'.[1] At the very least, it complicated and exacerbated his physical and mental condition considerably in his maturity.

After the removal of *L'equivoco stravagante* from the season's repertoire, Rossini still had two more operas to rehearse, namely *Il trionfo di Quinto Fabio* by Domenico Puccini (1771–1815), grandfather of Giacomo Puccini, and Mayr's *Ginevra di Scozia*. There were problems with the chorus, who seem to have been upset by Rossini's treatment of them, and the rest of the season does not appear to have ended on a particularly happy note for the young composer. In later life he was never inclined to suffer fools gladly, especially in a professional context, and even in his early years he quickly grew impatient with what he perceived as incompetence.

However, this was only a passing irritation for Rossini, for the Venetian success of *La cambiale di matrimonio* almost exactly a year before (November 1810) had prompted a further invitation from the Teatro San Moisè, and in December he left Bologna and had the new work, *L'inganno felice*, ready for its first performance on 8 January 1812. The libretto provided for him was by Giuseppe Foppa, based on Giuseppe Palomba's libretto for Paisiello's opera of the same title (Naples, 1798). Rossini's *L'inganno felice* was a hit, and was the opera chosen to close the season on 11 February. Portraits of the *prima donna* Teresa Giorgi-Belloc and poems in her honour were sold at the theatre, and doves, canaries and even wild pheasant were said to have been set free from the boxes into the auditorium.

Although designated a *farsa* (the title means 'The happy deception'), the comic element in this work is but a minor part of what is essentially a melodrama with strong romantic interest. The plot tells how, some years before the opera begins, Isabella, wife of Duke Bertrando, repulsed the amorous attentions of Ormondo, her husband's friend, who thereupon made an attempt on her life. Fortunately she survived and floated out to sea, where she was rescued by Tarabotta, the leader of a mining community situated on the coast. When the opera opens, Isabella is living in the mining village, when the duke, her husband, Ormondo and his henchman Batone arrive. Husband and wife are reconciled, and the former, in league with Tarabotta, devises a plan to trap Ormondo and Batone at night in the mines. This last part of the plot is elaborated in a finale of considerable proportions, given the fact that the opera is in one act, and also how relatively inexperienced Rossini was at this time, and yet the whole work, including the overture, points to what is to come in Rossini's developing style.

In the overture there is the first essay in what was to become the composer's hallmark, the extended crescendo; and in the opera itself, in addition to the finale already mentioned, there is, on the one hand, a markedly lyrical element in Isabella's music and, on the other, the *buffo* or comic element, here restricted to the villains. It is also remarkable that three of the five principals in the opera are basses.

With such a rich variety within the space of its one act, it is easy to see why the work enjoyed considerable success, not only in Venice, but also throughout Italy, then in Paris, Vienna, London and New Orleans; it even reached Mexico. Certainly its immediate success inspired Cera, the impresario of the San Moisè, to commission another *farsa* from Rossini, for the spring season that same year (1812). The new Venetian opera was to be *La scala di seta* ('The silken ladder'), but before that, and within a month or so of the close of the opera in Venice, Rossini was ready with an *opera seria* for Ferrara, for which a local dilettante, Conte Francesco Aventi, provided the libretto.

Hitherto the Rossini operas which had been staged were all *farse*: the two one-act commissions for San Moisè in Venice and the two-act failure in Bologna. Although his first opera was an *opera seria*, it had not yet been heard in performance. He was known primarily as a composer of comic opera, therefore, and the Ferrara opera represented something of a departure both for Rossini himself, and also in the eyes of those who followed his career. For Rossini's next opera, *Ciro in Babilonia*, his point of departure was not only serious, but also biblical in origin.

This opera, one of only two that Rossini wrote on a sacred subject, was the composer's version of Belshazzar's Feast, and was effectively a means of circumventing the laws then in effect controlling the use of theatres in Lent. Similar laws in England, one may recall, though in a slightly different context, had been in part responsible for the birth of Handelian oratorio in the previous century.

Baldassare (Belshazzar) is depicted as a bullying tyrant, who has in his power the wife, Amira, and son of the Persian king, Ciro. In his attempt to free his wife and child, Ciro is in turn imprisoned and condemned to death, and Baldassare prepares to marry Amira. The prophet Daniel appears, and in a short scene tells Baldassare that he has been weighed in the balance and found wanting, and that his kingdom has been divided and given to the Medes and the Persians.

Unfortunately, despite the appearance of Marcolini in the *travesti* role of Ciro, the work became one of Rossini's *fiaschi*, as he told Hiller many years later.[2] On his return to Bologna he was invited to go and eat with friends, so he ordered from the confectioner a marzipan ship with a pennant bearing the name *Ciro* on it. However, the mast was broken, the sail torn, and the ship itself, listing badly to one side, was afloat in a sea of cream: so much for *Ciro*. Nevertheless there was much laughter and good spirits as the friends consumed the wreckage. This may, of course, have been mere bravado on Rossini's part. As his career progressed he taught himself to conceal his real feelings in such circumstances, which was then interpreted as insouciance, especially by whose who would have preferred to see him devastated.

It is from Ferdinand Hiller that we have Rossini's recollection of how he came to write for *Ciro* the *aria del sorbetto*, literally the sherbet aria, sung by a lesser character whilst the audience talked and took refreshment. The aria in question, 'Chi disprezza gl'infelici', was written for the *seconda donna* at Ferrara, Anna Saivelli, and has a vocal part which consists of only one repeated note, a B flat. Not only was Saivelli terrifyingly ugly, according to Rossini, but she also had a dreadful voice, and when he listened to her carefully he decided that she had only one good note – the famous B flat – so he determined to restrict her to that. The orchestra made up for the rest. 'The piece gave pleasure, and was applauded,' said Rossini, 'and my unitone singer was highly delighted with her triumph.' On this occasion, we may be sure, there were no complaints about heavy orchestration or 'Germanic' tendencies.

Such amusing anecdotes, however, ought not to allow us to pass over the rest of *Ciro*, since there are things of note in it. Rossini wrote no overture, but used that from *L'inganno felice*. Since a particular feature of the opera was its employment of a chorus – which, as we have seen, was by no means usual at this time in opera, whether *seria* or *buffa*, though it was suited to oratorio – Rossini wrote some good music for it, including one section that looks forward melodically to 'Ecco ridente', sung by Almaviva in *Il barbiere di Siviglia*. Amira has two pleasing arias: 'Vorrei veder lo sposo', which Rossini was to use again in his other religious opera, *Mosè in Egitto*, and the prayer 'Deh, per me non v'affligate'. Less successful is his music for Baldassare, which is certainly taxing for the singer, and was in fact written for the tenor Eliodoro Bianchi, the teacher of the Russian tenor Nicholas Ivanoff, who became a particular protégé of Rossini's. At this time, however, Rossini would not have expected the high notes to be sung in a chest voice by the tenor – a development which did not please the composer. Even so, Baldassare's dazzlingly ornate music tends merely to hold up the action and adds little or nothing to the audience's perception of character as Rossini portrays it.

It is in the last two scenes of *Ciro* that the young composer produced moving and impressive music that ought to have kept the work alive longer. In the penultimate scene Ciro, now condemned to death, takes his leave of his family, and although Rossini used themes taken from *Demetrio e Polibio* (as yet unperformed) he constructed a scene which looks forward to the apple scene in *Guillaume Tell* where the same testing of family ties and affection is involved. In such a situation, where Rossini drew on direct first-hand experience, the composer produced a touching and indeed impressive effect. And, of course, he had the collaboration of Marcolini.

The final banquet scene contains Rossini's first exposition of storm music, at which he was to excel, as well as the appearance of the prophet Daniel, and brings to its close a work which may indeed be flawed but which at the same time would repay closer investigation. It reached Munich in 1816, and Vienna the following year, and was also produced in Weimar and Dresden. Its appearances were mainly confined to Italy, however, where it survived for some fifteen years – no mean achievement if one bears in mind that very few operas had hitherto found their way into a standard international repertoire of the sort to which we are accustomed today. Audiences almost invariably preferred new music, hence the enormous number of operas written in the eighteenth and early nineteenth centuries. It was only with the Romantic movement that certain works were enshrined in the repertoire and at the same time revered as sacrosanct entities. In fairness to the Romantic composers, such as Mendelssohn with his revival of Bach's *Matthäus-Passion* in 1829, they also resurrected the music of the past; but then they had to confront the embarrassing problem of self-plagiarism or, even worse, plagiarism of other composers. When Rossini began working in Italian opera houses, the spirit of the eighteenth century was still very much alive. When *Ciro in Babilonia* was given in Milan in 1818, an aria by Nicolini was introduced at the behest of one of the singers and a duet from

Rossini's own *Otello* (1816) was inserted into the second act, prompting the description of 'un vero guazzabuglio' ('a real mess') from the writer in *La gazzetta di Milano*. No wonder, then, that the same writer declared that, in his opinion, *Ciro* did not merit inclusion among the finer compositions of Rossini; and it is not surprising that it was not repeated in the city, where the audiences had been treated already to the ebullient side of Rossini with his very first opera there in 1812.

Fortunately the failure of *Ciro in Babilonia* did not dampen Rossini's creative enthusiasm. At this point in his career he had seemingly boundless energy and optimism, aided by the inspiration and encouragement of family and friends such as Marcolini, and of course the motivation, not to say economic necessity, of providing both for himself and his parents. Furthermore, Venice had so far been kind to him, so whether it was wise of him to have accepted the commission from Cera to compose *La scala di seta* for the Teatro San Moisè would hardly have come into Rossini's considerations. The implicit danger in being associated with failure is something that rarely affects artists on the threshold of a career. In the event, the opera, burdened by a feeble libretto, was not the hoped-for success, though it would be wrong to imply that *La scala di seta* was an outright fiasco.

As far as *La scala di seta* is concerned, it is one of the Rossini operas (along with *La gazza ladra*, 'The thieving magpie') seemingly condemned to be known almost solely by its overture, and it must be admitted that much of what follows is something of an anticlimax. However, one must bear in mind that it is essentially a *farsa*, and that it would be inappropriate to look for profundity of expression or depth of character in the music. Indeed, at its first performance at the Teatro San Moisè in Venice on 9 May 1812, it shared a triple bill with an act of Pavesi's *Ser Marcantonio* and a ballet! In the event, Rossini brought to the work a freshness which Giuseppe Foppa's stale libretto was hardly calculated to inspire in a composer. Indeed, critics noted the echoes in the plot between Foppa's intrigue and that of Cimarosa's *Il matrimonio segreto* (1792), which in any case gave more than a backward glance to George Colman and David Garrick's *The Clandestine Marriage* (1766) as well as to Madame Riccoboni's novel *Sophie ou Le Mariage caché* (1768). Its immediate source, however, was Planard's libretto for Gaveaux's *L'Échelle de soie* (Paris, 1808).

The plot concerns the way in which the heroine, Giulia, manages to find her way out of the dilemma created when her guardian wishes her to marry a young army officer, Blansac, when she is already married in secret to his friend, Dorvil. The solution is to encourage Giulia's cousin, Lucilla, to fall in love with Blansac, and after many ruses, including the silken ladder of the opera's title, the heroine is successful. There is considerable rhythmic skill – another important aspect of the mature Rossini – deployed in the work as a whole, including Lucilla's 'Sento talor nell'anima', which Rossini reworked for the gypsy chorus at the opening of *Il turco in Italia*, and there is particularly sympathetic writing for the old servant, Germano, a *basso buffo*.

Although, as we have seen, *Demetrio e Polibio* was Rossini's first opera to be written, its first performance, in Rome, did not take place until nine days after that of *La scala di seta* in Venice. It is therefore highly questionable whether Rossini was present at the Rome première, since it was usually a contractual requirement that the composer directed from the pit for the first three performances of a new opera. Certainly Rossini told Hiller that he had not been present.

At all events, his career was soon to take a dramatic step forward, and when he returned to Bologna that summer (1812) he received a commission from La Scala in Milan for what turned out to be his first undoubted comic masterpiece. The libretto that he was to set was *La pietra del paragone* ('The touchstone'), by one of the theatre's house librettists since 1799, Luigi Romanelli, whose collected works ran to no less than eight volumes. Rossini's own reputation played its part in the commission – for which he was to receive six hundred lire – though Marcolini and the bass Filippo Galli also had a hand it it.

La Scala was at that time Italy's most important opera house, so naturally Rossini wanted to ensure – as far as he was able – that the work he put before the sophisticated Milan audience was a sure hit; and to his relief he achieved exactly that. It was heard no less than fifty-three times during its first season, beginning on 26 September 1812; and, although Pavesi's *Ser Marcantonio* had achieved one more performance there in 1810, it was not until 1842, when Verdi's *Nabucco* achieved fifty-eight performances during its first season, that *La pietra del paragone*'s record total was surpassed. At all events, the composer, still only twenty, was henceforth able to consider himself a *maestro di cartello*, one whose name alone was deemed of sufficient stature to draw the public. Of more relevance to Rossini's immediate career prospects, his success helped to gain him exemption from military service, for which he was now eligible.

La pietra del paragone might well be held up as an example of how much a good libretto may inspire a composer, just as an indifferent one may have the contrary effect. Designated a *melodramma giocoso*, it lays no claim to being a profound exploration of human character; but in it Rossini portrays in scintillating fashion a world of sophistication with which the Milanese audience would readily identify. It is a remarkable achievement for a twenty-year-old, deploying intellectual and musical brilliance to dazzling effect.

Count Asdrubale has recently inherited a fortune, and has invited a group of friends to spend the *villeggiatura*, or holiday season, with him at his house at Viterbo, outside Rome. Chief among the guests are his friend Giocondo, a poet, and the Marchese Clarice, a young widow. This trio, then, provides the love-interest, since Giocondo is in love with Clarice, though he suspects what is in fact true: namely that she favours Asdrubale, and he is in love with her. However, Clarice is reluctant to reveal her affection for Asdrubale, since in view of her widowhood and his recent good fortune her behaviour might be capable of misinterpretation. As a foil to the romantic trio, there is a quartet of guests: the poetaster Pacuvio and his companion Donna Fulvia, the journalist Macrobio and Baroness Aspasia.

Asdrubale, assisted by his servant Fabrizio, decides to put to the test the genuineness of his friends' feelings for him by announcing that he has lost all his money. He then appears disguised as a Turkish emissary to claim possession of his own estate in exchange for a bond which has not been honoured. His famous aria 'Sigillara . . .', sung as he prepares to set seals on the count's possessions, became so popular that it provided the opera with what virtually became its alternative title. Because of her genuine affection for Asdrubale, Clarice remains loyal to him, and in an addition to the original plot she disguises herself as her own brother, who then appears to take Clarice away. At the request of Marcolini, who created the part, Clarice was able to dress up as a Captain of Hussars, thus repeating her success in a *travesti* part that she had had in *L'equivoco stravagante* before it was closed down. This is now Clarice's chance to test the genuineness of Asdrubale's professed affection for her, and in his response to the 'brother's' appearance – 'Lasciami, amico, a qual destino in preda' – she is convinced that his love is in fact genuine.

Musically, the opera abounds in good things, right from the opening ensemble sung by Asdrubale's guests, which includes a hint of Pacuvio's 'Ombretta sdegnosa/Del Missipipi', which is to appear in its fullness later in the act. Pacuvio represents the typical critic of the day, ignorant and presumptuous, and yet at the same time evincing literary aspirations. There is a duet between the journalist Macrobio and the poet Giocondo, in which the former boasts of the power of the press, and in total contrast an echo duet between Clarice and Asdrubale, accompanied by horns. There then follows Pacuvio's 'Ombretta' aria which, he tells Donna Fulvia, is an example of how a maid, in language that is at once both 'pathetic and burlesque', talks to a wise man. The act ends with a splendid finale, which Stendhal maintained was the best *buffo* finale Rossini ever composed.

Act II opens with another ensemble, there is a hunting chorus and storm music, leading into a song for Giocondo to the beauty of his loved one, Clarice, though his love is destined to remain unrequited, for Asdrubale's deception is revealed, and we know that all will be resolved happily – though not before Macrobio becomes involved in a duel with Asdrubale and Giocondo, and Clarice appears as a Hussar to round off the evening with a bravura aria.

La pietra del paragone looks both forward and backward, in that it borrows from both *Demetrio e Polibio* and *L'equivoco stravagante*, while Rossini took with him ideas that he would use in his next opera, *L'occasione fa il ladro*, as well as *La gazzetta*. On a more fundamental plane, however, as far as his development as an opera-writer was concerned, he showed amazing facility both in setting words – as in Pacuvio's *canzonetta* – and responding to the opportunities presented by words – as in the echo duet – and from there to the portrayal of types and genres of personality and character, even if these are not yet fully rounded characters. It was, after all, basically a *farsa*. Rossini juxtaposed romance and foolishness, charm and stupidity, genuine affection and affectation, in a way which recalls the aspects of a work such as *Così fan tutte* that lovers of Mozart's music found so hard to come to terms with, especially as the nineteenth century advanced. This happy mixture of styles was to be very much a part of the nature of the mature Rossini – and, indeed, it was something he affirmed to the end of his life: 'Tous les genres sont bons, hors le genre ennuyeux' ('All kinds of music are valid except the boring kind').

It seems staggering that *La pietra del paragone* was the fifth Rossini opera to be first heard in 1812, and yet there was still one more to come, for he received two more commissions for the Teatro San Moisè in Venice, the first of which, *L'occasione fa il ladro* ('The opportunity makes the thief'), opened on 24 November that year. It seems only to have had five performances, and never became a favourite. When it was offered at the Teatro Carcano in Milan in April 1820, for example, it was noted that a one-act work had been split into two so as to make it last longer, there were echoes of other works, which is not surprising, since operas such as *La cenerentola* had been heard in the mean time (though it was not true that 'entire sections' of *La cenerentola* had been lifted and included), and an unknown singer, Signora Melas, who was only sixteen years old, had been entrusted with the leading role. In the words of *La gazzetta di Milano*, the public had little faith in either the impresario or the singer, so that the house was very thin for the first night, and as a result Signora Melas was virtually wasting her sweetness on the desert air.

L'occasione fa il ladro was the last of the six Rossini operas to have their first performance in the year 1812, and the first of a pair for the San Moisè in Venice which were to complete Rossini's apprenticeship as an opera-composer.

The opera opens with a storm, which enabled the composer to forgo an overture. In the event he took the storm music from his previous opera, *La pietra del paragone*, to which he added a slow introduction, so that as the storm recedes the scene opens straight away in an inn near Naples. We are introduced to Don Parmenione, who is fond of wine and women, but penniless. The storm has driven another man to the inn, namely Count Alberto, who is travelling to Naples to claim the hand of his bride, Berenice, whom he has never met but is able to imagine in his mind's eye because her uncle, Don Eusebio, has sent Alberto her portrait.

The way in which the plot now develops is indicated by the subtitle of the opera, *Il cambio della valigia* ('The change of suitcase'), since Alberto's servant picks up the wrong one and, as the count makes for Naples, Parmenione and his servant examine the contents of the remaining suitcase. To Parmenione's unbelievable good fortune, he discovers money and the portrait of a beautiful young woman, who is of course none other than Alberto's Berenice. Parmenione cannot resist the temptation, and decides to present himself at Don Eusebio's house in Naples as the intended bridegroom.

In the next scene we meet Berenice. When her supposed lover is therefore announced, she decides to put him to the test by changing clothes with her servant, Ernestina, and it is to her that Parmenione makes his first utterance, which is deftly suggested by Rossini in an opening phrase that begins with hesitating alternate quavers and rests and then plunges into a downward rush of semiquavers. Alberto, on the other hand, addresses the genuine Berenice in an elegant $\frac{6}{8}$ melody that foreshadows Donizetti. An ensemble follows which provides Rossini with the opportunity to explore all the implications of such deliberately created confusion and its effect on the parties involved. Effectively this brings to an end the first half of the opera.

Parmenione proves no match for Berenice, and she soon unmasks him. Not surprisingly, Alberto is thereupon quite happy to stick with the supposed maid and let his rival have the supposed mistress. The resolution is not to be quite so slick, however, for although Berenice is impressed by Alberto's genuineness she is still irritated by the mistaken identity. As Rossini embarks on the finale, he begins with a recitative in which Berenice emerges as the one who finally assumes control, which is underlined musically by giving her an imposing *cabaletta*. Thus dramatically and musically she becomes the focus of interest in the resolution of the opera, and Rossini was to repeat the effect subsequently on several occasions. Despite some good moments, however, the work was not a success, and it only received five performances on this occasion, though it was revived later and had further performances abroad.

The second opera, *Il signor Bruschino*, commissioned for the Teatro San Moisè was a very different sort of work, though this pendant to *L'occasione fa il ladro* (in so far as they are both one-act *farse* written to commission for the same theatre) enjoyed little more immediate success than its predecessor. Yet it is from many points of view a more considerable work, and as a result enjoyed more esteem in later years. The libretto was by Giuseppe Foppa once again, based on a French comedy, *Le Fils par hazard* (which provided the subtitle for the opera), by Alisan de Chazet and E.-T. Maurice Ourry, of 1809.

The plot tells of the love of Florville for Sofia, whom her guardian, Gaudenzio, has promised in marriage to the son of Signor Bruschino. Because no one has yet seen the young Bruschino, he decides to impersonate him, and presents himself at Gaudenzio's house. By the time Signor Bruschino himself arrives, everyone is convinced that Florville is his son, and that the father is acting very strangely indeed when he denies him recognition. Bruschino's anger is a source of amusement, no doubt, to those who are in the know, and a source of incomprehension to those who are not, but both reactions only serve to heighten his frustration and anger. At this point there is a very definite element of human cruelty and suffering which Rossini captures splendidly in the music. Bruschino's melodic line is dislocated and fragmented as his sanity seems to collapse, and Sofia reacts with a figure that snakes upwards in rising fifths and minor sixths.

From the musical point of view the opera is significant not only for the way in which Rossini delineates various emotions and facets of personality, but also in the incisive, sometimes almost mechanical rhythmic patterns he employs and the touches of originality in the orchestration. Sofia's 'Ah! donate il caro sposo' has a telling use of the cor anglais, and rhythm and orchestration are combined when the young Bruschino finally arrives on the scene and is given a march-like introduction on flutes, oboes and clarinets, underpinned by dotted rhythms from bassoons and horns. He is chastened and repentant, 'Padre mio son pentito', though the atmosphere is quickly and deliberately undermined by Rossini when he removes the first syllable from 'pentito', and the son's penitence degenerates into vain repetition of '. . . tito . . . tito . . . tito . . .'.

Eventually Signor Bruschino is able to get the better of Gaudenzio, at least, by insisting that Sofia marry Florville, who is in fact the son of an old enemy; and, although hero and heroine are to be married, one is left feeling – rather as at the end of *Twelfth Night* (and, for that matter, *Così fan tutte*) – that too much has happened for everyone simply to subside into general euphoria at the wedding celebrations.

Not long after the first performance of *Il signor Bruschino*, Rossini made his début at Venice's leading opera house, La Fenice. This took place on 6 February, but so far it has not been possible to be precise about the date of the first performance of *Il signor Bruschino*. We know that it was in late January 1813, and there may have been as little as a week between the two. Rossini had received the commission from La Fenice during the latter part of 1812, no doubt after he had already committed himself to Cera at the Teatro San Moisè. In the light of this, the triumph that was to come was all the more remarkable.

CHAPTER THREE

Triumph in Venice

Opera may be said to have been created at two of the great courts of northern Italy, Florence and Mantua, around the year 1600, and for almost the next forty years it remained more or less exclusively a courtly entertainment, presented only on an occasional basis. It was in Venice, however, that the first public commercial opera houses were opened in 1637, so that city may justly claim the credit for having made opera such a regular and important feature of Italian musical life. The Venetians had long enjoyed the theatre, and had a most distinguished tradition of church music, so the implantation of opera was a swift and successful operation. The buildings were there, many of the necessary musicians were there, and Venice had the prestige and the financial resources required to draw to it the stars – singers and composers – who would consolidate its position.

As Venice's political power declined, she had found a new role as one of the obligatory highlights of a visit to Italy – in short as a tourist resort. Outwardly the illusion of power and pomp was kept up, and the social and cultural life of the city seemed to go on as it always had done. Artistically, however, Venice gradually died of anaemia, and it ceased to have its own healthy living tradition. It continued to act as a source of inspiration to artists from all over the world, as it does today, but the artistic life of the city came to depend on outsiders to generate the activity. There were native composers still working in Venice in the early years of the nineteenth century but, as so often happens when people are heirs to a once-great tradition, they were incapable of arresting the decline of that tradition, let alone reviving it, and yet at the same time they resented the advent of outsiders such as Rossini. Their resentment was made more acute, of course, when the ordinary Venetians and the visitors took him to their hearts.

★

'I want to see Venice, and the Alps, and Parmesan cheeses, and look at the coast of Greece. . . .' So wrote Byron to Thomas Moore from Newstead Abbey on 15 September 1814.[1] Yet another in a long line of those for whom Venice, over the centuries, has held such a potent fascination, Byron did eventually get to Venice, and he attended the opera as a matter of course. Later he was to hear Rossini's *Otello*, though as one who responded far more to words than to music, and to Shakespeare rather than to Rossini, Byron is not a source for perceptive criticism of opera. Nevertheless he bears witness to the enormous popularity of Rossini in Venice in the second decade of the nineteenth century.

Rossini, too, was essentially a visitor to Venice, even though he came from only a relatively short distance away down the coast of Italy. For him, however, it was not some exotic romantic city where fantasies might be lived out and dreams fulfilled, but the traditional home of opera. Although other Italian cities had flourishing opera houses at this time, and Milan and Naples were rapidly overtaking Venice in importance, the latter still retained its prestige. It might be regarded, therefore, as a necessary stage on the journey to graduation as a fully fledged opera-composer, or, if not that, at the very least a source of commissions and employment.

Tancredi, Rossini's new opera for La Fenice, was to constitute both a commission and a graduation, and marks an important stage in his career, signalling the end of his apprenticeship and his emergence as a mature composer of serious opera. Although Gaetano Rossi took Voltaire's *Tancrède* (1760) as his immediate source for the libretto, the plot goes back much further to Tasso's *Gerusalemme liberata* (1580–93). A certain amount of background detail is necessary to explain what has happened prior to the beginning of the opera, to aid understanding of what is at stake in the plot.

The opera is set at the time of the Crusades, in Syracuse, which was then a city-state. Two families – those of Argirio and Orbazzano – quarrel, much as did the Montagues and Capulets in Verona. Eventually Orbazzano and his clan gain control, and Argirio's wife and daughter, Amenaide, are sent into exile to the court of the Emperor of Byzantium. The Saracen leader, Solamir, thereupon falls in love with Amenaide, but she has already given her heart to another exile from Sicily, Tancredi, and Amenaide's mother, on her death-bed, has given her approval to their marriage. Meanwhile, Solamir has been attacking Syracuse, Orbazzano has been replaced by Argirio as leader, and in an attempt to heal the self-inflicted wounds of the city-state Argirio offers the hand of his daughter Amenaide (now back in Syracuse) in marriage to Orbazzano. At the same time he condemns Tancredi to death in his absence and seizes his family estates. Amenaide knows virtually nothing of all this past history except where it touched her directly, and as the opera begins she sends an anonymous letter to Tancredi, encouraging him to return home to Syracuse.

After the overture, taken from *La pietra del paragone*, the opera opens with a chorus of knights of Syracuse who celebrate the ending of the internal feuding in the state, singing of peace, honour, faith and love. Stendhal thought it all rather insipid, hoping rather to find something more virile, more akin to the idea of medieval chivalry as portrayed in *Ivanhoe*.[2] Scott's novel, one must point out, was not published until 1819 – six years after *Tancredi*. Nevertheless Stendhal identified an important aspect of Rossini's treatment of the story, even if he arrived at it by the 'wrong' route.

Tasso had long been a source of opera plots, but hitherto it had simply been for the characters and situations; and, since *opera seria* dispensed with a chorus usually, the focus lay firmly on the principals and the somewhat artificial way in which they expressed their emotions and reactions. Furthermore, because of the average plot, with its tendency to impose situations arbitrarily, rather than that they should be the result of individual character, the portrayal of emotion and sentiment in music was highly stylised. In this scheme of things, it would have been difficult indeed to express in music the broad concepts of peace, honour, faith and love as they were understood by mankind in general. Rossini was by no means unique in that he subscribed to these concepts, but what he achieved in *Tancredi* was. Through his extensive use of the chorus and the music he writes for it, he gives those concepts a much broader appeal, painting them in altogether larger brushstrokes, and in so doing became what Julian Budden described as 'the reluctant architect of Italian romantic opera', handing on to Verdi forms which the latter developed, giving them more popular appeal, and infusing them with psychological realism.[3] Since Rossini never set down any kind of manifesto, one must assume that it was his 'instinct' at work, aided no doubt by his 'facility', to use his own words.

After we have met Amenaide at the beginning of *Tancredi*, it is the turn of Tancredi himself, who is seen arriving in Syracuse. A gentle barcarolle is the signal for his boat to appear, then in his recitative 'O patria' Tancredi expresses his feelings on his return. This leads into a *cavatina*, 'Tu che accendi questo', which in turn leads to the famous *cabaletta*, 'Di tanti palpiti'. The role was written for a coloratura contralto *en travesti*, and the first Tancredi was Adelaide Melanotte-Montresor, but subsequently Giuditta Pasta made the part very much her own. Such was the popularity of the *cabaletta*, Byron mentioned it in *Don Juan*:

> Oh! the long evenings of duets and trios!
> The admirations and the speculations;
> The 'Mamma Mia's!' and the 'Amor Mio's!'
> The 'Tanti palpiti's' on such occasions:
> The 'Lasciami's,' and quavering 'Addio's!'
> Amongst our own most musical of nations;
> With 'Tu mi chiama's' from Portingale,
> To soothe our ears, lest Italy should fail.[4]

As we have seen, Byron was not particularly gifted musically, and *Don Juan* dates from 1819–24, when the initial freshness and exhilaration offered by *Tancredi* had – in Venice at least – become a somewhat uncritical adulation of Rossini.

Byron's own footnote to the stanza predicted that the tide would turn against Rossini eventually:

> Who would imagine that he was to be the successor of Mozart? However, I state this with diffidence, as a liege and loyal admirer of Italian music in general, and of much of Rossini's: but we may say, as the connoisseur did of painting, in the *Vicar of Wakefield*, 'that the picture would be better painted if the painter had taken more pains'.

If nothing else, Byron's reference to 'Di tanti palpiti' indicates its phenomenal success in Venice, where people whistled it in the streets and a judge was said to have been obliged to suspend a hearing in court because he unwittingly used some of the words from it, causing an uproar. It also became known as the *aria dei risi*, or Rice Aria, because Rossini was said to have written it in four minutes – the time taken to cook rice. It is true that he wrote *Tancredi* speedily, but there is no evidence for the incidence of the rice. Moreover, such anecdotes have only served to compound the simplistic image of

Rossini as a somewhat blasé *bon viveur*. What is generally true about the music for *Tancredi*, however, is that it has an engaging fluency and freshness, and offers the singers wonderful opportunities for *bel canto*. In fact the poet and critic Giuseppe Carpani (1752–1825) described it as 'cantilena, always cantilena, beautiful cantilena, new cantilena, magical cantilena, rare cantilena. . . . This pearl of great price, this difficult virtue . . . this sun . . . shines at noonday in Rossini's music.'[5]

Such emphasis on long lyrical lines should not, however, lead one to imagine that the opera lacks excitement. The finale to Act I is a case in point. Amenaide, now promised in marriage to Orbazzano, is wrongly accused of sending a letter to the communal enemy, Solamir. A slow sextet in D major begins the finale, leading to a fast section with two discernible orchestral motifs, one expressing Amenaide's anguish, and the other the general surprise and amazement, and then Amenaide's impassioned 'Padre amato'. But she pleads in vain, first to her father, then to Tancredi and Orbazzano, trying to assert her innocence; the climax comes in the final *stretta*.

For the *stretta* of the finale Rossini makes a striking key change, and within the *stretta* itself modulates rapidly through a wide range of tonalities. This is a pattern Rossini will subsequently use in the finales of first acts of both *opera seria* and *opera buffa*. For example, there are very close harmonic similarities between the Act I finale *stretta* of *Tancredi* and that of *Il barbiere di Siviglia*.

Amenaide's prison scene in Act II is in C minor, one of the few minor-keyed passages in the whole opera, with touching use of oboe and violin in the introduction, and cor anglais for the *cavatina*, and a fine duet between Amenaide and Tancredi 'Lasciami! non t'ascolto'. Tancredi then has an accompanied recitative and the *cavatina* 'Ah! che scordar non so', which are prefaced by an orchestral introduction notable for the chromaticism in the bass and the broad melody above it.

Although the first performance of *Tancredi* was given on 6 February 1813, both the leading ladies were unwell, and at both that and the next performance the opera had to be abandoned during the second act. It was not until 12 February that the work was heard in its entirety, and in all received some fifteen performances at La Fenice that season. It was not an immediate hit during its first Fenice season; that only came after it had been revived at the theatre in the autumn of 1815. Immediately after the first Venetian performances, however, Rossini was asked to take *Tancredi* to Ferrara, and he used the opportunity to make some important changes to the first version of the opera.

In the earlier version, Rossini and Rossi gave the opera a happy ending, which was not only contrary to Voltaire's original, but did not really convince the composer, either. Given the chance, therefore, to do something different for Ferrara, Rossini turned to Luigi Lechi, Adelaide Melanotte-Montresor's lover, who went back to Voltaire and prepared a new, tragic ending for the opera. Unfortunately this did not please the audiences – the hero or heroine was not yet expected to die at the end of an opera, let alone on stage – so the original ending had to be restored, and it was in this version that *Tancredi* gained its international reputation.

Rossini subsequently salvaged some of the new music (for example, in his opera *Aureliano in Palmira*), but one cannot help but wish that he had either stuck to his instinct or worked with Lechi on the opera earlier. It is almost certain that a greater work of art would have emerged as a result, and that Rossini would have had an even greater impact on Italian opera than he did at this time – despite the audience's reaction to the tragic ending. Therein lies the problem, however, for Rossini was emphatically no Beethoven or Wagner, determined to press ahead regardless of whether he could carry his audiences with him. He had no manifesto to publish and propagate. He had only his instinct and his as yet unquenchable desire to write opera. As the Romantic movement took shape, to allow the audience to dictate to the composer became tantamount to selling one's soul to the Devil.

Tancredi finished its first season at the Fenice on 7 March 1813, and after the visit to Ferrara Rossini soon had to be back in Venice, for he had promised the Teatro San Benedetto an *opera buffa*, entitled *L'italiana in Algeri* ('The Italian girl in Algiers'), for the middle of May. The libretto was a revised version of the one Angelo Anelli had provided for Luigi Mosca's opera of the same name for Milan in 1808, though it is not clear who was responsible for the revision. Certainly Rossini himself must have had a hand in shaping it. It is interesting to note that, whereas previously Rossini had been paid 250 lire for a *farsa* at the Teatro San Moisè, for this new work, which was eventually described as a *dramma giocoso*, he was to receive 700 lire, though there was something of a crisis at the Teatro San Benedetto at the time, and he was in a strong position to dictate terms. In between, he had asked for 600 lire for *Tancredi* at the Fenice, had been made a counter-offer of 400, and had ended up with 500. If such bargaining seems somewhat undignified, one must bear in mind the fact that there was a long tradition of haggling over opera contracts, especially for the star performers. The size of the fee was important for the price it set on one's status as much as for what it represented in cash terms, and it was alleged that at times false contracts were agreed between singers and impresarios, fixing fees that were much higher than the ones paid in reality.

L'italiana in Algeri was particularly well received at its first performance on 22 May, though Marietta Marcolini, the first Isabella, fell ill and the second performance had to be postponed for a week or so. Rossini is said to have commented, after the first performance: 'I thought that after having heard my opera, the Venetians would treat me as a madman; they have shown themselves to be madder than me.'[6] Once again, it is the sort of remark which was probably made in all innocence, when he was in reality delighted, and at the same time relieved, at the reception of his music. It was taken, however, as yet another example of his vanity, self-satisfaction and contempt for the Venetian audiences. Had he said it of one of his later offerings, such as *Edoardo e Cristina*, the criticism would have been justified.

The Venice *Giornale* maintained that Rossini had written the opera in twenty-seven days, and the Venice correspondent of the *Allgemeine musikalische Zeitung* of Leipzig affirmed that the composer had told him that he had written it in eighteen days. Zanolini, whom Rossini himself is said to have commended as a reliable source for the earlier part of his career, asserted that when, as the opera became popular, Giuseppe Malerbi enquired of Padre Mattei what he now thought of his erstwhile pupil he received the answer: 'He has emptied his sack.'[7] Even so, Rossini had, by any standards, pulled off a remarkable double of a *melodramma eroico* and a *dramma giocoso* with *Tancredi* and *L'italiana* in such a short space of time. Nor was his sack empty yet, by any means.

L'italiana opens in the palace of the Bey of Algiers. A chorus of eunuchs (tenors and basses, somewhat inappropriately perhaps) bemoans the lot of women, and then the bey's wife, Elvira, with her confidante Zulma, informs the audience that her husband no longer loves her. Rossini's setting of 'Ah, comprendo, me infelice' is suit-

L' Italienne à Alger–

Annotated sketch for Elvira's costume for the first Paris production of *L'italiana in Algeri* (1817), the first Rossini opera to be heard in the French capital.

ably sobbing with its snatched rests and rising and falling intervals; but when her husband, the bey, arrives on stage he shows no sympathy, and replies with a suitably vigorous tirade against the arrogance of women: 'Delle donne l'arroganza'. To his wife's pleading he complains that his eardrums have burst, and a boisterous quartet, with the addition of Haly (=Ali), captain of the bey's corsairs, then ensues. At the end of it the bey tells Haly to go and find him an Italian wife.

It happens that the bey has in his service an Italian man, Lindoro, and in a charming *cavatina*, 'Languir per una bella', Lindoro sings of his loved one, from whom he is separated. When the bey asks Lindoro if he would like to marry, the latter answers that he would.

The scene changes and Isabella (the Italian girl of the title), who has been searching for her lost lover, Lindoro, is conveniently shipwrecked on the shores of Algeria, where she is discovered by Haly and his men, along with Taddeo, her elderly admirer. Isabella sings of the cruel fate, 'Cruda sorte', that has brought her, through her devotion to her loved one, into this situation – a Rossinian twist if ever there was one. Haly is particularly pleased to find that he has two Italians among his prisoners. With the woman, at least, he will be able to fulfil the bey's command.

In the duet 'Ai capricci della sorte' Isabella and Taddeo quarrel about their situation, but eventually agree to pose as niece and uncle. The vigorous rhythms, both here and in the *cabaletta* to 'Cruda sorte' previously, establish Isabella as a woman well able to take care of herself.

We return to the bey's palace, where Elvira and Zulma are attempting to persuade Lindoro to accept the bey's offer of freedom and money if he will marry Elvira and take her off his hands. Haly then arrives with the news that he has taken Isabella prisoner. The act is now brought to its close. At first the eunuchs sing of Mustafa the bey, 'the scourge of women, who changes them from tigresses into lambs', though when Isabella is brought on stage she is highly amused at the bey's appearance and is in no way intimidated. They have a duet, followed by a quartet with the addition of Taddeo and Haly, which in turn becomes a septet when Elvira, Zulma and Lindoro enter. Isabella and Lindoro recognise each other, though when Isabella discovers that Mustafa intends to dispose of Elvira in such a fashion she protests. With witty, scintillating orchestration Rossini creates a marvellous finale, using onomatopoeic words for each character – din-din, bum-bum, cra-cra, tac-tac – to increase the effect of total but carefully controlled chaos.

At the beginning of Act II the chorus of eunuchs observes how love has altered Mustafa. Isabella is unhappy at the prospect of Lindoro's marriage to Elvira, and tells him so. She is convinced, however, by his affirmation of undying love for herself, and they plan their escape. As the plot advances, the fantasy increases, though kept carefully under control – and, indeed, meticulously engineered – by Rossini, which is why Padre Mattei was of the opinion that he had squandered his talent on such an unworthy undertaking.

We now see Isabella in front of her glass as she finishes off her dressing 'alla turca'. She sings 'Per lui che adoro' about the one she loves, watched by Lindoro, Taddeo and Mustafa from behind, each one of whom thinks that the sentiments are intended for him. In a typical Rossini crescendo, the quintet which follows develops into pandemonium as Mustafa's frustration breaks into anger. As in all successful comedy, it is the fine line between reality and fantasy, tears and laughter that gives the work its appeal. Moreover Rossini has by now made his characters more probable, more human in fact, so that the interplay itself is an important factor contributing to the impetus and ultimate success of the opera.

Mustafa complains of the way Isabella is treating him, but Lindoro explains that she is only waiting for him to be received into the ancient Italian order of the Pappatacci. The nonsense name implies a complacent husband who is prepared to eat, drink and sleep. Mustafa is of course unaware of the implication, and readily agrees to be enrolled. The following trio is one of the delights of the opera, and was a hit from the outset. Haly has begun to be suspicious, however, and asks Zulma why Isabella gives the eunuchs so much to drink. She tells him that it is to help them enjoy the celebrations.

For Mustafa's admission into the order of the Pappatacci, Isabella gathers together all the Italians in the palace, with the intention of making good their escape during the ceremony. Her patriotic rondo 'Pensa all patria' was banned in Naples as being too inflammatory in the days when consciousness of Italian identity was a spur to liberation movements. Isabella has chartered a ship to return home, and even when she and Lindoro prepare to go on board Mustafa accepts this as part of the ceremony. Eventually, however, he is convinced of his mistake by Elvira, Zulma and Haly, and returns to his wife as his real love, declaring that Italians were only a fad in any case. Fundamentally, therefore, it is a very moral tale.

Giuseppe Radiciotti, Rossini's great biographer, commented: 'As with *Tancredi* in the field of *opera seria*, so with *L'italiana* in the field of *opera comica*, Rossini still had not completely acquired his own personality: here and there some trace of imitation is still evident.' Having cited examples of where he detected this imitation – from Mozart, Cimarosa, Pietro Generali and Pietro Carlo Guglielmi – Radiciotti continued: 'At least in part, then, we are still in the field of Neapolitan *opera buffa*, but on the verge of emerging from it shortly.'[8] At this stage in his career Rossini had not set foot in Naples, though there would have been performances elsewhere that he might have seen. In general, however, where the *buffa* tradition was as specialised in character as it was in Naples and Venice – in its earlier days, at least – and had a very local flavour it tended not to travel. In broader terms, however, Radiciotti's comment is apt in so far as *L'italiana* looks ahead to the peaks of *Il barbiere di Siviglia* (1816) and *La cenerentola* (1817).

L'italiana went on running in Venice through the month of June, after which it was taken to Vicenza, though without Rossini, for he appears to have gone back to Bologna to see his parents. Composition now proceeded at a rather less frantic pace than hitherto, with three operas completed between June 1813 and December 1814. By most standards, of course, this would have been a considerable achievement; but, as we have already seen, Rossini was capable of working with phenomenal speed. He was also capable of better writing, too, for there is a noticeable falling-off in musical quality after the two Venetian successes.

Of the two operas commissioned by La Scala, the first was a *dramma serio, Aureliano in Palmira*, written for the opening night of the Carnival season on 26 December 1813, though before that Rossini had to supervise the production of *Tancredi*, which had been chosen to open the new Teatro Rè in Milan during the Advent season. Because *Tancredi* had so recently been seen in the city, therefore, the critics were able to make direct comparisons between that and *Aureliano*, and the latter did not come off at all well, though such was Rossini's stock at the time that he was let off somewhat lightly by the writer in *Il giornale Italiano*:

> Rossini, in whom so many hopes reposed, slept on this occasion like good Father Homer, with the difference, however, that the Greek lyricist slept from time to time, whereas the Pesarese composer fell asleep for a long time. Joining the name of the young maestro to that of the sovereign poet, it was my intention to temper in part the bitterness of a truth that I could not hide, without betraying the calling of historian and critic. *Tancredi in Siracusa* is the most beautiful musical composition of our time; *Aureliano in Palmira*, as far as effect is concerned, is simply nothing like an opera by Rossini. The former ravishes and enchants me, the other tires and bores me; but what does it matter? Even if the sleep of Rossini were not that of Homer, it would be the sleep of the eagle; this noble mind, reinvigorated with new breath, will take off again, whenever it might be.

More succinctly, perhaps, the *Allgemeine musikalische Zeitung* declared: 'The music has many beauties; but one is aware of the want of inner vitality in it.' After a somewhat reserved initial reception the work was given fourteen times that season at La Scala, and Rossini received a fee of 800 francs (= lire) for it. Nor did it harm his reputation with the Milanesi, for he paid a return visit to the Teatro Rè for the first performance in Milan of *L'italiana in Algeri* on 12 April 1814.

Doubtless part of *Aureliano*'s initial lack of impact was its somewhat old-fashioned format – *castrato* and all. To a degree it was a backward step for Rossini in terms of what he had created for Venice. True, it had a chorus, which traditional *opera seria* would not have had, but it is a small one at that, and on the whole it seems to have been the size and scale of the work, which was simply not big enough for La Scala, which increased the impression of lack of vitality. It was almost as if Rossini had deliberately thought himself back into an earlier mode, and the face that he showed was very different from that of *La pietra del paragone* of 1812.

The plot centres on two historical figures – the Roman Emperor Lucius Domitius Aurelianus (*c.* AD 215–75) and Zenobia, Queen of Palmyra – and one fictitious character: Arsace, King of Persia (though the Arsacids provided the royal dynasty of Parthia). In the opera Aurelianus (tenor) offers Zenobia (soprano) both glory and love, but she finds Arsace more to her taste. The part of Arsace was written for the *castrato* Velluti, which gave Rossini more satisfaction in later years, it would seem, when he talked about the *castrato* voice and the fact that he had written for it. At the time, however, the work failed to arouse much enthusiasm, and one of the stories put about was that Rossini had been angered by Velluti's embellishment of his vocal lines. Rossini was to take issue with singers who behaved in this way, but there is no documentation for any quarrel with Velluti. *Aureliano* never achieved great popularity, let alone many performances outside Italy, but there is considerable charm in the music, and Rossini thought sufficiently highly of some of it to salvage it later – not least the overture, which came to rest, via *Elisabetta, regina d'Inghilterra,* in *Il barbiere di Siviglia.*

Rossini returned to La Scala on 14 August 1814 for the first performance of a new opera, *Il turco in Italia.* Although it was given twelve times, and Rossini's fee was again established at 800 francs, its initial reception was somewhat cool, and once again the proximity of another Rossini opera in the calendar – namely *L'italiana in Algeri,* which had preceded it – must have made unfavourable comparisons inevitable. On this occasion, however, they were ill-founded. As the writer in *Il giornale Italiano* put it: 'I examine, I think, I recognise, and I say in the ear of my neighbour, a very discreet man, "C'est du vin de son cru [in other words, 'the same old stuff']." "A new, uncorrected edition," he added, rather loudly.' Because of the similarity between the plots of *L'italiana* and *Il turco,* the audience convinced themselves that there was similarity in the music, too. Seven years later in Milan, Rossini was vindicated, for *Il turco* was heard during both the Carnival and spring seasons at the Teatro Lentasio, and also at the Teatro Carcano during the spring season.

The libretto, by Felice Romani, was taken from an existing one of the same title by Caterina Mazzolà that had already been set by Franz Seydelmann (1788) and Franz Süssmayr (1794). The opera opens on a beach near Naples, where the gypsy fortune-teller Zaida is relating her adventures to Prosdocimo, a dramatist or poet in search of characters for a comedy. Zaida was once a slave, beloved of a Turk, Selim Damelec, but was unjustly accused and condemned to death, only to be saved by the faithful Albazar, who took her into his gypsy tribe and brought her to Italy. The plot appeals to the poet, who promises to help Zaida by introducing her to a Turk who is even now on his way to Italy. In fact the Turk (who is, of course, none other than Selim) soon arrives. However, he falls in love with the first beautiful Italian woman he encounters, Donna Fiorilla, who is already married to the elderly Don Geronio, and has an admirer, Don Narciso, both of whom bore her. The duet between husband and wife, 'Per piacere alla Signora', shows Rossini at his best in comic realism. Fiorilla is set to depart with Selim, who is waiting for her on the beach, when Zaida arrives instead. He once more falls in love with her, to the satisfaction of the poet. Fiorilla now arrives on the scene, and the act concludes with a brilliant finale in which the mixture of emotions rises in a typical Rossini crescendo.

In Act II, Selim and Don Geronio meet, and in the course of a duet Selim asks the husband to sell him his wife. Fiorilla, however, proposes that Selim should first choose between herself and Zaida, but the latter declines to compete. A masked ball is to take place that evening, during the course of which Selim is to carry off Fiorilla. The poet informs Geronio and Narciso, and suggests that Zaida should dress as Fiorilla, and Geronio as Selim, at which point Narciso also decides to appear disguised as Selim. In an effervescent quintet, 'Ah! guardate che accidente! Non conosco più la mia moglie!', between Fiorilla, Zaida, Narciso, Geronio and Selim, the plot is worked out. Fiorilla's plan is unmasked, but all ends well. Selim returns to Turkey with Zaida, and Fiorilla decides to remain faithful to her husband. The poet has his resolution for his play, and Narciso is left with food for thought. The final statement of the moral, 'Restate contenti, felici vivete', is not by Rossini. Despite its initially cold reception, the opera eventually made its mark.

Whilst he was in Milan this year (1814), Rossini wrote a cantata, *Egle ed Irene*, dedicated to Principessa Belgiojoso, for soprano, mezzo-soprano and piano, most noteworthy, perhaps, because of the final section which Rossini took for the trio for Rosina, Count Almaviva and Figaro in Act II of *Il barbiere di Siviglia* two years later.[9] The composer then left for Venice, to fulfil another commission for La Fenice. The next opera was a *dramma* or *opera seria* entitled *Sigismondo*, for which the composer was to receive 600 lire. The libretto was by Giuseppe Foppa, with whom Rossini had already worked on three operas – *L'inganno felice*, *La scala di seta* and *Il signor Bruschino* – which were all one-act *farse*. However, one cannot lay the blame for *Sigismondo* solely on Foppa's libretto.

Despite Marcolini in the cast, the work was a failure, though it was politely received by the Venetians at its first performance on 26

Teatro alla Scala, Milan, as depicted by Angelo Inganni (1807–80). The previous theatre on the site, Teatro Ducale, had burned down in 1776, and the architect of the new building, Giuseppe Piermarini (1734–1808), had to produce no less than five versions of the façade before he was able to satisfy the owners of the boxes, who insisted on the addition of the classical pediment and – what was much more of an innovation at the time – the *porte cochère* to allow patrons to alight from their carriages under cover. This is the exterior which is still largely preserved today, and which Rossini would have known when his *La pietra del paragone* was acclaimed there in September 1812.

Felice Romani (1788–1865), one of the most celebrated and prolific librettists of his day. For Rossini he provided *Il turco in Italia*, first heard at La Scala on 14 August 1814, which was adapted from an existing libretto by Caterina Mazzolà that had already been set by Franz Seydelmann (1788) and Franz Süssmayr (1794).

December 1814, when it opened the Carnival season. Even Rossini himself realised that the work was not up to standard, and when some of his friends politely applauded he said to them: 'Whistle, whistle.' The *Nuovo osservatore Veneto* described the libretto as 'the unfortunate offspring of a writer who now offers the hundredth proof of his incompetence', but Rossini knew that he must bear the blame for the failure. When he wrote to his mother about it he is said to have drawn a flask (*fiasco*) on the outside of the letter. There were some redeeming features in the music, which Rossini, characteristically, salvaged later, but there is at the same time a certain impression of boredom, of lassitude, as if Rossini needed stimulus, over and above that of a good libretto, to inspire him to new achievements. The Venetian triumph seemed to have evaporated. Happily, that badly needed inspiration was soon to come, from a centre of musical excellence, and of opera especially, for which Rossini had not hitherto composed: Naples.

After the débâcle of *Sigismondo*, Rossini returned to Bologna, where he gave music lessons to a niece of Napoleon, the daughter of Elisa Bacchiocchi, lover of Paganini and former Grand Duchess of Tuscany. Then, on 5 April 1815, Joachim Murat, Napoleon's brother-in-law, and since 1808 *de facto* King of Naples, issued a proclamation in Rimini in which he declared Italian independence from Austria. This inspired an uprising in Bologna, and Rossini set to music the *Inno dell'indipendenza*, 'Sorgi, Italia, venuta è già l'ora'. The words were by his old literature teacher Giambattista Giusti. Murat was present in the Teatro Contavalli in Bologna when the work was heard for the first time on 15 April; but the euphoria of the previous ten days soon evaporated, for the Austrians returned to Bologna the very next day, and it seemed as if independence was to remain nothing but a dream.

Louis Hérold, who was to compose *Zampa* and *Le Pré aux clercs*, was in Bologna from 12 to 24 April 1815 and met Rossini, whom he described as 'a young composer who at that time was making a dickens of a reputation for himself in Italy'. With the return of the Austrians, however, things could have been very difficult for Rossini, and there were rumours about an abrupt volte-face on his part, and capitulation to the Austrian camp. Although at first he denied it hotly, he later claimed that he was in any case in Naples by then. Clearly he was not, for not only did Hérold meet him, but in mid-May Rossini also wrote to the Venetian librettist Luigi Prividali, who had provided the libretto for *L'occasione fa il ladro* (1812), about a possible oratorio commission. This seems to have come to nothing; but in the same letter Rossini indicated what was to be for him one of the most momentous turning-points in his career: 'I shall leave the day after tomorrow for Naples.'

CHAPTER FOUR

The Lure of the South: Naples and Rome

The Naples to which Rossini made his way in 1815 had not been isolated from the stirring events which had so affected the rest of the peninsula, though on the surface, at least, all had now been restored to what it had been before the war. After more than two hundred years of existence as a province of Spain and Austria, Naples had become an independent kingdom under Charles of Bourbon in 1734, thanks to the efforts of his Italian-born mother, Elisabeth Farnese, second wife of Philip V of Spain. On the death of his half-brother, Ferdinand VI of Spain, in 1759, Charles returned to become King of Spain, where his mother was still alive to welcome him (born in 1692, she lived until 1766). Ferdinand's son now became King Ferdinand IV of Naples, which he ruled until his death in 1825, apart from two periods, the first in 1799, when the Parthenopean Republic was set up by the invading French, and a somewhat longer one between 1806 and 1815, when Napoleon installed first his brother Joseph as King of Naples, and then in 1808 his brother-in-law Joachim Murat, when Joseph Bonaparte was made King of Spain.

On the day that Rossini had decided to set out from Bologna for Naples, 17 May 1815, King Ferdinand left Sicily (he was also ruler of that island, and later the title became King of the Two Sicilies), where he had taken refuge during the French occupation of Naples, and on 7 June landed at Portici, the port of the ancient city of Herculaneum, along the bay to the south of Naples itself. His first wife, Maria Carolina, had died in 1814, whereupon he married his mistress Lucia, Duchess of Floridia. She did not arrive from Sicily until 24 June, so that when he entered his box at the Teatro San Carlo on 19 June he did not have the support of a wife. He was moved to tears by the reception he received, and the applause and cheering lasted for half an hour. His bust was shown on stage in the midst of the banners of the allied powers; and it was this moment, more than anything else, that set the seal on his return.[1] It is significant that it should have taken place in the opera house. The king was described by Sir William Hamilton as, 'without exception, the most educated sovereign in Europe'. After the giddy carousel of the Napoleonic adventure, things were back to normal in Naples, with opera restored to its rightful pre-eminence.

Neapolitans regarded their city as the operatic – and that meant, in their eyes, the musical – centre of Italy and, by extension, of Europe itself. The city boasted no less than three houses at this time: San Carlo, the Fondo (later known as the Mercadante) and the Nuovo. In addition, opera was given at the Teatro dei Fiorentini until 1820, and sometimes at the San Carlino until 1849. It was of course San Carlo which was, and remains, one of the great opera houses of the world, and it was the impresario of the theatre, Barbaia, who decided that Rossini would enhance the musical life of the city, as well as boosting the profits. Unfortunately we do not know how, or even when, contact was established between the two men. Presumably Barbaia wrote a letter which was subsequently lost, or sent an intermediary to Bologna during the first half of 1815, and it is just possible that Rossini had already made a preliminary visit to Naples in late April or early May, though if he did it is surprising that there was no reference to it in later years, particularly in view of the part that Barbaia had played in shaping this next, most crucial phase of Rossini's career.

Domenico Barbaia (1778–1841) was born into a poor family in Milan, and started his working life as a waiter. As Giuseppe Rovani wrote in *Cento anni*: '. . . driven by his genius . . . he discovered the lofty secret of mixing whipped cream with coffee and chocolate, hence the immortal word *barbajata*, which raised him a monument more solid than granite.' Of course, fortunes have been made out of such benign items as patent beverages, and it would have been appropriate that such a fortune should be applied – at least in part – to encouraging the arts, and opera in particular. The truth, however, was somewhat different in Barbaia's case. He may well have made the beginnings of his fortune from *barbajata*, but the real wealth came from gambling. As Rovani went on: 'This man, then, except for his special knowledge concerning cocoa and mocha, was of a legendary ignorance; but he had a genius for making money, without paying attention to the means, and with no idea of honesty.'

It may seem somewhat surprising that opera and gambling should be thus closely allied, but it had been so almost from the start in Venice, where the authorities were always mulling over the problem. It was not until 1774 that they finally closed down what had been the original casino of the *ridotto* at San Moisè. Because opera houses had been the social centres in Venice and other Italian cities as the art form became more popular, so the patrons took there all things necessary for their enjoyment – and that included gambling. Hence the generous amount of space allocated for such activities in relation to stage and auditorium if one looks at the ground plans of almost any of the opera houses at this time. There was a great deal of money to be made, and monopolies were often granted to the impresarios who organised opera seasons in any given theatre. Although the tendency was gradually to abolish these monopolies during the course of the eighteenth century, they were reintroduced from 1802 onwards by the new Napoleonic states in Italy as a means of raising money to finance themselves. Milan and Naples in particular offered opportunities for the impresario prepared to exploit the gambling 'facility' offered by the theatre, and it is significant that those were the two cities where Barbaia first operated.

Nor should it come as any surprise that building contracting followed in the wake of such activity – with remarkable results in the case of Barbaia in Naples. He had a nose for money-making opportunities. When the roulette wheel, a French invention, appeared in Italy, it was Barbaia who introduced it to La Scala in the Carnival season of 1805. Initially he had subcontracted from the titular impresario of the theatre, Francesco Benedetto Ricci, who had failed to appreciate the potential of the new device, and within a year Barbaia had money and property. He also joined forces with another impresario, Carlo Balochino, who had been excluded from La Scala when the gambling started up in 1802, but had then organised it in a house used by Joachim Murat, Napoleon's brother-in-law and, as we have already seen, a future King of Naples. Murat himself was at this stage attempting to set up a gambling operation. In 1807, Balochino went on to become impresario of the Teatro La Fenice in Venice, whereas in 1809 Barbaia took over the Teatro San Carlo and other royal theatres in Naples.

Out of this dubious activity, however, came artistic benefits, and at both La Scala and San Carlo audiences were offered productions which might otherwise have been financially impossible. Nor was Barbaia's flair entirely commercial. As Rovani put it: 'In his position as impresario . . . he was an inexorable usurer of composers, singers and dancers. In this way he sniffed the scent of true merit, like a fox that, when still a long way off, raises its muzzle in the air, and catches the scent of the chicken.' Or, as Rossini himself commented on his agreement with Barbaia to go to Naples in the first place, the impresario would also have put the composer in charge of the kitchen had he been able.

In the La Scala Museum in Milan there is a striking anonymous portrait of Barbaia painted after he had left Naples and taken over La Scala itself, therefore some ten or fifteen years after Rossini first worked with him. In the background, to the right of the picture, are three figures – Bellini and Pasta behind, Rossini in front; together they occupy almost the same area of the canvas as Barbaia's head. Admittedly only their busts are shown, whereas Barbaia is a three-quarter-length standing figure; nevertheless the proportion says a great deal about the fundamental role played by the impresario in the careers of these three artists, and many more besides. A list of composers includes Carafa, Mercadante, Weber, Pacini, Donizetti, Bellini and of course Rossini himself. Barbaia's taste was by no means entirely for the modern and Italian. He brought the operas of Gluck and Spontini (by then settled in Paris, and almost a French composer) to Naples; and of course he engaged the best singers of the day, such as Pasta, David, Garcia, Nozzari, Donzelli and Benedetti. To this list must be added Isabella Colbran, who became his mistress, and afterwards Rossini's first wife, in a sequence whose very ease and facility is of the essence of the operatic milieu down to the present time.

Rossini had had the opportunity to see and hear, and possibly even meet, Colbran in Bologna in April 1807, from where she went on to make her début at La Scala in 1808. The following year she returned to sing in Bologna, at the Teatro Comunale, as well as in Venice that year, and in Rome in 1810. She made her début at the San Carlo on 15 August 1811, as Giulia in Spontini's *La vestale*. She had a vocal range of almost three octaves, from soprano bottom G (below middle C) to top E, and the sort of words used by the Bologna newspaper *Il redattore del reno* to describe her voice at her first appearance there in 1807 were 'smoothness, strength, evenness, mellowness, energy'. Her stage presence, too, was worthy of note, and from Stendhal's description quoted earlier she was clearly much more impressive on stage than off. Vocally, however, she could do little right in Stendhal's opinion, to the point where one feels that she simply could not have made an international career if she had been that bad, even if her vocal powers clearly did decline latterly. This was, after all, the soprano for whom Rossini wrote ten of his eighteen operas composed between *Elisabetta, regina d'Inghilterra* (1815) and *Semiramide* (1823) – in other words, between his arrival in Naples and his last Italian opera, written for Venice.

Rossini's contract with Barbaia has been the subject of some exaggeration. He himself told Hiller that it was worth some 8,000 francs, whereas Stendhal said that it was worth 12,000, some of which probably came from gambling. What is certain is that it came into effect in the autumn of 1815, that Rossini was to be responsible for the music at both the San Carlo and Fondo theatres, and compose two operas a year for Naples. However, Rossini was to be permitted to take unpaid leave so as to undertake engagements elsewhere.

The composer's arrival in Naples was not hailed there as the most exciting event to have taken place in the operatic world for years. On the contrary, there was a perceptible lack of enthusiasm in the report in the *Giornale del Regno delle Due Sicilie* on 25 September: 'A certain Signor Rossini, *maestro di cappella*, who has arrived, it is said, to give an *Elisabetta, regina d'Inghilterra* on the stage of the Teatro San Carlo. . . .' Readers were left in no doubt that Mayr's *Medea* and *Cora*, recently heard there, would be used as yardsticks by which to judge Rossini's offering.[2]

In the event he chose wisely for his début in Naples. The average opera-goer knew little of his work hitherto, so that he was able to incorporate some of his earlier music, whilst simultaneously providing a suitable vehicle for Colbran. Nor must one underestimate the appropriateness of the subject-matter. This was the year of Waterloo, and things English were in fashion. There had, of course, been a strong English presence in Naples for some time, which the Napoleonic interval had done nothing to attenuate. *Elisabetta* had its first performance when it opened the season at the Teatro San Carlo on 4 October 1815, and later that month *L'italiana in Algeri* opened at the Teatro dei Fiorentini, though minus 'Pensa alla patria', which was regarded as potentially too sensational.

Barbaia was justified in his decision to bring Rossini to Naples, in the event, and the king is said to have liked his first opera so much that he told Zingarelli, the Director of San Sebastiano, the Royal

School of Music, to withdraw his ban on allowing students to study Rossini scores.[3]

The libretto for *Elisabetta* was by Giovanni Federico Schmidt, taken from a play by Carlo Federici of 1814 based on the English novel by Sophia Lee (1783–5) entitled *The Recess*. The plot turns on the relationship between Elizabeth I and the Earl of Leicester, her favourite, who has secretly married – a fact which he unwisely confides in the Duke of Norfolk. Leicester returns victorious from wars in Scotland, bringing with him some of the sons of the nobility as hostages. To his surprise his wife Matilde is amongst them, disguised as a boy, and her own brother Enrico (Henry) is also one of the hostages. Both are children of Mary, Queen of Scots. Elizabeth takes all the hostages into her service as pages but, informed of Leicester's marriage by Norfolk, she calls the former's bluff by offering to make him her consort. She has recognised his wife by her uneasy manner. The first act ends with a stirring finale.

At the beginning of the second act the queen sends for Matilde and requires her to sign a document renouncing any claim upon her husband, in return for which she will obtain the safety of both her husband and her brother. Leicester appears and defies the queen, tearing up the document. The married pair are taken away, under arrest, but the queen, realising Norfolk's treachery, orders him to be banished. Outside the Tower of London, Norfolk attempts to stir the crowd to revolt, but they are more concerned about the fate of Leicester.

Norfolk comes to the dungeon in the Tower where Leicester is imprisoned, and promises to bring help. As the queen arrives to visit Leicester before his execution, Norfolk hides. By this time Matilde and Enrico have already found their way into the dungeon. Leicester now learns that it was Norfolk who betrayed him, and the queen herself now realises the full extent of Norfolk's treachery. The latter draws a dagger to stab the queen, but Matilde interposes herself. In the ensuing finale the queen condemns Norfolk to death, but frees Matilde and Leicester in gratitude. The queen shows the latter to the crowd outside, since they have been begging for his life from the queen, and they now acclaim her.

Despite the liberties taken with historical truth, the libretto set out for Rossini a series of basic human situations clearly and simply, giving him the opportunity to express the resulting emotions with a directness that signalled for the first audiences that a change had come over *opera seria*. It had, in a way, suddenly sprung to life as far as Neapolitan audiences were concerned. Yet Rossini had no desire to overturn convention simply for the sake of doing so. His approach was rather to use the means at his disposal – singers, orchestra, libretto and the forms of *opera seria* – at that time. He was, after all, still only twenty-three. *Elisabetta* marks the second stage in the series of *opere serie* spanning the decade from 1813 to 1823 that began with *Tancredi* and was to end with *Semiramide*.

The overture was written for *Aureliano in Palmira* (1813), and was subsequently to serve for *Il barbiere di Siviglia*. As to the opera in general, it already looks forward to *grand opéra* in the style of Meyerbeer. It seems strange, therefore, that it should soon have been disregarded and dismembered by Rossini himself, for it contains much fine music and testifies to Rossini's developing theatrical sense. It reached Milan in the summer of 1817 (Carcano), was played again in the spring of 1825 (Rè), and in the 1828 Carnival season had no less than thirty-one performances at La Scala. Within a decade, however, its popularity had waned to the point where the composer himself, writing to Bandini, impresario of the Pergola Theatre in Florence, on 18 August 1838 about the staging of *Elisabetta*, had this to say:

> Just a line to thank you for all the kind things that you said to me in your most esteemed letter. I am unable to give you any information about *Elisabetta*, since any recollection of the costumes, scenery, etc., has been erased from my mind. Such operas ought to be left in peace. Give modern music to the public, who are so fond of novelty, and do not forget the old-fashioned composer, and your friend. . . .

At the time of composition of *Elisabetta*, Rossini had been relatively free from what by now had become the usual pressures he worked under, and was certainly able to lavish more care on the instrumentation, for example; and in the role of Elizabeth herself he created a splendid part for Isabella Colbran. With this his first opera for Naples, he also sought to win over the regular audience of the San Carlo. It would have been unwise, therefore, to offer anything too original, and there is much that is faithful to the conventions of the day – the happy ending, for example. The opera also has its *longueurs* and imbalances. Even so, it marks the decisive emergence of

Rossini's individual dramatic voice, which would expand and develop with succeeding operas.

That Rossini was perfectly capable of using existing material in enhancing ways, and ways that are totally consistent with, and indeed part of, his developing dramatic sense, may be seen in Leicester's prison scene in Act II. There is an orchestral introduction by way of a prelude, taken from *Ciro in Babilonia* (1812), leading into the recitative 'Della cieca fortuna', then an *andante*, where the melodic interest is entirely in the orchestra, while the monologue 'Sposa amata' unfolds over it. Then comes an *andantino arioso*, 'Fallace fu il contento', and finally an aria, 'Saziati sorte ingrata'. The sequence represents an extraordinary, even avant-garde, development of, and flexibility in handling, traditional components, with the orchestra playing its part to the full in reflecting the meaning of the words and the evolution of the state of mind of the character.

One particularly important point of development is the abandonment of *secco* recitative throughout the opera; for, although Gluck had made considerable advances both in the use of accompanied recitative and in the use of the chorus, by and large his reforms had made little impact in Italy. By using accompanied recitative Rossini conferred on it a much greater role in Italian opera on Italian soil than it had enjoyed hitherto – certainly throughout the previous century – in enhancing the overall dramatic action, not only in the Leicester passage just mentioned, but also in the scene in Act I in which Norfolk reveals to the queen that Leicester has married Matilde. The chorus, too, was given a much more important part to play, and a more effective one dramatically. In the average *opera seria* there was no chorus at all, but where it was used its role was minimal. Rossini increasingly developed its dramatic and musical potential. At the end of Act I, for example, the chorus, as the Court of Elizabeth, adds dramatic and musical dimension to the finale by throwing the plight of the main characters into prominence, and the soldiers have a substantial chorus in Act II, mostly accompanied by strings with brass intervention, as they enter the courtyard of the Tower where Leicester is imprisoned.

From the purely vocal point of view, Rossini – for the first time – kept under his control the florid ornamentation required by contemporary fashion by writing it out himself, rather than allowing the singers to introduce their own, as was customary. In this way he at least ensured stylistic consistency, which is evident, for example, in the duet between Leicester and Matilde, 'Incauta che festi'. In the wider context, this duet is important for the way in which Rossini conveys the mixture of surprise and fear, as well as the mutual love of husband and wife, against the anxiety and unease of the situation, reflected in the orchestral writing. It is marked 'Allegro agitato', and Rossini's subtle use of chromaticism heightens the effect, anticipating Bellini or Verdi. There follows a recitative, then Matilde's aria 'Sento un interna voce', the first section of which is one of the most lyrically inspired passages in the whole of the opera. Possibly the most remarkable aspect of it, seen in the context of its time, is the virtual independence of the vocal line from the accompaniment, and indeed the vocal line itself, with its flattened intervals which enhance the pathos. It is a pity that the second section then indulges in vocal acrobatics, thereby mitigating the effect created.

Despite its inequalities, *Elisabetta* was in a sense ahead of its time. It reveals the twenty-three-year-old Rossini in confident control, playing a decisive part in the creation of music drama: one could even argue that after it opera would never be quite the same again. But, as always with Rossini, practical considerations were never far away. The choice of tenors for both Leicester and Norfolk, when a bass or baritone would have seemed preferable for the latter, was called into question. Rossini's response, according to Stendhal, was pithy and to the point: 'I happened to have two tenors at my disposal, whereas I had no bass to play Norfolk.'[4]

It is Stendhal who gives us the flavour of that first performance in Naples, and the effectiveness of Colbran in the title role. She was every inch the queen herself, and the overall effect and impression created by the opera was 'prodigious'. Despite the borrowings, he found it original and fresh. Rossini had been fairly successful, therefore, when choosing his ground for his Neapolitan début, as he was to exercise care, and achieve comparable success, when making his début as a composer of 'French' operas in Paris.

Rossini quickly took advantage of the terms of his contract with Barbaia, for within a month or so of the opening of *Elisabetta* he was in Rome, at the beginning of November 1815, where he had been engaged by the impresarios of the Teatro Valle, Pietro Cartoni and Vincenzo de Santis, for the staging of *Il turco in Italia* and the composition of a new *dramma semiserio*, *Torvaldo e Dorliska*, which opened the Carnival season on 26 December. The librettist was Cesare Sterbini (1784–1831), who was to be the common denominator between this, one of Rossini's least successful operas, and *Il barbiere di Siviglia*, in the opinion of many people his best. *Torvaldo* was not a success, and the composer is said to have drawn another *fiasco* on a letter to his mother, though admittedly a somewhat smaller one than that for *Sigismondo* the previous year, according to Geltrude Righetti-Giorgi. The opera is, of course, overshadowed by its successor, and to some extent the lack of success of the first opera may be attributed to the protracted negotiations required for the second, though it is highly likely that most of the work of composition had in fact been completed on *Torvaldo* – apart, perhaps, from adjustments made during rehearsal – well before Rossini committed himself to *Il barbiere*. A more likely factor was Sterbini's libretto, which offered little scope for drama until the second act.

Torvaldo e Dorliska has a rescue plot, and concerns the designs of the Duke of Ordow on Dorliska, the wife of Torvaldo. Before the opera begins, the duke has ambushed the pair, but Dorliska has escaped, and Torvaldo is left for dead. As fate would have it, Dorliska has taken refuge in the nearest dwelling, which happens to be the duke's castle. Torvaldo revives and disguises himself, and goes to the castle with a letter which, he says, was given him by a dying knight to give to Dorliska. She immediately recognises her husband, and in her surprise betrays his identity to the duke, and so the first act ends.

The rescue takes place in the second act, thanks largely to the duke's steward, Giorgio, a *buffo* role which was still unusual in *opera seria* at this time. However, Rossini reverted to *secco* recitative, and the orchestration is much less interesting than what had become his usual standard by now. Oddly, perhaps, he provided a new overture for *Torvaldo*, rather than press an existing one into service. The new overture was unable to save the opera, however. The Rome *Notizie del giorno* for 18 January 1816 stated quite categorically that the opera had not lived up to expectation: 'It ought to be said that the subject of the very gloomy and uninteresting libretto has not awakened Homer from his sleep; for that reason only the introduction and start of the trio identified the famous composer of *Tancredi*, *La pietra del paragone*, etc.' Rossini salvaged some of the music subsequently for *Otello*, though when it was heard in Milan in 1818 critics detected echoes not only of *Otello*, but also of *La cenerentola* and *L'inganno felice*, whereas only the last-named had actually preceded *Torvaldo e Dorliska*.

Fortunately the failure of one opera did not bring Rossini to a standstill, and it may well have been the sheer pressure to produce another which spurred him into such fruitful activity. On 15 December – eleven days before the opening night of *Torvaldo* at Teatro Valle, Rossini signed a contract with Duca Francesco Sforza-Cesarini, owner and impresario of the Teatro di Torre Argentina in Rome, for an opera to be composed 'on that libretto, whether new or old, that will be given him by the above named . . . [lord duke, impresario]'. Rossini was under the obligation to hand over the score by the middle of January, and to carry out, if need be, 'all those changes that will be thought necessary both for the good success of the music and the convenience of the singers'.

Rossini had, therefore, one month for the composition and orchestration of an entire two-act opera, the subject of which – let alone the libretto – was undecided at the time the contract was signed. Moreover, Rossini was involved, as we know, until 26 December with preparations for *Torvaldo* at the Teatro Valle. In all, therefore, he would have had about twenty days at his disposal, and estimates as to the actual time he took to compose *Il barbiere* vary from twelve or thirteen to nineteen or twenty. The contract went on:

> Maestro Rossini will, moreover, be obliged to conduct his opera according to custom, and to be present in person at all the vocal and orchestral rehearsals, every time this is necessary, and also undertakes to be present at the first performances given consecutively, and to direct the performances from the keyboard, etc., because it must be thus, and no other. In recompense for his labours, Duke Sforza-Cesarini undertakes to pay him the sum of 400 Roman scudi [the *prima donna* was to have 500 for each performance], once the first three performances have taken place, which he will direct from the keyboard . . . in addition the impresario will provide lodging for maestro Rossini for the time of the duration of the contract.

None of these conditions was particularly unusual, but it is of considerable interest as a document in its own right because it relates to such an important opera and has survived intact.

Rossini agreed to the conditions and signed the contract, but neither the duke nor, one assumes, Rossini liked the libretto provided by the first choice of librettist, Jacopo Ferretti (1784–1852), doubtless chosen because he was much in fashion at the time. Rossini and

Ferretti were to work together later on *La cenerentola* and *Matilde di Shabran*. It was said that it was Rossini himself who then suggested the idea of *Il barbiere*, since Paisiello's setting of the same tale had been composed ten years before Rossini's birth, and he may well have had it in mind as an opera for himself one day. Eventually Sterbini was prevailed upon to provide the new libretto, for which he went back to the original Beaumarchais play, *Le Barbier de Séville* (1775), as well as Petrosellini's libretto for Paisiello's opera (St Petersburg, 1782).

To avoid potentially invidious comparisons with Paisiello's still popular and revered setting, the alternative title of *Almaviva, ossia L'inutile precauzione* was initially chosen. Rossini later (in 1860) said that he had written to Paisiello at the time (Rossini was still not yet twenty-four years old, it must be remembered) and begged forgiveness for setting the same subject, and that the older composer readily accorded it. Neither letter has survived. What we do have, however, is the 'Notice to the Public' on the printed libretto, which points out that the title had been changed out of 'feelings of respect and veneration which motivate the composer of the present opera towards the very famous Paisiello, who has already set this subject to music under its original title'.[5] Had it been left there, Paisiello's supporters (he was to die in June 1816) might have accepted the situation, but the text ran on:

> Called to take on the very same difficult task, signor maestro Gioacchino Rossini, so as not to incur the bad reputation of a foolhardy rivalry with the immortal composer who has preceded him, has specifically asked that *Il barbiere de Siviglia* should be entirely reversified, and that there should be added to it several new situations of musical pieces which were, moreover, called for by modern theatrical taste, so greatly changed from the period in which the famous Paisiello wrote his music. Another difference between the plot of the present drama and that of the French play mentioned above was caused by the necessity to introduce into the same subject choruses, either because required by modern usage, or because indispensable to the musical effect in a theatre of considerable size. From this the kind public will therefore understand and exonerate the author of the new drama, who, without the existence of such weighty circumstances, would not have dared introduce the slightest change into the French

work, already given the accolade by the applause of all the theatres of Europe.

Although Sterbini would have ostensibly written the foregoing, there can be little doubt that Rossini would have had a large part in its composition.

We may also assume that it was under Rossini's influence, if not his actual direction, that the libretto derived so much more vitality from the original Beaumarchais play than Petrosellini had for Paisiello. There are plenty of cues for music in the original play, and frequently the diction – as, for example, in the heaping-up of adjectives by Figaro to describe Bartolo – almost cries out to be set to music. On the other hand, Sterbini and Rossini deliberately moved away from Beaumarchais at certain points, and for different reasons. One is the creation of Rosina's governess, Berta, in place of Bartolo's two male servants, the old man by name of Youth, and the sleepy young simpleton called Wideawake, who have a marvellous trio with Bartolo in Paisiello's version. Rossini was clearly anxious to avoid too many potential points of comparison with his predecessor.

There is a more fundamental move away from Beaumarchais in the conception of the role of Figaro. Gone are the reflections on the deeper issues that made the originals of both *Il barbiere di Siviglia* and *Le nozze di Figaro* such controversial social and political plays. Figaro becomes much more a character in the *buffo* tradition, with recognisable roots in the *commedia dell'arte*, and although in the process he loses his Beaumarchais conception he gains in musical and dramatic terms, for Rossini is able to portray him in broader, if less subtle, strokes. It certainly gives Figaro a dynamism, shared by all the characters. Their motivation is straightforward, and they are perceived as 'real' people. What gives *Il barbiere de Siviglia* its impact at Rossini's hands is the fact that the characters pursue their aims clearly and with determination. This is not to imply that they are devoid of subtlety, by any means, or that Rossini does not deploy a wide array of musical effects to achieve his end. Quite the contrary.

Reference has already been made to some of Rossini's self-borrowing in *Il barbiere* – notably in connection with 'Una voce poco fa' and the section from *Elisabetta*. There are more of these, but they are mostly fragments, and in no way would indicate large-scale liftings of entire arias. The speed of completion makes the opera all the more remarkable, and gives it more cohesion in the spirit of its conception and composition.

Then there is the matter of the lost overture, and what was originally intended by Rossini for Rosina to sing during the singing lesson. When Léon Escudier wished to publish the opera in Paris, he approached Rossini there, who then wrote to Domenico Liverani in Italy to ask him to try to find the missing music in Bologna. Liverani was unable to produce it, though the manuscript is now in the *conservatorio* in that city. As ever, Rossini was philosophical about the fact that the music seemed lost for ever and, in thanking Liverani for his pains in a letter of 12 June 1866, Rossini was content to accept that Fate had decided that it was to be thus. Some have assumed that Rossini wrote an overture on Spanish themes provided by Garcia; but, if this had as little success as Garcia's own serenade on the first evening in Rome, Rossini may well have decided that oblivion was a better fate for it, and that the *Aureliano/Elisabetta* overture was as good as anything.

As to the singing-lesson music, the libretto states: 'Rosina sings an air, *ad libitum*, for the occasion.' It may well have been Righetti-Giorgi herself who chose 'La biondina in gondoletta', which was often used by Italian *prime donne* in the early days, though later 'Di tanti palpiti' from *Tancredi* was inserted. Later exponents seemed to forget that it was a lesson, after all, and turned it into an additional 'turn' for the benefit of the audience – and the singer, too, no doubt.

What is certain about the opera is that it usually made a dazzling impression when it was first heard. Rossini's youthful spirits positively explode from the music, and the work dashes along. It was this that seems to have struck most people who heard it for the first time – like Hegel in 1824, for example, in Vienna – and it never lost its appeal throughout the century, though in Paris its reception was at first mixed. Perhaps one might leave the last word to Verdi, writing in 1898 to Camille Bellaigue, who affirmed that *Il barbiere di Siviglia* was, in his opinion, for the abundance of its ideas, its comic verve and the truth of its declamation, the most beautiful *opera buffa* in existence.[6] It is all the more surprising, therefore, and somewhat ironic, that this reception of *Il barbiere* into the sacred canon of opera took place when Rossini's reputation was in decline.

The original choice for the part of Rosina was Elisabetta Gafforini, but Duca Sforza-Cesarini decided that she was too expensive, so turned instead to Geltrude Righetti-Giorgi, a contralto who had been recommended to the impresario previously, having made her Rome début in 1814. Her memoirs, though not entirely reliable – for example she categorically denied that Rossini had written to Paisiello – provide us with a vivid account of the first night of *Il barbiere* and the events before and after it.[7]

Almaviva was taken by Manuel Garcia, and Figaro by Luigi Zamboni (?1767–1837) whom Rossini had known previously in Bologna. He had made his début in 1791 and became a highly regarded *buffo cantante*. Bartolo was Bartolommeo Botticelli, who does not seem to have been especially well thought of, though the Basilio, Zenobio Vitarelli, was a singer in the Sistine Chapel who went on to create the role of Alidoro in *La cenerentola*. He was also supposed to be a *jettatore*, a possessor of the evil eye. Berta was taken by Elisabetta Loyselet, and Fiorello by Paolo Biagelli – neither of whom was regarded with any degree of admiration at the time.

The first night was, for a variety of reasons, a disaster. We have mentioned the Paisiello supporters' claque, and it is clear from contemporary references that the ploy of having given the work a different title simply had not worked. It seems to have been referred to as *Il barbiere di Siviglia* right from the start. Conte Cesare Gallo noted in his diary on 20 February 1816: 'A new opera by Rossini entitled *Il barbiere di Siviglia* whistled at the Argentina'; and Principe Agostino Chigi-Albani noted in his diary on 21 February: 'Yesterday evening a new *burletta* entitled *Il barbiere di Siviglia* by Maestro Rossini went on to the stage at the Argentina – an unhappy event.'

Things got off to a bad start when Garcia came on stage with a guitar to accompany himself in the serenade under Rosina's balcony, and proceeded to tune it. Geltrude Righetti-Giorgi maintained that Rossini had allowed him, out of respect for his talent, to compose his own serenade, which he did, based on Spanish love-songs. Righetti-Giorgi said that she was 'ready for anything' when she went up the steps behind the scenery to appear on her balcony. The audience, however, were not ready for the fact that she did not launch into an entrance aria, but merely had the words: 'Segui, o caro, deh segui così' ('Carry on, dear, carry on like that'). She knew then that things would go from bad to worse, and 'Largo al factotum' and the duet between Figaro and the count were simply drowned in whistles and shouts. She maintained that she received bursts of applause after 'Una voce poco fa', but that was only a brief respite in the general catastrophic chain of events.

From Azevedo's account, Rossini's initial appearance in a Spanish-type jacket, hazel-coloured with gold buttons, to direct from the keyboard had been a source of amazement before a note of music had even been played or sung.[8] Then, when Vitarelli came on as Basilio, he tripped on a trapdoor and cut his face badly, and almost broke his nose. He was in no condition to sing the aria 'La calunnia', nor was the audience in any condition to give it a hearing. In Azevedo's account the final blow came when a cat wandered on to the stage in the finale. Zamboni (Figaro) chased it off, but it then reappeared from the opposite side and threw itself at Botticelli (Bartolo). Elisabetta Loyselet (Berta), in an attempt to avoid the animal, began jumping about the stage, whilst the audience cheered it on and assisted with miaowing.

Righetti-Giorgi recorded that when they had reached the words 'Quest' avventura' someone shouted from the audience, 'Here they are at the funeral of D[uke] C[esarini]', who had died on 6 February after attending a rehearsal of the opera that morning. That was just about the last straw. Rossini sat, impassive, at the keyboard, as if he were saying: 'Forgive these people, Apollo, for they know not what they do.' She went on:

> When the first act was over, Rossini chose to applaud with his hands, not his opera, as was commonly believed, but the performers, who had in truth done their duty. Many took offence at it. That is sufficient to give you an idea of what happened in the second act. Rossini left the theatre as if he had been there as an indifferent spectator.

She added that she went to his lodgings to comfort him, but that when she got there he needed no consolation; he was sleeping peacefully.

The following day, however, she said Rossini took out of the score what he himself felt had been justifiably disapproved of, and then pretended to be ill, possibly so as not to have to appear at the next performance. After that, the Romans decided that they ought at least to hear the music, so they were attentive at the second performance, and greeted the work with applause at the third. Presumably one of the changes Rossini made was to insist on Garcia singing 'Ecco ridente in cielo' as Almaviva's serenade, instead of his own Spanish confection.

As to the second evening, Rossini is supposed to have told Salvatore Marchesi di Castrone that he remained in his apartments on his own, trying to forget what was possibly taking place in the theatre by doing some composition, but it was difficult. He even took out his watch and played and sang the overture and the first act, but eventually he could bear it no longer, so dressed, and was about to go out when he heard a commotion in the street. This could be made to tie in with Geltrude Righetti-Giorgi's account, for she said that when she went to visit Rossini after the second performance she found the 'feigned invalid' in bed, surrounded by many distinguished Roman gentlemen, who had gone to compliment him on the excellence of his work. It is just possible that he had decided, on hearing the noise below, to return to bed quickly, and that is where the well-wishers – and Righetti-Giorgi – subsequently found him.

Edmond Michotte, it must be said, gave a slightly different version, though purporting to be reproducing Rossini's own words.[9] The composer claimed that he was sleeping peacefully when he was awakened by a noise in the street, and when he realised that the crowd was carrying torches he feared that they were going to set fire to the building and took refuge in a stable. It was Garcia who finally found him there, and told him of the success of the opera, and the crowd's desire to see the composer. 'F*** them, their cheers, and everything else. I'm not coming out of here.' It was left to Garcia to phrase Rossini's words appropriately, though even when they were rephrased someone in the crowd expressed his dissatisfaction by throwing an orange at Garcia, who had a black eye for the next few days. Next the proprietor of the building came, pleading with Rossini to come out because the crowd were breaking the windows and threatening to set fire to the house. Finally the crowd dispersed, and Rossini returned to his bed, though with two broken windows opposite it he did not have a very satisfactory night.

In all there cannot have been more than seven performances of *Il barbiere* at the Argentina that year, since the theatre closed on 27 February; and the opera was not given in Rome for a further five years. In the mean time it was heard in Bologna and Florence towards the end of 1816, and arrived in London, beginning at the King's Theatre in the Haymarket, on 10 March 1818, New York (Park Theater) on 3 May 1819 (in English). When the Garcia family gave it as the opening opera of a season – also at the Park Theater – on 29 November 1825, it became the first opera to be sung in Italian in New York.

CHAPTER FIVE

Years of Industry

Whilst Rossini was busy in Rome, in Naples fire had destroyed the Teatro San Carlo during the night of 12–13 February, only a week before the first performance of *Il barbiere di Siviglia*. This would inevitably involve changes in existing plans, so Rossini was obliged to return to Naples, but before he did so he signed a contract on 29 February, his twenty-fourth birthday, with Pietro Cartoni for an opera for the Teatro Valle to open the Carnival season on 26 December 1816. That opera was to be *La cenerentola*, though it did not have its first performance until 25 January 1817.

After the fire at the Teatro San Carlo, the king visited the ruins and said that he wished to attend the theatre on his next birthday, 12 January 1817. Barbaia determined to fulfil the royal request, and brought in his own building contractors and the architect Antonio Niccolini in order to do so. The cost, some 200,000 ducats, was to be met by Barbaia himself against a concession from the Government on the gambling monopoly. Tradition had long asserted that Barbaia had magnanimously footed the whole bill.

Rossini's first official task in Naples was the provision of a cantata, *Le nozze di Teti e di Peleo* ('The marriage of Thetis and Peleus'), to celebrate the wedding between Maria Carolina Ferdinanda Luiga, grand-daughter of King Ferdinand I, and the duc de Berry, second son of the comte d'Artois, the future King Charles X of France (1824–30). It was for the coronation of the last in 1825 that Rossini was to provide his first opera for Paris, *Il viaggio a Reims*. In *Le nozze di Teti e di Peleo*, Isabella Colbran sang the role of Cerere (Ceres) and Margherita Chabrand that of Teti (Thetis), while Giovanni David was Peleo (Peleus); though 'role' implies dramatic action, whereas the work was more in the style of an oratorio, with costumes and décor. Because of the fire at the San Carlo, what seems to have been the only performance took place on 24 April at the Teatro del Fondo, where *Tancredi* would be given later in the year. Of the eleven musical numbers, eight are partial or complete borrowings from earlier works.

In Pesaro, on 30 April, Rossini's paternal grandmother, Antonia Olivieri Rossini, died at the age of eighty-one. Together with his maternal grandmother, she had looked after him in the early days whilst his parents were touring, and he must have felt her death deeply. However, he was unable to leave Naples at this time, for he had two new works in hand, the first a *dramma* or *opera buffa* for the Teatro dei Fiorentini, and the second a *dramma* or *opera seria* which was to have been put on at San Carlo but in the circumstances had to be given in the company's temporary home at the Fondo. The fact that both a *buffa* and a *seria* work are now designated *dramme* shows how the old hard-and-fast distinctions are becoming blurred, at least in the composer's mind.

Although basically the work of Giuseppe Palomba, from Goldoni's *Il matrimonio per concorso* (1763), the libretto for the *opera buffa La gazzetta* was revised for Rossini by Andrea Leone Tottola, about whom a rhyme was written, to the effect that, since he was not an eagle, he was either a bat or an owl (*nottola* rhymes with Tottola), neither of which is complimentary.[1] Expectations ran high in Naples for this new work, and by August 1816 the local papers were looking for some novelty instead of what they had hitherto been offered, namely endless repetitions of existing operas.

La gazzetta is another Rossini opera to have its own overture, though he borrowed a good deal from previous works such as *La pietra del paragone* and *Il turco in Italia* for the main body of the opera, and when it failed – 'una caduta strepitosa', 'a resounding flop', according to one commentator[2] – Rossini salvaged the overture for *La cenerentola*, in which guise it is much better known today.

The unoriginal plot concerns the efforts of Don Pomponio Storione to find a husband for his daughter Lisetta, by advertising in the local newspaper, *La gazzetta*. There is a brisk opening scene in which the travellers and visitors to the hotel where father and daughter are staying quarrel over who should have the newspaper first. Lisetta has already fallen in love, it should be noted, with Filippo, the owner of the hotel. There now arrive Alberto, who is looking for a wife, and is wealthy but somewhat useless, and Anselmo with his daughter Doralice. She has an elderly admirer, Monsù Traversen, and the cast is complete with Madame La Rose, whose business is to know everybody's business.

The opera would repay revival, though there is a language problem. Neapolitan dialect is used in the *secco* recitative, especially for the part of Don Pomponio, and the libretto would benefit from a good witty translation into the language of the listener. The use of dialect in Naples and Venice (the original Goldoni play on which *La gazzetta* was based was, of course, Venetian) is one of the reasons why *opera buffa* tended not to travel outside the immediate locality of its origin. Furthermore, an exceptional *buffo* is needed for the part of Don Pomponio. Stendhal saw the original, Carlo Casaccia, or Casacciello as he was known in Naples, and said of him: 'If you have ever laughed in your life . . . go to Naples and see Casaccia.'

Lisetta was sung by Margherita Chabrand, who had sung Teti in the wedding cantata earlier in the year; and Alberico Curioni, who played Alberto, was known as the most handsome tenor in Italy. He was still singing at San Carlo as late as 1855. The talents of the singers, however, were unable to redeem the work, and it sank from sight. However, as so often happened with Rossini, a failure was succeeded by a success, and his new opera, *Otello*, was to be just that, despite a mixed reception at its first performance at the Fondo on 4 December 1816.

Rossini's new librettist was Marchese Francesco Berio di Salsa (1767–1820), who kept a brilliant salon in his *palazzo*. He was described by Stendhal as a 'charming . . . companion in society', but 'an unfortunate and abominable . . . poet'. In the specific context of *Otello*, he referred to him as 'the unmentionable literary hack', which was something of an irony coming from the pen of Stendhal. One must add that Berio and Stendhal were friends, but that did not mean that the latter would permit Berio's deficiencies to go unrecorded.

The Rossini version of *Otello* has inevitably suffered unfavourable comparison with both Shakespeare's original play and Verdi's subsequent opera. There is no doubt that the libretto provided for Rossini by Berio di Salsa was of inferior quality. Stendhal suggested that, out of somewhat misguided patriotic zeal, the librettist had gone back to Shakespeare's source, G. B. Giraldi Cinthio's *Hecatommithi* (1565), though it is not clear whether this was added in an attempt to deflect some of the blame away from Shakespeare, or simply to increase Berio di Salsa's condemnation for ineptitude. Either way the result was pretty much the same, for in Stendhal's opinion the libretto was 'an orgy of blunders'.

One must bear in mind that in 1816 Shakespeare was little-known to the average opera-goer in Italy, or indeed to the public at large; one suspects that even those who had read him might well have echoed Voltaire's view, expressed in 1765, that Shakespeare was a barbarian. Indeed, Berio di Salsa was complimented for having toned down 'the tremendous catastrophes of the ferocious Shakespeare'.[3] On 20 February 1818, Byron wrote in a postscript to a letter to John Murray that he was going the following evening to Rossini's *Otello*. He thought that it would be curious to see the Venetian story represented in Venice, as well as to discover what they would make of Shakespeare in music. In the event, when he wrote to Samuel Rogers on 3 March, he declared that Shakespeare's play had been 'crucified', though the music was 'good but lugubrious'. Did he really expect the music of this tragedy to be lighthearted?

It is true, however, that the score only takes off in the third act, which is where Rossini was most in control; and from that point of view it is rightly to be regarded as his own achievement. Above all, it is Rossini's conception of the role of Desdemona which makes the opera remarkable and something of a landmark, reaching its peak in the third act. Desdemona and Emilia are suddenly interrupted by a gondolier singing in the distance. The words he sings are taken from Dante: 'There is no greater pain than to recall happiness in sadness.' Both this tune and the setting of the Willow Song which follows shortly afterwards were Rossini's own tunes, and he had to insist on his own better judgement for the choice of Dante for the gondolier's words. Berio di Salsa had objected that no Venetian gondolier would have aspired to Dante; but Rossini replied – or so he told Moscheles[4] – that he had stayed in Venice several times and he *knew*. In any case, he felt instinctively that he needed some words from a poet of the stature of Dante for this particular scene. For the Willow Song, the scoring of harp, strings and woodwind is a particularly happy choice. Far more than in Shakespeare, Rossini's whole conception centres on Desdemona. Her role was a gift to Isabella Colbran, who was by now almost certainly Rossini's mistress.

It is all the more surprising, therefore, that both Giuditta Pasta and Maria Malibran seem, at one point, to have found the part too insipid and switched to that of Otello, which they sang *en travesti*. In the case of Malibran, it was opposite Wilhelmina Schröder-Devrient in 1831, though two years later, in London, they exchanged roles, and it was as Desdemona that Malibran was remembered by Alfred de Musset in the verse that he wrote at her death in 1836:

> Ces pleurs sur tes bras nus quand tu chantais le *Saule*,
> N'était-ce pas hier, pâle Desdémone?
> (These tears on your naked arms when you sang the Willow Song,
> Wasn't it [only] yesterday, pale Desdemona?)[5]

There is no doubt whatsoever that Rossini conceived Otello as a tenor role, created by Andrea Nozzari, as were those of Rodrigo (written for Giovanni David) and Iago (probably Manuel Garcia, Malibran's father). Barbaia's company was nothing if not stocked with tenors, and Rossini had no intention of deliberately putting back the clock as far as *travesti* roles were concerned.

It is intriguing to read the reaction of Giacomo Meyerbeer, who attended a performance at the Teatro San Benedetto in Venice, and wrote about it on 17 September 1818 to his brother Michael in Berlin.[6] After the first two acts 'the thinking part of the audience openly expressed its displeasure [at Rossini's self-plagiarism] . . . the habitués actually uttered the word "fiasco", especially since they knew that the last act had only three pieces, two of which . . . were quite small'. But, as Meyerbeer went on to explain, it was those two pieces which not only saved the opera, but which also created a furore unheard of in Venice for twenty years. Thirty performances were entirely sold out, and Nicola Tacchinardi (the tenor) and Francesca Maffei (the soprano) were supposed to have been offered large sums to sing in a continuous three-month season. Meyerbeer put his finger on what made the opera so firmly entrenched in the repertoire – it was given in Milan as late as 1873 – when he wrote:

> The third act of *Otello* established its reputation so soundly that a thousand mistakes were unable to shake it. But this third act is really divine, and what is so amazing is that its beauties are totally un-Rossinian. First-rate declamation, endlessly impassioned recitative, mysterious accompaniment full of local colour, and, in particular, the style of old romance at its utmost perfection.

This sort of reaction enables us to appreciate how it was that the opera held its own – especially when there were performers of the calibre of Malibran to take the part of Desdemona. For the generation that first knew Verdi's *Otello* (1887), there could be no doubt, however, that Rossini's had been brushed aside, possibly for ever.

However disappointing the initial reaction to *Otello* in Naples (the opera's success there dated only from the following year, 1817), the pace of Rossini's life at this time did not provide time for reflection. As we saw earlier, he had a contract to provide an opera for Rome; and in theory the deadline was 26 December – little more than three weeks after the first performance of *Otello*. Not surprisingly, work on the new opera still had not started on 23 December, if only because there was as yet no libretto. In this case, Cartoni could hardly invoke the penalty clause in the contract for non-delivery. In fact he and Rossini were friends; the composer was staying in Cartoni's apartment in Palazzo Capranica, close to the Teatro Valle, so there was no question of animosity over the lack of progress.

The chosen libretto, entitled *Ninetta alla corte*, by Gaetano Rossi, had run into difficulties with the ecclesiastical censor, so Jacopo Ferretti was called in to help. He was of the opinion that at least part of the reason for his being selected was that he had already begun work on a libretto previously, which had then been rejected in favour of *Il barbiere di Siviglia*. So Rossini, Cartoni and Ferretti found themselves in the impresario's apartment on a cold evening two days before Christmas, drinking tea. According to a memoir that Ferretti left at his death in 1852, he proposed some twenty or thirty subjects, all of which were rejected as being either too serious, too complicated, too expensive to mount, or not suitable for the cast already engaged.[7] By this time Rossini had got into bed, and the exhausted Ferretti, almost in desperation, murmured 'Cinderella'. This galvanised Rossini, who shot up in bed and asked when he could have the libretto. Ferretti said that if he went without sleep Rossini would have it in the morning. Thereupon Rossini said 'Good night' and went to sleep. Cartoni and Ferretti agreed on a price, shook hands on it, and the latter hurried home, exchanged tea for coffee as his beverage and next morning produced the outline for Rossini, who accepted it.

Ferretti was, of course, writing the memoir after the event, and no doubt in the spirit of how it ought to have happened in view of Rossini's subsequent career and reputation. It is the sort of story that fuelled, and was in turn fuelled by, the myth of Rossini as the insouciant composer of whatever – more or less – was put before him. And yet one cannot help but feel in this particular example that there is present, at the very least, an element of the truth that Rossini responded directly to the idea, and that he was spurred on to composition. Ferretti said that he completed the libretto (from existing sources) in twenty-two days, and Rossini set it in twenty-four. Even so, Rossini had to have help for three items and a good deal of the recitative from Luca Agolini, and for the overture he turned to *La gazzetta*. Otherwise there is only one self-borrowing in the opera: Cenerentola's rondo and variations at the end of Act II, based on Almaviva's 'Cessa di più resistere' in *Il barbiere di Siviglia*.

La cenerentola finally had its first night on 25 January 1817. It belongs, together with *L'italiana in Algeri* and *Il barbiere di Siviglia*, to a trio of comedies from Rossini's maturity, and might well have been a second *Barbiere* but that it lacks the mingling of dramatic action, pungent wit and psychological insight that so distinguished the earlier opera. Of course, Rossini took a very conscious decision to make the characters believable people, and not simply fairy-tale figures, and he was combating the long tradition of such a well-known story. Ultimately Ferretti's libretto went back to Perrault's *Cendrillon* (1697), as well as those by C. G. Étienne for Isouard's *Cendrillon* (Paris, 1810), and Felice Romani for Pavesi's *Agatina* (Milan, 1814). Moreover, it is interesting that the subtitle of the last-named opera – *La virtù premiata* ('Virtue rewarded') – has a strong echo in the subtitle of Rossini's opera, namely *La bontà in trionfo* ('Goodness triumphant').

Ferretti took some pains to explain what he and the composer had intended in his preface to the libretto, alluding at the same time to the fact that the shoe dropped by Cinderella at the ball was altered to a bracelet because in the Papal States it was likely that the censor would intervene.[8] Actresses on stage – already something of a revolution – could not be seen lifting their skirts to try on shoes, and thereby expose their ankles. However, this detail becomes part of the larger issue of the changes brought about in the fairy-tale. If Cinderella, the preface runs,

> does not appear in the company of a magician or a talking cat, and does not lose a shoe at the ball (but rather consigns a bracelet) as in the French theatre, or in that great Italian theatre [La Scala], this ought not to be considered as a crime of disrespect, but rather a necessity on the stage of the Teatro Valle, and an act of respect to the delicacy of Roman taste, which does not tolerate on the stage what is diverting in a tale told by the fireside.

All of which may well seem totally gratuitous today, but one must remember that there were several people, such as Stendhal, who felt that there was something intrinsically vulgar in the tale being promoted to the substance of the opera, though of course his prejudice blinded him to some of the subtleties in Rossini's music, and indeed his handling of the story altogether.

The role of Cinderella (Angiolina) was created by Geltrude Righetti-Giorgi, though she seems to have been the only singer on form on the opening night – or, indeed, during any of the early performances – for Ferretti described Andrea Verni (Don Magnifico) as being by then in the twilight of his glory; Giuseppe de Begnis (Dandini) shouted rather than sang, while Giacomo Guglielmi (Don Ramiro) was no longer what he had been, and sang lots of wrong notes. He made no adverse criticisms of the others – Clorinda and Thisbe, the two step-sisters, and Alidoro – but he said nothing complimentary, either, except that Clorinda (Caterina Rossi) was pretty. The first night was emphatically not a success, but Rossini was philosophical, recalling the première of *Il barbiere di Siviglia.* He prophesied that the work would catch on, and it did. It even became the first opera to be staged in Australia, when it was sung in February 1844.

At the start of the opera Cenerentola is by the fire, cooking, and singing her 'usual' song, which so irritates her step-sisters. It is in a minor key, in $\frac{6}{8}$ time, almost a folk-song: 'Una volta c'era un re, che a star solo s'annoio' ('Once upon a time there was a king who was bored by being on his own'). It is prophetic of the whole plot, of course, but Clorinda and Thisbe are too busy prettying themselves, and so unlikely would it be ever to happen to Cenerentola, they simply mock her in their irritation. To her 'once upon a time' they interrupt with 'twice' and 'thrice' and 'Are you going to finish it or not?', and their shrill soprano contrasts with her mellow contralto. Their father, Don Magnifico, enters and has to stop their bickering, and in his *cavatina* describes a dream he has had, in which a winged donkey flew up to the top of a church tower – a prefiguration of his wealth and rise in social status. It gives Rossini scope for lots of musical onomatopoeia in the word-setting.

There is a wonderful moment at the conclusion of the first scene when Alidoro, tutor to the prince (Don Ramiro), enters, produces his list of eligible girls and asks where the third daughter is. After a pregnant pause, observed by the orchestra, too, Don Magnifico announces that she has died. The orchestra descends chromatically, to land on E flat; and then silence. There follows a typical *buffa* ensemble, in which the characters, with a studied detachment, try to decide who is lying. The juxtaposition of genuine sentiment with such detachment is one of the high points, not only of the opera as *buffa*, but also of Rossini's own musical response to, and handling of, human nature. In this context the role of Dandini, which almost outdoes the prince, his master, in dramatic interest, is one of Rossini's most notable conceptions. Finally, however, it is Cenerentola – as it must be, both dramatically and musically – who plays the pivotal part in resolving the plot and forgiving those around her with the rondo 'Nacqui all'affanno'. Cenerentola shows that, in the words of the opera's subtitle, goodness triumphs after all.

It seems extraordinary that *La cenerentola* (1817) should have virtually marked the end of Rossini's career as a composer of *opera buffa* when he was not yet twenty-five years old. There were another nineteen operas still to come, but the one-act *farsa Adina*, written for Lisbon in 1818 (though not performed there until 1826), was the only other comic opera to an Italian text, unless one counts *Il viaggio a Reims* as comic, for it is designated as a *dramma giocoso*. It was written for Paris (1825), as was *Le Comte Ory* (1828) which is to a French text, and is either an *opéra* or *opéra comique*. In abandoning a genre virtually at the moment he had mastered it, Rossini was setting himself a precedent that he would follow in twelve years' time with *Guillaume Tell*.

Still taking advantage of his permitted absence as enshrined in his contract with Barbaia, Rossini left Rome on 11 February in the company of a wealthy Bolognese friend, Marchese Francesco Sampieri, who was also a composer of sorts. They went to Bologna via Spoleto, where they took part in a performance of *L'italiana in Algeri* which, by chance, was being given in Spoleto on the evening of 12 February. Sampieri sat at the keyboard while Rossini played the double bass in the orchestra. We do know exactly how long Rossini stayed in Bologna with his parents, but he was bound ultimately for Milan, which he had reached before 19 March, for on that day he wrote to his mother and told her that he was lodging with Francesca Maffei-Festa and her husband. The soprano had been the first Fiorilla in *Il turco in Italia* in the city in 1814. On that occasion the opera had not been a great success. In fact Rossini had not had a first-night triumph in Milan since *La pietra del paragone* in 1812. He was therefore determined that his new opera would be the best he could provide, and he told his mother that the subject was wonderful – 'il soggetto e bellissimo'.

The new opera was *La gazza ladra* ('The thieving magpie'), to a libretto that had been prepared by Giovanni Gherardini (1778–1861) for Ferdinando Paër, but which the latter had rejected the previous year (1816). Gherardini had based his libretto on *La Pie voleuse* (1815) by D'Aubigny and Caigniez, in turn based on a true incident in which a French peasant girl was wrongly hanged for a theft which turned out to be the work of the thieving magpie of the opera's title. In Rossini's *semiseria* opera or *melodramma*, the wrongly accused heroine, Ninetta, is reprieved from execution at the last minute through the discovery of the magpie's nest and the missing silver. A potentially tragic conclusion is therefore averted, and the opera ends in triumph.

Rossini certainly took great care with the composition of the opera. There is a minimum of self-borrowing, and the orchestration is particularly carefully laid out, though the use of the snare drums caused some critics to protest. The ever pragmatic Rossini retorted that if the opera involved foot soldiers, then of necessity it would require drums, too. The overture has found its way into the classical repertoire, even if the opera itself has not; but the overture epitomises the glittering brilliance of the scoring of the whole opera, and ought to encourage more frequent performance of the work.

In fact, some critics found the instrumentation *too* brilliant, even strident ('strepitosa'), and hard work for the singers to compete with. There was a feeling, too, that the vocal music was rather too sophisticated for what were basically peasants. It was declared more suitable for Caesar and Trajan than Pippo and Ninetta. At the end of the first performance, however, Rossini and the baritone Filippo Galli, who created the role of Ninetta's father, embraced each other on stage in front of the audience. As one of those present observed: 'This made a river of tears flow from the eyes of all the spectators.'[9]

From Milan, Rossini set out on the return journey to Naples, possibly spending some time in Bologna on the way, and early in August the Neapolitan newspapers informed their readers that the composer had returned to the city and was at work on a new opera for the autumn season at the rebuilt Teatro San Carlo. Described as an opera 'a grande spettacolo', *Armida* was precisely that. Naturally, Barbaia wanted something spectacular for his new theatre, and he probably had to prevail upon Rossini to accept the subject-matter, and in so doing he would no doubt have been assisted by Isabella Colbran, for temperamentally the composer was not well disposed towards magic and the supernatural, as we saw in his declared approach to *La cenerentola*. As he subsequently wrote to the librettist Carlo Donà: 'If I were to give you advice, it would be to return within the bounds of the natural, rather than go further into the world of wild fancies and devilishness from which modern philosophers say that they have laboured so hard to free a too credulous mankind.'

The libretto that Barbaia provided for Rossini was by Giovanni Schmidt, who had collaborated on *Elisabetta*, based on the story of Armida and Rinaldo from Tasso's *Gerusalemme liberata*, which had also been the ultimate source for *Tancredi*. Armida was a subject that Lully, Handel, Gluck, Jommelli and Haydn – amongst others – had already essayed, and it certainly provided plenty of scope for spectacle, lavish scenery, ballet and chorus – the standard ingredients of grand opera in Paris in later years.

Naturally there was a leading role for Isabella Colbran (the title role, in fact), but the music is perhaps more notable for the duets between Armida and Rinaldo, especially 'Amor! possente nome' in Act I and the *terzetto* for tenors, 'In quale aspetto imbelle', in Act III, when Carlo the Dane and Ubaldo, sent to try to bring Rinaldo back to his senses and save him from Armida's witchcraft, hold up the miraculous shield in which he sees his own reflection. The conclusion of the opera took the audience completely by surprise at its first night on 11 November 1817. Rinaldo departs, Armida is bereft, then suddenly rouses herself to vengeance. She orders the destruction of the magic palace and rides off in her chariot in order to deliver what, we assume, must be suitable punishment for the fleeing knights.

Stendhal assigned it to his chapter on 'eight minor operas by Rossini'.[10] The duet 'Amor! possente nome' was particularly singled out for praise, however, and in his 'final word' he described it as resembling 'nothing so much as dreamed of before'. One does not sustain a whole opera with one duet, however, and more immediately the critics in Naples (as in *Il giornale delle Due Sicilie* of 3 December) saw conflict between the harmony and the melody, which they attributed to the Germanic influences in the opera. The following year *Il nuovo osservatore Veneto* observed that at the conclusion of the opera 'The Rossinians, with slow and heavy step, left the theatre in pensive mood'.

Temperamentally Rossini was not inclined to fantasy and the supernatural, as we have seen; so it was not the opportunity for exoticism that appealed to Rossini when undertaking the task. But he did respond with some richly scored music – the colourful brass writing in Act II, for example, which contrasts vividly with the following duet, 'Dove son io?', accompanied by solo cello. It is the love-duets that inspire the most sensuous music in the opera, as it is Armida herself that inspires the most florid and taxing virtuosity.

Here was a role in which Colbran might indeed dazzle her audience. At the same time, it has made the opera extremely hard to revive – that and the fact that it requires no less than six tenors. Maria Callas was the first soprano in this century to allow us to gain an impression of what Armida could sound like in performance, and one wonders whether there was not a strong similarity between the two singers. One recalls Callas in her later years, especially as Medea, when the voice no longer responded in the way that it had done before, but her very presence on stage almost made one forget. She was Medea, as Colbran seems to have been Elisabetta or Armida.

The pace of Rossini's life at this point did not permit him time to conduct a post-mortem on *Armida*, for he had a contract to fulfil for the Teatro Argentina in Rome by the end of the year, and Schmidt was again the librettist. In the event, the opera that opened on 27 December was described by Radiciotti as 'the worst of Rossini's *opere serie* . . . one encounters only banality from start to finish'. *Adelaide di Borgogna* was the choice of Pietro Cartoni, who had assumed the management of the Teatro Argentina after the demise of Sforza-Cesarini. Rossini used the overture from *La cambiale di matrimonio*, had recourse to *secco* recitative, and compositional help from Michele Carafa (1787–1872), who was a Neapolitan prince and had some ability as a composer. It would be wrong, however, to assume that the work was merely thrown together, and if it lacks notable arias or ensembles the orchestration has moments of striking originality. On the one hand, Rossini uses plenty of drums, for the plot has plenty of warring and feuding; but, on the other, the woodwind writing is of great delicacy and subtlety, as in Adelaide's final aria. At other times Rossini uses what is another of his hallmarks, namely pizzicato strings contrasted with either woodwind in their lower register or sustained violas.

Once again, the sheer momentum of Rossini's existence at this time did not allow pause for recrimination or regret. He returned to Naples, where he had a new opera to compose for the beginning of March 1818, but he still found time to carry on negotiations for a staging of *La gazza ladra*, which was to celebrate the reopening of the renovated Teatro del Sole in Pesaro that year.

Easter fell very early, on 22 March, in 1818, which meant that the Carnival season had also ended early. A biblical subject, *Mosè in Egitto*, had therefore been chosen, so that it could be given in the theatre during Lent. Hence its designation as *azione tragico-sacra*, which does not put it in the category of oratorio, strictly speaking, for it is effectively an opera in three acts, composed to a libretto which Tottola (librettist of *La gazzetta* of 1816) had based on Francesco Ringhieri's tragedy *L'Osiride* (1760). The love-interest is taken from this last work, whereas the basic action is the Old Testament story of the Exodus of the Jews from Egypt. It was given on 5 March to great acclaim, though one of its most famous passages, the prayer for chorus 'Dal tuo stellato soglio', was not added until its revival for the Lenten season at San Carlo the following year (1819).

Elcia, a Jewish girl (sung by Colbran), falls in love with Osiride, Pharaoh's son (sung by the tenor Andrea Nozzari). Moses was sung by the bass Michele Benedetti, which was an unusual choice for the time, since the audience would have expected a tenor, but Rossini's instinct told him that Moses needed to be given to a bass. Moreover, Benedetti looked the part, and Stendhal vividly described his appearance and his costume, 'sublime in its very simplicity', which had been copied from Michelangelo's statue of Moses in the church of San Pietro in Vincoli in Rome.

Unfortunately Rossini expanded the original three-act opera into a four-act work for Paris in 1827, as we shall see, and in so doing radically altered its nature. At the heart of both, however, is a story of conflict between love and duty, and the demands of family and country. It is a work of contrasts, then, and Rossini reflects this in the music. The original Naples version opens with the Plague of Darkness in progress. No overture prepares the ground, simply a succession of three repeated Cs, which are followed by a transition to the minor and then, after a pause, the semiquaver passages over which the plagued Egyptians' prayers are heard. Stendhal began to laugh when the curtain went up, but 'before I had heard twenty bars of this superb *introduzione* I could see nothing less profoundly

Right: Giuditta Pasta (1798–1852) in the title role in *Tancredi*, which had its first performance at Teatro La Fenice in Venice in 1813. Although Rossini wrote the part for Adelaide Melanotte-Montrésor, Pasta came to make the role her own. She sang in the first performance of Rossini's *Il viaggio a Reims* in Paris in 1825, and went on to create a number of title roles for both Bellini and Donizetti.

Left: An engraving by Filippo Pistrucci of the three principal characters from Rossini's opera *L'inganno felice*, which had its first performance on 8 January 1812, at Teatro San Moisè, Venice.

The interior of Teatro San Carlo, Naples, by Cetteo di Stefano (1835). It was here that Rossini made his Neapolitan début on 4 October 1815 with *Elisabetta, regina d'Inghilterra*, starring Isabella Colbran. The opera being given in the painting is *Lara*, by the forgotten Frenchman, Henri de Ruoloz (1808–87).

moving than a whole population plunged into deep misery'. He claimed that he could still recall the overwhelming impression made by the first hearing of Moses' words 'Eterno, immenso, incomprensibil Dio!'

There are two particular moments in the original version of the opera where Rossini uses a change from minor to major with telling result. It is, of course, an effect one cannot use too often, since it simply kills the effect ultimately. The first occurs early in the opera, when Moses restores light to the Egyptians, and the second is in Act III, when the prayer 'Dal tuo stellato soglio', first stated in G minor, is eventually heard in the major. Carafa wrote an aria for Pharaoh which Rossini subsequently replaced, perhaps less happily, with 'Cade del ciglio il velo'.

Rossini was said to have received 4,200 lire for the opera. For *Tancredi* he had received 600, it will be recalled, and for *Otello* 100 louis, which was twice the agreed fee, according to Silvestri; an act of spontaneous generosity on the part of Barbaia inspired by the success of the first night.

On 2 May 1818, Ester Mombelli sang, for the first time in public, a cantata with chorus entitled *La morte di Didone*, which Rossini had composed for her in Bologna in 1811. It was her benefit night at the Teatro San Benedetto in Venice; but according to the critic of *La gazzetta privilegiata di Venezia* she would have done better to have kept the cantata to herself. He quoted some words of Virgil, describing Dido, from the *Aeneid*, book 4: 'Quaesivit coelo lumen, ingemuitque, reperta' ('She sought light from heaven and, having found it, she groaned'). Subsequently some of the music was salvaged and published in Milan two years later.

More satisfying for Rossini from the artistic point of view was the opening of the reconstructed opera house in his birthplace of Pesaro on 10 June that year (1818). At the beginning of the year he had started what turned out to be protracted negotiations with Antaldo Antaldi, *gonfaloniere* (chief magistrate), and Conte Giulio Perticari, a local aristocrat, who were supporting the reopening of the theatre. The opera eventually chosen for the occasion was *La gazza ladra*. On 27 January, Rossini wrote from Naples to Antaldi that he would like to have Isabella Colbran and Andrea Nozzari as principals, but it eventually became clear that they would be too costly. Rossini expressed a certain amount of frustration to Luigi Achilli in Rome, protesting that it was all very well for the people in Pesaro to prevaricate, but he could not be expected to ask singers of calibre to keep themselves at his disposal for six months in the hope that they might eventually be asked to sing in a town which could clearly afford to pay very little. So Nozzari and Colbran faded from view, and Rossini had to try at least four more sopranos. Eventually the soprano Giuseppina Ronzi de Begnis was engaged, with Alberico Curioni as tenor and Raniero Remorini as bass. Camillo Landriani and Alessandro Sanquirico would provide the sets.

Understandably, for his home town, Rossini was at pains to ensure that everything was as well organised as possible, but what emerges from the correspondence is the extent to which he was prepared to go, and the attention he gave to minutiae. He concerned himself with the orchestral layout and lighting, administration, rehearsals, and – almost inevitably – the whims of the singers. Remorini successfully claimed an entrance aria, which Rossini lifted from *Torvaldo e Dorliska*, and Ninetta and Giannetto were given the love-duet 'Amor! possente nome' from *Armida*. There was a certain calculation on the composer's part, of course, that the majority of the citizens of Pesaro had not yet had the opportunity to hear these other operas. At the same time, he had a flair for what would go down well. He was, after all, now working with the major opera houses of Italy, and despite his mere twenty-five or twenty-six years he had already evolved a highly developed sense of what constituted professional standards at a national level. Pesaro was clearly not in this league; but Rossini wanted to demonstrate that he certainly was.

Perticari invited Rossini to be a guest in his house during the time that he would be in Pesaro; the composer would have declined the offer, but was prevailed upon to accept. Possibly Rossini had had premonitions of what was to ensue, for he told Filippo Mordani that, although Perticari himself was civil and hospitable, his wife (whose father was the poet Vincenzo Monti) was a curious character. She would fly into a rage and fight with her husband, who then appealed to Rossini to mollify her. Rumour soon established a relationship between hostess and guest. It was even suggested that Rossini was watched, that Costanza Perticari got her maid to tell her when he got up and left the house in the morning, whereupon she leaped, naked, into his bed, in an endeavour to absorb by contact, she maintained, a small particle of his genius.

Present in the audience in Pesaro on 10 June was Caroline of Brunswick, estranged wife of the future George IV of England. No longer a young woman (she was in fact fifty-six at the time), she had taken up with an Italian, Bartolomeo Bergami, who was assumed to be her lover, and was living outside Pesaro. At first she was welcomed into the community, but gradually her way of life alienated the more conservative members of society. Rossini, no doubt influenced by his hosts the Perticaris, refused invitations to the Princess of Wales's receptions. On one occasion he maintained that rheumatic pains affected his ability to bow according to etiquette. This was to have serious repercussions the following year.

Rossini had advised Perticari, once the composition of the company had been decided on, not to promise more than twenty-four performances, though he felt that they could run to thirty if necessary. In fact twenty-four performances of *La gazza ladra* were given, but after that Curioni refused to take part in two planned performances of *Il barbiere di Siviglia*, and the festival began to disintegrate. Rossini fell ill with such a serious throat inflammation that his death was reported in both Naples and Paris, and then had to be denied. In reality this was an indication of his standing and growing international reputation. Clearly he was thought to be of sufficient importance now for his death to be considered worth reporting! Before his departure for Bologna the Perticaris gave a banquet in his honour; he claimed to remember their hospitality to the end of his life.[11]

In Bologna that August, Rossini received a commission from a son of the prefect of police and inspector of theatres in Lisbon for a one-act *opera buffa*. The point of departure for the libretto was Felice Romani's *Il califfo e la schiava*, which Marchese Gherardo Bevilacqua-Aldobrandini revised and entitled *Adina, o Il califfo di Bagdad*. Since no overture was specified in the contract, Rossini did not provide one, which may possibly have contributed to the delay in its production, since it was not given in Lisbon until 1826 at the Teatro São Carlos, and remained unpublished until 1829. It seems, however, that the lack of an overture is a rather specious excuse in the circumstances.

Despite rumours that Rossini was negotiating to provide operas for Paris, contained, for example, in a letter from Meyerbeer, who was then in Milan, to his brother in Berlin, dated 27 September 1818, the composer returned to Naples at the beginning of that month and set to work on a new opera for Barbaia, *Ricciardo e Zoraide*.[12] The libretto was by Marchese Francesco Berio di Salsa, which Stendhal said was based on a poem in thirty cantos entitled *Ricciardetto* by

Niccolò Forteguerri (1674–1735), published posthumously in Paris in 1738. Ricciardo, the Christian knight, was a part written for Giovanni David, and Zoraide was of course Colbran. She is loved by King Agorante (Andrea Nozzari), who has taken prisoner her father Ircano (Michele Benedetti).

The opera as a whole shows Rossini continuing to use existing *opera seria* forms, whilst adding or developing ingredients. Accompanied recitative, for example, is not used merely for its own sake; but, as one would expect by now from Rossini, is very carefully handled, especially with regard to the balance between vocal line, orchestration and underlying harmonic treatment. In other words, it is an essentially expressive element in the overall structure. The chorus is used effectively, and the deployment of an onstage band is particularly colourful. Stendhal stated quite categorically that one of the features of the opera was the absence of an overture: 'Rossini shows a distinct tendency to become bored with the chore of writing overtures, and so has demonstrated, with a fine display of logic and reason, that they are unnecessary.' In fact, as one might expect, the truth is otherwise. There is an opening *largo*, only eleven bars long, which serves as an introduction, the curtain rises, and there is a march, played by the onstage band. This is followed by an *andante* with variations, the march is repeated, then the chorus is heard. Such a carefully thought out scheme is hardly indicative of having 'become bored with the chore of writing overtures', especially when such an opening could not be used subsequently in another opera. Moreover, the orchestration is richly varied, and shows Rossini consciously seeking out new effects.

In this respect Rossini was a victim of his own success. Because overtures such as *La gazza ladra*, *La scala di seta* and *Guillaume Tell* became popular in their own right, detached from their operas, of course, it was assumed that Rossini was perfectly capable of writing overtures when he felt like it, and the fact that he chose not to do so was taken as a sign of his laziness. As specifically composed overtures, often using thematic material from the works themselves, became an obligatory feature of nineteenth-century operas, the fact that some of his operas did not have an overture, or that he used overtures apparently indiscriminately, again confounded audiences and critics. One has a certain amount of sympathy with them, but Rossini was never convinced that an overture was imperative, and when the fashion grew for introducing thematic material from the body of the opera he was by no means in favour of it. As the majority of his operas fell out of the repertoire, however, the majority of people who heard the overtures alone had no idea that they were not related to the music of the operas; but at least they kept alive some of Rossini's orchestral achievement at a time when the operas themselves were not being heard.

Ricciardo e Zoraide opened at the Teatro San Carlo on 3 December 1818, and was so successful that it was repeated the following spring. Rossini had plenty of tasks on hand, however, during these winter months. He had work to do on *Armida* to turn it into a two-act opera (the original was in three) for San Carlo in January 1819. Then there was the revision of *Mosè in Egitto*, which he had completed by 7 March, and added the prayer 'Dal tuo stellato soglio'.

There were also two occasional pieces. A cantata entitled *Omaggio umiliato*, to a text by Niccolini, for soprano, chorus and orchestra, was given at the Teatro San Carlo on 20 February 1819, in celebration of King Ferdinand's recovery from an illness. Colbran was the soprano, Taglioni the choreographer, and the newspapers enumerated no fewer than 120 wind instruments on stage. Some of the music was used again for another state occasion, when a cantata was performed to celebrate the visit of Emperor Francis I (the king's father-in-law) on 9 May 1819. This time, in addition to the soprano, there were two tenors (David and Rubini), though Rossini himself was not present, since he was on his way back to Naples from Venice. The text on this last occasion was by Giulio Genoino, with whom Rossini was to collaborate again.

In between the two cantatas Rossini had had a new opera, *Ermione*, given at the San Carlo for the first time on 27 March. For the libretto the much despised Tottola turned to Racine's *Andromaque* (1667), which provided, if nothing else, a taut human situation with lots of scope for dramatic interplay of character on the stage. Pirro (Pyrrhus) is loved by Ermione (Hermione), the title role of the opera, whereas he is in love with Andromeca (Andromache). To complete the quartet, Oreste (Orestes) is in love with Hermione. This last was a role for Colbran again, with David as Oreste and Nozzari as Pirro. During the course of the opera she experiences a rich variety of emotions towards the last, from intense admiration and infatuation to bitter jealousy when his betrothal to Andromeca is announced. In this mood she induces Oreste to kill Pirro, and her long *scena* in the second act makes great demands, vocally and dramatically, on the soprano, who carries the whole sequence.

With such strongly delineated characters and such powerful emotions involved, it is hardly surprising that Rossini should devote more attention to the arias and duets in *Ermione* than he did, for example, in *Ricciardo e Zoraide*. By the same token, the chorus has much less to do than in the earlier opera. However, Rossini uses a similarly imaginative opening for *Ermione*, and the overture comprises a chorus lamenting the fall of Troy.

The opera had its first performance on 27 March, but was not revived subsequently during Rossini's lifetime. Stendhal attributed its lack of success to the fact that it was too German, which usually meant too much orchestration at that time; then he said that Rossini had tried to imitate Gluck's French declamatory style, which does not carry much conviction. He then went on to say something which may well have been nearer the truth, however, certainly as far as his contemporaries were concerned (which makes Stendhal such a frustrating source at times):

> Music without direct sensual appeal to the ear is condemned to half-hearted appreciation by the Neapolitans. Moreover, in *Ermione*, the *dramatis personae* spent all the time they were on stage in losing their tempers with each other, so that the whole opera was fixed in one relentless mood of anger, which ultimately proved very boring. *Anger*, as a theme for music, is only valid as a contrast to something else. There is a popular saying among the *dilettanti* of Naples, which states that in opera, the angry explosions of a bad-tempered tutor should always be used to set off the gentle aria of the pretty young ward.[13]

Into the crowded first three months of 1819, Rossini also had to fit a commission for the Teatro San Benedetto in Venice. Since it was virtually impossible for him to have produced a completely new opera in that time, he resorted to *pasticcio*. The libretto chosen was that for Pavesi's *Odoardo e Cristina* (Naples, 1810), which Schmidt, Bevilacqua-Aldobrandini and the ubiquitous Tottola all had a hand in. Rossini did contribute some new music, but he also had recourse to operas that had not been heard in Venice: *Adelaide di Borgogna*, *Ricciardo e Zoraide*, and the latest, *Ermione*.

Such an expedient gave, and still gives, plenty of ammunition to those who see Rossini as essentially an opportunist. The new opera,

Litho. de C. Motte, R. des marais

Théâtre Italien.

A caricature of Rossini in 1819, when *Il barbiere di Siviglia* was first heard at the Théâtre-Italien.

Eduardo (later *Edoardo) e Cristina*, opened on 24 April and was enthusiastically received. *La gazzetta* reported that 'It was a triumph like no others in the history of our music theatres'. The performance began at eight and went on until two o'clock in the morning because nearly all the numbers had to be repeated and the composer was called on to the stage several times. No less than twenty-five performances were given that season, and the following year, as *Edoardo e Cristina* now, it was repeated in Venice at La Fenice.

Byron was present during the first staging, and on 17 May 1819 wrote to John Cam Hobhouse:

> There has been a splendid Opera lately at San Benedetto – by Rossini – who came in person to play the Harpsichord – the People followed him about – crowned him – cut off his hair 'for memory', he was Shouted and Sonnetted and feasted – and immortalized much more than either of the Emperors. . . . Think of a people frantic for a fiddler – or at least an inspirer of fiddles.[14]

Rossini must have left Venice shortly after this, for he was due in Pesaro for a repeat performance of *La gazza ladra* at the Teatro del Sole on 24 May. The Princess of Wales had not forgotten Rossini's behaviour the previous year, and the events of that evening were recorded in a letter written three days later by Conte Francesco Cassi to Giulio Perticari, Rossini's host of the previous year, who was then in Rome.[15]

Apparently Rossini was virtually 'ambushed' the moment he entered the orchestra pit by the Princess of Wales's 'thugs', for they saw him first and, before the rest of the townspeople could register their pleasure at having the composer in their midst, began to whistle loudly. They also had confederates planted elsewhere in the theatre, who were said to have threatened those around them with physical violence. The Pesaresi were not to be so easily subdued, however, and began to applaud and shout 'Viva' once they had overcome their initial shock and surprise.

Clearly the 'thugs' were not going to be content, however, and in order to prevent any harm being done to Rossini one of the local councillors rushed down to the pit and escorted him to one of the boxes where he remained until the ballet that was part of the programme had ended. The composer then left the theatre via the directors' private entrance, and thence directly into the carriage of the lady in whose box he had taken sanctuary. So he was conveyed safely to his hotel.

This only served to increase the confusion, for the 'thugs' were waiting in the auditorium to renew their noise when he re-entered the box, whilst the pro-Rossini faction wanted to applaud him and escort him back to his hotel with a torchlit procession. In the event the latter party had its way – to some extent, at least – for when they all found out what had transpired they went off to Rossini's hotel. He left the place a few hours later, still escorted by torch-bearing citizens beyond the town gate. According to Cassi, these citizens had the temerity to shout 'Death to the whistlers' amongst their 'Evvivas', and so were arrested by the police as they returned into the city. Rossini never set foot in Pesaro again.

So incensed was he at what had happened, Cassi resigned from his position as one of the theatre administrators and wrote a strongly worded protest to the chief magistrate. In order to make amends, the Accademia decided to commission a marble bust of Rossini to adorn its meeting chamber, and decided to arrange a gala evening in the composer's honour. Cassi then prepared to deliver a speech to the town council in an endeavour to persuade it to take part in the celebration. This only served to rekindle the animosity between the supporters of Rossini and the Princess of Wales and her entourage. A war of pamphlets, threats and counter-threats broke out, so that the Papal Legate felt obliged to intervene, and forbade Cassi's speech to the town council, as well as the proposed Accademia gala. Matters only really settled down, however, when the Princess of Wales left for England. King George III died on 29 January 1820, and Caroline was now technically Queen of England. Subsequently the Accademia authorised Perticari to commission a bust of Rossini, and he chose Adamo Tadolini (1792–1868), a pupil of Canova working in Rome.

For Naples, in the autumn of 1819, Rossini composed *La donna del lago*, whose libretto was based by Tottola on Sir Walter Scott's poem in six cantos *The Lady of the Lake* (1810), which had reached Italy within some three years of its publication. It is not clear how Barbaia and/or Rossini came to choose the subject, though the composer Désiré Alexandre Batton (1798–1855), a pupil of Cherubini at the Paris Conservatoire and winner of the Prix de Rome, told Radiciotti that he had first introduced Rossini to Scott's poem when he was in Naples that year (1819). Whether this was true or not, the fact seems correct that it was via a French translation that Rossini came to the subject, and it seems that he responded to the lyrical and pastoral elements in the story, which almost inevitably lead one to think ahead to *Guillaume Tell* (1829), with which it has much in common from this point of view.

The plot takes certain liberties with Scott's poem, as Tottola observed in his preface to the libretto, though naturally the chief characters are the same. The central character is a knight, James Fitz-James, who is in fact King James V of Scotland. As a boy he had been held prisoner for two years by Archibald Douglas. When James escaped, Douglas fled to England, and the king punished his relations. At the start of the opera Douglas (bass) has returned to Scotland and is living under the protection of Roderick Dhu (Rodrigo, tenor), a Highland chieftain leading a rebel faction against the king. Out of gratitude, Douglas has promised the hand of his daughter, Ellen (Elena, soprano), to Roderick. She, however, is in love with Malcolm Graeme (Groeme, in the first printed libretto, mezzo-soprano), and in the first scene, in which she arrives by boat, she meets James Fitz-James (Uberto, tenor), who is much taken with her beauty. He has become separated from his hunting companions, and she takes him to her cottage, where she reveals whose daughter she is. The rest of the plot is the working-out of the fates of these characters. Ellen will marry Malcolm in the end, the king will accept that she loves another, and pardons both her father and her husband-to-be. Ellen's father, too, must accept that she will not marry the man he chose, Roderick Dhu.

Rossini again dispenses with an overture, and simply has a sixteen-bar orchestral prelude, followed by a chorus of Highlanders on the side of Loch Katrine. A hunt is in progress in the distance, which gives opportunity for effective use of horns on the stage. Ellen then arrives in her skiff on the loch, singing a charming *cavatina*, 'Oh, matutini albori!', which is used rather as a leitmotif in the early part of the opera. Accompanied recitative also plays an important part in Rossini's treatment, mingling with *arioso* in this early part of the opera, especially in the first encounter between Ellen and Fitz-James. Sadly the impetus then fades, however, and the opera never quite recovers. Ellen has a brilliant rondo, 'Tanti affetti in tal momento', right at the end, which was about the only section that pleased the San Carlo audience on the opening night, 24 September 1819, though it was much better received at the second performance and indeed, with Colbran (Elena), David (Fitz-James/Uberto) and

Nozzari (Rodrigo) as the principals, and the music Rossini gave them to sing in, for example, the trio in Act II, 'Alla ragion, deh rieda', the Neapolitans must have been fickle indeed not to respond.

There is an interesting letter from Giacomo Leopardi to his brother Carlo, written from Rome on 5 February 1823, about the current production there at the Teatro Argentina of *La donna del lago*:

> I congratulate you on the feelings and the tears that Rossini's music has occasioned you, but you are wrong in thinking that nothing comparable touches us. We have at the Argentina *La donna del lago*, the music of which, performed by surprising voices, is a stupendous affair, and even I might weep, if the gift of tears had not been taken away from me; I am aware, though, that I have not entirely lost it. But the length of the opera, which lasts six hours, is intolerable and killing . . . here it is not the custom to leave. . . .[16]

The hectic year 1819 demanded still one more opera from Rossini, commissioned for the opening of the Carnival season at La Scala, Milan. He was in the city by 1 November, if Stendhal is to be believed. The new opera, entitled *Bianca e Falliero, ossia Il consiglio dei tre*, was set in seventeenth-century Venice, though taken from a French melodrama, *Blanche et Montcassin*, by Antoine-Vincent Arnault. Felice Romani's libretto, or possibly simply the subject-matter itself, did not seem to inspire Rossini, though the quartet at the end of Act I, 'Importuno in qual momento', accompanied by chorus, made a considerable impact. Giovanni Pacini, whose *Vallace* was successfully given in the same season, admitted that the quartet alone was of more worth than the whole of his opera.[17] There is also a quartet in Act II, 'Cielo, il mio labbro ispira', which was later, with Rossini's approval, imported into the second act of *La donna del lago*. As 1819 drew to its end, and with it the second decade of the century that had seen such an amazing blossoming of Rossini's career, it seemed as if nothing could stop his progress. On the other hand, was he capable of maintaining such a frantic level of activity? It is a question that Rossini does not seem to have asked himself. But change was on the way.

CHAPTER SIX

The God of Harmony

After the opening performances of *Bianco e Falliero* Rossini left Milan for Naples, visiting his parents in Bologna *en route*, and whilst in Rome devoting some time to the sculptor Adamo Tadolini for the bust commissioned by the Accademia in Pesaro. The turn of the year and the start of a new decade therefore makes a convenient point at which to take stock of Rossini's career to date. The composer was not quite twenty-eight years old, but in the space of the last thirteen years he had composed no fewer than thirty operas, even if some of them owed varying degrees of indebtedness to each other, and in some cases to other composers. Indeed, if one excludes *Demetrio e Polibio*, composed before 1808, then the tally is a staggering twenty-nine operas in the space of nine years between late 1810 and the end of 1819. In addition, there were quantities of other sorts of music – liturgical works, cantatas, songs, and orchestral and instrumental pieces. Whether or not Rossini took a conscious decision at this time to slow down his rate of composition – as he did some nine years later when he decided to leave the operatic stage altogether – the fact remains that during the next four years he produced only one opera a year.

If, however, Rossini slowed down his rate of composing operas, he did not necessarily work any less feverishly. According to *Il giornale*, he returned to Naples on 12 January 1820 and immediately threw himself into rehearsing Spontini's *Fernando Cortez*, which had first been heard at the Paris Opéra in November 1809, and then revised by the composer for the same house in May 1817. Despite the strong cast at Rossini's disposal, which included Colbran and Nozzari *inter alia*, the work did not please at its first performance on 4 February. Such a reception may well have been salutary for Rossini as he considered the direction that he wished to take in his own music.

In the mean time, such composition as he undertook was not for the opera house, but for the church. For the Arciconfraternità di San Luigi in Naples he composed a Mass which was sung in the Church of San Ferdinando (the former Jesuit Church) on 24 March. It is scored for soprano, alto, two tenors and bass, with chorus and orchestra. As a *Messa di Gloria* it consists only of the 'Kyrie' and 'Gloria'.

It is a work of richly varied textures, both in the allocation of the text to the vocal forces and in the instrumentation chosen by Rossini. The chorus and orchestra open the 'Kyrie', in E flat, and the 'Christe' is a duet in G flat for two tenors. *Il giornale* called the music 'learned, grave, sublime', which may well have applied to the opening of the 'Kyrie', but the opening of the 'Gloria', for soloists, chorus and orchestra, has a very different character. A rising figure played pizzicato is followed by a descant-like theme with repeated falling arpeggios, and then a well-articulated dotted rhythm in a rising sequence which, according to one account, made the Neapolitans applaud. These two contrasting figures were seen by the same writer as symbolising a chorus of angels singing above the rejoicing of the shepherds. Rossini used the first theme again at the end of Act II of *Le Siège de Corinthe*. By contrast, the chorus passages in the 'Qui tollis', in E minor, have a much more restrained treatment, more in common with the Scene of the Shadows in *Mosè*. In between there is a succession of movements for soloists and orchestra. The 'Laudamus te', in A, is for soprano, the 'Gratias agimus', in F, is for tenor with cor anglais and orchestra, the 'Domine Deus' a trio in E flat for soprano, alto and bass and, lastly, the 'Quoniam', in E flat, is for bass with clarinet and orchestra.

Rossini may well have used musicians from the opera house, for the important woodwind solos reflect passages in the operas that he was writing for Naples at this time. Stendhal, of course, maintained that the music was simply all Rossini's best arias in slightly different guises, thus giving the listeners the chance to play a guessing game and lending a piquancy to the occasion. Nevertheless the opera house was never far away, and it was also suggested that Rossini had assistance with the composition from Pietro Raimondo, who was in Naples to assist him with the staging of *Ciro in Babilonia*, though there seems little reason why this should have been so. Although there are only autograph fragments in the Fonds Michotte in Brussels, the score in the Naples Conservatoire is an authenticated manuscript copy.

In the following month, April 1820, Giovanni Colbran, Isabella's father, died on his estate at Castenaso near Bologna, leaving her in a comfortable financial situation, irrespective of what she might earn as an opera singer. As an indication of the extent of Rossini's involvement with her by this time, it was he who wrote to the sculptor Tadolini in Rome, where Rossini had sat for his bust, about a monumental tomb for the man who, had he lived, would have become the composer's father-in-law. In a subsequent letter Rossini detailed what he had in mind: a figure on one side representing the daughter weeping for the loss of her father, and on the other a singer celebrating his glory. He enclosed two sketches to indicate what he had in mind. Tadolini did not carry out the commission in the end, but a monument corresponding to Rossini's sketches was placed in the Certosa at Bologna, the work of a sculptor from Carrara, Del Rosso.

Opera composition was not to be far from Rossini's thoughts for long, however. For one thing, he was still under contract to Barbaia to provide operas for him in Naples, and the experience of working on Spontini's *Fernando Cortez* may well have given Rossini the stimulus to think in new textures and on a different scale. According to *Il giornale* of 25 May 1820, he had already been presented with a new libretto, *Maometto II*, prepared by Cesare della Valle, Duca di Ventignano, from his own verse play *Anna Erizo* of that year. He may have drawn inspiration for his play from Byron's *The Siege of Corinth* (1816), whose subject-matter is similar, though the siege in question is a different one. When Rossini revised *Maometto II* for Paris in 1826 it was renamed *Le Siège de Corinthe*, which has given rise to some confusion.

In the original two-act Neapolitan version, Rossini elaborated much grander structures, deployed formidable orchestral effects, and in the second act provided plenty of scope for Colbran to show off her vocal talent. In between the Naples and Paris versions, Rossini made changes to the opera for the Venetian production at La Fenice on 26 December 1822, notably the addition of an overture and a happy ending. We shall return to the work in relation to the Parisian alterations, but it is one of Rossini's most impressive creations in either version.

If Rossini began work on *Maometto* soon after receiving the libretto in late May, then his routine was likely to have been upset by the political events that shook Naples and the monarchy during the summer of 1820. During the month of June dissatisfaction with the *status quo* as represented by Ferdinand I began to mount, a plot was hatched, and on 1 July members of the Carbonari, army deserters, and even the odd disaffected priest marched out to Avellino, to the north-east of Naples, thus marking the start of their campaign. On 5 July five members of the Carbonari arrived at the royal palace in Naples and demanded an audience of the king, with the aim of obtaining a constitution similar to the one granted to Spain in 1812, which few people in Naples seem to have even read. With remarkable ease, their demand was agreed to. On 9 July, General Guglielmo Pepe, leader of the Carbonari, entered the city with his troops, and the constitution was soon proclaimed.

The events in Naples did not please rulers and politicians in other parts of Europe, however. In Vienna, Metternich, for one, viewed the situation as a grave threat, and on 26 July, the day that complete freedom of the press was decreed in Naples, he announced to the German courts that Austria would not tolerate the revolution. His rationale, as reported in a despatch of 29 August 1820 from the comte de Caraman in Vienna to the duc de Richelieu, was that the revolution was the work of a subversive sect and was 'the product of surprise and violence'. If other courts sanctioned the revolution, then its 'germs' would spread to other countries that were still free from infection. It was therefore the duty of the foreign powers, and greatly in their interest, to nip the revolution in the bud.

In pursuit of his aim, Metternich invited the allies to a conference at Troppau in October. On the first day of that month the first constitutional parliament met in Naples, though the fact that the celebrations ended with a heavy fall of rain was regarded by some as a sign of divine displeasure. At this point General Pepe resigned as commander of the Army, but became inspector-general of the Militia and the Civic Guard. He was at loggerheads with the Minister for War, but still very much enjoyed the support of the Carbonari. Sir William A'Court, the British envoy, described him going about the city 'at the head of an immense mob of people armed with guns, knives, sticks, clubs, swords, etc., carrying a tricolour flag which had previously received benediction from Carbonari priests, filling the streets with tumult and changing the cry of "King and Constitution" to that of "Liberty or Death"'.[1]

The Duchess of Floridia, the king's morganatic wife, was fearful for the safety of the royal family, and had been in secret negotiations with Sir William A'Court. When two British frigates appeared in the Bay of Naples on 6 October, there was great relief in many hearts, though the Carbonari were outraged. The Minister for Foreign Affairs was obliged officially to request the withdrawal of the ships, but privately he told A'Court: 'For heaven's sake, take no notice of the letters I have to write to you about your squadron. If it leaves the bay we are all lost.'

If Rossini was aware of such goings-on, he may well have smiled, since the whole scenario would have fitted well into an *opera buffa*, as long as no one was killed. However, the Minister for Foreign Affairs, and many like him, were in a difficult situation, for they had in many cases only accepted appointments in an attempt to prevent anarchy ensuing. They were by no means committed to radical reform. They had to wait whilst Parliament debated such profound topics as whether God was, or was not, the Legislator of the Universe. As A'Court reported: 'The question was decided in favour of the Deity by a small majority.'

Under the Protocol of Troppau, the original members of the Holy Alliance effectively asserted their right to interfere in the internal affairs of the Kingdom of the Two Sicilies. Britain did not subscribe to this protocol, though accepted that Austria should have the right, as an individual state, to intervene if it so wished. Metternich wanted the king to escape, send in troops, and then let the king play the role of mediator between his people and the European powers. On 20 November the King of Prussia, the Tsar and the Emperor of Austria wrote to the king inviting him to meet them in Laibach. He communicated the news to Parliament almost as soon as he received the letters on 6 December, and after various deliberations Parliament gave its consent for his departure. A week later he boarded HMS *Le Vengeur*, and reached Laibach on 8 January 1821. Metternich observed: 'This is the third time I am putting King Ferdinand on his feet . . . he still imagines that the throne is an easy chair to sprawl and fall asleep in.'

On 23 March the Austrian troops entered Naples, and the Revolution quickly withered away. On 15 May the king returned to his capital. There had been remarkably little bloodshed, though a number of old scores were settled. On 18 May, three days after Ferdinand's return, Metternich praised a performance of *La cenerentola* that he had just attended in Laibach. Against these events Rossini may well have experienced some hitches in getting *Maometto* into production, for it did not have its first night until 3 December 1820. At one point it was just possible that he might not have had a theatre; for, as A'Court recorded, a motion was submitted to Parliament which might well have resulted in the abolition of what was described as 'the Asiatic pomp of the theatre of San Carlo, worthy only of a nation of slaves'. As A'Court observed, it was in fact a 'splendid establishment, the delight of the capital and the great attraction of strangers'.[2] Such was the appeal of the opera house that, even with events beginning to gather pace up to the point of the king's departure, the season went on. The cool reception accorded to Rossini's latest opera was not, therefore, necessarily due to the political situation, as Beethoven experienced with *Fidelio* in 1805 when the French entered Vienna only a week before the first performance. *Maometto* simply failed to please the Neapolitans.

However, Rossini did not take it too much to heart, and indeed did not remain in Naples for long after the opening night. He was bound for Rome, where he had a commission for the Teatro Apollo. Also at this time, Rossini came into close contact with Paganini, who conducted the first performance of the new opera, *Matilde (di) Shabran*, on 24 February 1821. It is not clear when the two musicians first met, or even where they met. It may have been in Milan, or it may have been in Bologna, for when Rossini spent some time there in August 1818, after his first 'operatic' visit to Pesaro, the violinist gave a concert in the city. Paganini told a friend that Rossini was unable to accompany him, though it is not evident from the letter whether Rossini actually did offer to accompany the violinist and was then unable to, or indeed whether he even knew that Paganini was hoping that he would do so.[3]

The following year (1819), Paganini visited Naples, entered into negotiations with Barbaia for a theatre, and wisely chose the Teatro del Fondo for his opening concert on 31 March, rather than set his sights too high on San Carlo. In fact one of the critics said that, even in the Teatro del Fondo that evening, 'the first audience was more select than numerous'. Rossini's *Ermione* had had its first performance on 27 March, and if the two men had not met already, then it is almost inconceivable that they should not have done so now. Paganini went back to Rome, but planned to return to Naples for concerts in June and July, all being well. In fact he was back there in May, and spent more than a year between Naples and Palermo, and witnessed the events of July 1820; though as we found with Rossini the Revolution – such as it was – does not seem to have made a great deal of difference to the life of musicians.

The libretto for *Matilde di Shabran* was prepared by Jacopo Ferretti from an existing one which F. B. Hoffmann had written for Méhul's *Euphrosine* (Paris, 1790–1), and also drew on the play *Mathilde* (1799) by J. M. Boutet de Monvel. The Teatro Apollo in Rome was the old Teatro Tordinone which had been bought and renovated by the banker Giovanni Torlonia, Duca di Bracciano. The theatre's impresario was Luigi Vestri, and the music director Giovanni Bollo, from Turin, who unfortunately died of apoplexy on the day of the dress rehearsal. It was Paganini who stepped in to fill the breach, and conduct the first performance, which by all accounts he did admirably. He had, after all, directed the music in Lucca when Napoleon's sister Elisa was sovereign there.

Matilde di Shabran betrayed its rather scrambled genesis, however, and it was even said that Rossini had to call in Giovanni Pacini to help him out with its composition. The reception on the first evening was mixed, to say the least, though it was by no means a flop, and was mounted in other Italian opera houses, as well as in London, Paris and New York. However, after the events leading up to the first night and the rumours circulating about the opera not being all Rossini's own work, culminating in the reaction of the audience, Torlonia refused to pay Rossini the 500 scudi stipulated in the contract. Rossini reacted by removing the score and band parts from the theatre, and on 27 February wrote to Cardinal Bernetti, the Governor of Rome, who was also responsible for theatres, explaining his action. Since performances seem to have gone on until 6 March, when the season closed, presumably Rossini eventually received the sum due.

Before returning to Naples, Rossini joined with Paganini – according to the memoirs of Massimo d'Azeglio – in dressing up as blind female musicians and singing in the streets of Rome.[4] The figures of Rossini and Paganini, already quite well differentiated, were accentuated by the fact that Rossini padded himself out, while Paganini remained painfully thin. They never developed a close relationship, however, which is not entirely surprising, given the two very different personalities. Although some critics see certain characteristics common to the two musicians, in particular an eye to commercial success, there is little doubt that Rossini was much the more fastidious of the two, and by far the better composer.

From Rome, Rossini returned to Naples, though it was not the end of his association with Paganini. Their respective careers took them to several foreign cities where they found themselves simultaneously. Paris was one such, and London another. And it was to these two cities that Rossini's mind was now turning. He was known there, and his operas were being performed there. Louis Hérold, writing from Naples to his mother on 10 April 1821, told her that Rossini was 'burning to come to Paris', and at about that time Rossini must have received what seems to have been a second invitation to compose an opera for the King's Theatre in London, for he replied on 23 April that he wanted to create the definite impression that he was contracted for London. It is interesting that he singled out Barbaia as one of those he particularly wanted to be convinced.

During the course of April, Rossini conducted Haydn's *Die Schöpfung* at the San Carlo, and invited Hérold to attend the rehearsal and give his advice. One may assume, then, that Hérold knew that Rossini was sincere in his desire to leave Naples, and indeed events were in train that would begin to make his departure all the more likely. Barbaia had been negotiating to become impresario of the Kärnthnertortheater in Vienna and eventually, on 1 December 1821, signed the contract. As a consequence, Rossini's contract was renegotiated, giving him the freedom to travel to Vienna, London and Paris, though it was implicit that he would eventually return to Naples. As *Il giornale* for 5 January 1822 indicated: 'Rossini, a name which in itself is worthy of a thousand eulogies, the honour of Pesaro, the ornament of Italy – Rossini is about to abandon the city . . . returning from the banks of the Seine, [he] will stay among us again for more years, according to an agreement reached with the impresario of the royal theatres.'

Under the terms of his contract, Rossini was entitled to a benefit night at the San Carlo, so for the occasion he composed a cantata, *La riconoscenza* ('Gratitude'), to a text by Giulio Genoino, for soprano, alto, tenor and bass soloists, chorus and orchestra. Subscription tickets were suspended for the evening – 27 December 1821 – so that Rossini would derive the maximum benefit from the occasion. He is said to have received some 3,000 ducats on that night. The cantata turned out to be one of Rossini's more enduring occasional pieces, and was repeated in Naples in 1822, in Verona the same year, as *Il vero omaggio*, and in Bologna in 1829, as *Il serto votivo*, to welcome a new papal legate.

Almost two weeks before the benefit performance, on 14 December 1821, Rossini wrote to his uncle, Giuseppe Guidarini, and asked him to obtain a baptismal certificate and proof of his bachelor status, for he was going to marry Isabella Colbran. He asked his uncle not to break the news yet, and that the banns should not be published. He subsequently maintained (to the painter Guglielmo de Sanctis) that if he had had only himself to consider he would have remained single, but that he married largely to please his mother, who was fully aware of the rumours linking his name with Isabella's.

It seems a curiously detached way of having embarked on the matrimonial state, but Rossini was no fool, nor did he fool himself. He certainly seems to have enjoyed the company of women, and enjoyed being in a relationship. On the other hand, despite his youthful precociousness, he was no great romantic lover, either, and Isabella had been Barbaia's mistress, by all accounts, before she became his. Through their common bond in opera they were drawn together, and as Rossini approached his thirtieth birthday (she was thirty-seven), and was set to embark upon a completely new phase of his existence, marriage no doubt seemed a very sensible step to take. After all, Isabella was a fairly wealthy woman, with both her parents dead; and, since she was clearly going to spend a good deal of time in Rossini's company in the future, why not set the seal on what had proved to be a very successful working relationship by making it acceptable to the world at large? This led to the accusation that he had merely married her for her money, a claim it would be difficult to refute completely; but his subsequent treatment of Isabella was not the behaviour of a man who had only seen matrimony as a means to a more comfortable existence. On the other hand, whether Rossini saw it as a marriage of true minds, let alone true love, is equally open to question.

Before the departure of Rossini and Colbran for Vienna, however, there was one last opera for Naples, *Zelmira*, which was to be given a trial run at the San Carlo on 16 February 1822. On the final evening, 6 March, King Ferdinand attended and, as *Il giornale* reported, the run ended in triumph: 'His Majesty gave the departing *maestro* and the singers flattering indications of his gratitude at the end of the performance; the entire vast auditorium then resounded to *viva* and continuous applause; the performers were called back on stage, and received from the approving audience that farewell, which is the dearest and most desired reward of generous souls.'

In reality *Zelmira* was only moderately successful in Naples, and it seemed as if, for the moment, Rossini was not concerned to break any new ground, despite the fact that this was to be given in Vienna, where several of his operas had already been heard. The libretto, it is true, cannot have provided a great deal of inspiration, having been an adaptation by Tottola of Dormont de Belloy's *Zelmire* (1762). In Vienna, as indeed in Milan, the work had a much greater success; and, whilst a certain amount of obloquy was heaped on the libretto, the music was taken seriously and considered worthy of a composer of the status Rossini now enjoyed there. Indeed, one is tempted to speculate that, with Rossini about to leave Naples, *Zelmira* was tailored more to northern Italian and, especially, Viennese taste than to the Neapolitan public.

There is an interesting letter from Donizetti, written not long after his arrival in Naples, to his teacher Giovanni Simone Mayr (Johann Simon Mayer) in Bergamo, dating from 4 March 1822.[5] Six days after the first performance of Rossini's *Zelmira*, *Il giornale* announced that a new opera by Donizetti would be performed during the summer season; and on 12 May his *La zingara*, to a libretto by Tottola, had its first performance at the Teatro Nuovo. As Rossini was preparing to depart, therefore, a new star was already in the ascendant. Donizetti was twenty-five, almost six years Rossini's junior, and he had some rather tart remarks on the way in which the *maestro* was preparing a performance of Mayr's oratorio *Atalia* for the San Carlo. He reported that Atalia herself was not being sung by Isabella Colbran, but by Giuseppina Fabré, who had not sung for two years, and was simply not good enough. In fact Rossini had 'edited' the music to suit her. Rossini seemed far too relaxed, in Donizetti's opinion, if the singers were not keeping up with him in the soloist's rehearsals, and when it came to the orchestral rehearsals, instead of conducting, Rossini was chatting with the *prime donne*. Then there were several other omissions of the music which Donizetti noted. In his opinion they (Rossini and Barbaia in particular) were such dogs that they ought to be out looking for bones, rather than performing Mayr's music. However, when Donizetti took issue with Barbaia, who planned to give the oratorio as part of his Viennese programme, Donizetti was assured that the oratorio would be given in its original version, as the composer intended.

From another source, which appeared in the *Journal des débats* of 11 March 1822, and which related specifically to the final rehearsals of *Zelmira*, it was observed that although Rossini appeared outwardly unconcerned, and said very little, this was a definite policy on his part.[6] Initially it was to demonstrate his confidence in Giuseppe Festa, the conductor, but also so as not to upset the orchestra or make the singers look foolish. However, he stored up in his memory all the points he wished to make, and then communicated them individually, in private, after the rehearsal. He was also capable of detecting copyists' errors in the score without even looking at the music, it was claimed. This was an aspect of Rossini's working practice that Donizetti could not have been aware of in these first weeks – or, rather, days – in Naples, but which were the product of the great practical experience that Rossini had by now accumulated in his work with singers and instrumentalists all over Italy. Gone were the days when he laughed out loud at a *prima donna*'s cadenza, when he upset the chorus, or alienated the orchestral players in his youthful zeal.

The day after the last performance of *Zelmira* in Naples, on 7 March 1822, Rossini left the city with Isabella Colbran, the bass Antonio Ambrosi and the tenors Giovanni David and Andrea Nozzari, *en route* for Vienna. They did not go straight there, however; for, on 16 March, Rossini and Colbran were married at Castenaso, in the presence of his parents. The witnesses were Francisco Fernándes, servant to Isabella, and Luigi Cacciari, who lived in the parish. It was noted that the wedding had taken place without the banns having been published.

Under the terms of the marriage settlement, Isabella Colbran was said to have brought to Rossini a dowry worth 40,000 Roman scudi. In addition to the villa at Castenaso, which Giovanni Colbran had bought in 1812, Isabella inherited land in Sicily. The size of the dowry, in addition to the disparity in their ages, made for malicious gossip. Stendhal, in his *Correspondance*, exaggerated her age, saying that she was forty or fifty years old, and portrayed Rossini as the recipient of Barbaia's largess, to the extent of a free carriage, food and lodgings, and a cast-off mistress.[7]

As in most situations of this sort, the truth probably lay somewhere in the middle. As we saw earlier, with the benefit of hindsight Rossini said that he ought not to have married. Certainly, if it was said to have been done purely for Isabella's money, then he was on the verge of a new stage in his career, which might well take him to great wealth, but which by now had its own impetus. Her money may certainly have been useful, but he no longer needed her – if he ever had needed her – as a protectress. Moreover, her voice was in decline, and her days as a *prima donna* were numbered. From a purely practical point of view, as Rossini's career developed and his wife's declined, great strains would be put on their marriage because of his long periods of absence abroad, unless she chose to accompany him everywhere. In the event she chose to remain at home, and so the deterioration of the marriage set in. They lived together for about eight years, but after that Isabella lived alone, or with Rossini's father, and she developed a passion for gambling. As long as she lived – and she did not die until 1845 – Rossini behaved correctly towards her, but it was usually his father who had to bear the brunt of her temperament, especially after the death of Rossini's mother in 1827.

The party of musicians had reached Vienna by 22 March 1822, for on that day Rossini wrote to Giovanni Battista Benelli, impresario of the King's Theatre in London, and announced his recent marriage.[8] He then stated quite categorically that neither he nor his wife wished to return to Naples after their season in Vienna, and that if Benelli had not already engaged a *prima donna* for the next year, then they would come together, though he asked Benelli to keep all of this secret for the time being, because he had other irons in the fire. Colbran was to make her Viennese début in *Zelmira*, which opera, Rossini claimed, was his property, and would therefore be the opera in which Colbran would make her London début also. Barbaia, however, seems to have thought otherwise about the ownership of *Zelmira*, and for this reason he is said to have withheld money which Rossini had invested in Barbaia's gambling enterprises – both the capital and the interest due – which ought to have been handed over to Rossini when he left Naples. It is interesting to observe how Rossini absorbed Barbaia's business methods, becoming a much more redoubtable adversary in financial and legal matters over the years.

Five days after writing to Benelli, Rossini attended a performance of Weber's *Der Freischütz*, conducted by the composer, at the Kärnthnertortheater. The role of Agathe was sung by Wilhelmine Schröder-Devrient. The first performance of the opera had been in Berlin the year before (1821), on 18 June, and Barbaia was well aware of the impression that it had made on the German-speaking world. He therefore asked Weber to compose an opera for Vienna, which was to be *Euryanthe*, with its first performance on 25 October 1823. There is no record of a meeting between Weber and Rossini at this time, and from what we know of Weber's opinion of Rossini it is more than likely that he went out of his way to avoid any such meeting. It was probably not so much the music as Rossini's popularity which incensed Weber. Four years later, however, the latter sought Rossini out in Paris, as Rossini recalled for Wagner in 1860.[9]

Weber was on his way to England, and presented himself unannounced. Rossini said that his feelings at that moment were close to those experienced when he found himself in the presence of Beethoven. Weber was very pale, and breathless from climbing the stairs to Rossini's apartment, and was indeed to die within the year. He began to make amends for the articles he had published against Rossini, but the latter would not let him continue. 'Come on, let's not talk about that. In any case, I never read them; I don't speak German.' He then went on to tell Weber that the only German he ever remembered or was able to pronounce – and that 'after heroic application' on his part – was 'Ich bin zufrieden' ('I am satisfied'), which went down very well in Vienna. This made Weber smile, and Rossini was able to close the incident by telling him how much honour he had done him in discussing his operas at all, when he was so insignificant alongside the geniuses of German music.

Rossini embraced him, and declared that if his friendship could be of any use to Weber he offered it completely and with all his heart. Rossini said that he was appalled at the thought of the strain that the journey to London would put on Weber in his state of health, and when Weber came back to see him a few days later Rossini begged him not to go. It was, however, his contractual obligation to produce *Oberon* for London which obsessed Weber. Rossini gave him a letter of introduction to the king, with whom he had got on well, he said, and embraced him for the last time.

The linking of Weber and Beethoven by Rossini at that point in his talk with Wagner subsequently led the latter to ask Rossini whether he had ever met Beethoven, since various rumours were in circulation by this time. Even before he arrived in Vienna, Rossini (according to Michotte's account) had heard some Beethoven string quartets in Milan, and said that he knew some of the piano music.

It was only on his arrival in Vienna, however, that he heard a Beethoven symphony, the 'Eroica'. 'This music overwhelmed me,' said Rossini. 'I had only one thought, to meet this great genius, to see him, if only once. I sounded out Salieri on the subject, since I knew that he was in contact with Beethoven.' Beethoven had studied Italian vocal style with Salieri when he first came to Vienna, and Salieri warned Rossini that Beethoven had such a 'shadowy and fantastical' character that it would be very difficult to realise Rossini's wish.

Rossini then interpolated into his conversation with Wagner the suspicion that had fallen on Salieri of having been responsible for Mozart's death by slow poisoning. He told Wagner that he had joked with Salieri about this, and said: 'It's lucky for Beethoven that, out of an instinct for self-preservation, he doesn't invite you to his table, for you might well see him off into the next world, as you did with Mozart.'

'Do I look like a poisoner, then?' retorted Salieri.

'Oh, no,' he answered. 'You look more like an utter coward.'

According to Rossini, that is precisely what he was. Moreover, when it came to seeking a meeting with Beethoven, all Salieri could do was go through Giuseppe Carpani, the Imperial Poet Laureate, who was in any case acting as something of a publicist for Rossini in Vienna, and since he was *persona grata* with Beethoven was able to arrange the meeting.

It appears that, before this approach through Carpani, Rossini had tried to visit Beethoven in the company of the publisher Artaria, but that when Artaria came back to Rossini, who waited outside in the street, he told him that Beethoven was unable to receive him because the cold had affected his eyes and he was unable to receive anyone at all. This gave rise to many apocryphal stories that Beethoven had simply refused to see Rossini when he went with Artaria not once but twice, according to Schindler, because he so disapproved of him, and it was given substance by such factors as an entry in one of Beethoven's conversation-books for August 1826 in which someone asks: 'It is true, is it not, that Rossini wanted to visit you, but you refused to see him?' There is no written answer.[10]

What Rossini said to Ferdinand Hiller in 1856 was: 'During my stay in Vienna I had myself introduced to him [Beethoven] by old Calpani [sic], but between his deafness and my ignorance of German, conversation was impossible. But I am glad that I at least saw him.'

Then, in 1867, Eduard Hanslick visited Rossini in Paris and asked him to confirm that Beethoven had refused to receive him, as Schindler and other biographers asserted:

> On the contrary. I got Carpani, the Italian poet with whom I had already called upon Salieri, to introduce me, and he received me immediately, and very politely. True, the visit did not last very long, for conversation with Beethoven was nothing less than painful. His hearing was especially difficult on that day, and in spite of my shouting very loudly, he was unable to understand me; his little experience of Italian may have made conversation more difficult.

Of course none of this gainsays the fact that Rossini was far from being Beethoven's favourite composer. To Seyfried he is supposed to have answered the question 'What is Rossini?' with the reply 'A good scene-painter'.[11] And, again, in Seyfried's account, Beethoven said:

> The Bohemians are born musicians; the Italians ought to take them as their models. What do they have to show for their famous conservatories? Look at their idol, Rossini! If fortune had not given him a pretty talent and pretty melodies by the score, the things that he learned at school would only have provided him with potatoes for his big belly.

Beethoven told Rossini to stick to *opera buffa*. He had read the score of *Il barbiere di Siviglia*, he told Rossini, and that was clearly his *métier*. It is interesting that Beethoven's pupil, Archduke Rudolph, had written a set of variations on an aria from *Zelmira*, which Beethoven had corrected. Nevertheless, according to Beethoven, Italians lacked the technique to write any other kind of opera than *buffa*, and how were they to acquire that technique in Italy? They simply did not have the nature required for *opera seria* – which is somewhat surprising in view of the fact that they invented it, Rossini might have pointed out.

In view of Beethoven's strictures on the Italian conservatoires, however, it is interesting, if not ironic, that Rossini told Wagner that because of the deficiency of musical education in Italy in his youth he absorbed what he could from the scores, the property of a friend in Bologna, of *Die Schöpfung*, *Le nozze di Figaro* and *Die Zauberflöte*. That was when he was fifteen years old, he said, and since he had

had no hope at that time of obtaining the works for himself directly he slaved away at copying them. Often he only transcribed the vocal part, and did not look at the orchestral parts. He would then try to write his own accompaniment, which he would then compare with those of Haydn or Mozart, and in that way, he claimed, he learned more than from all the courses at the Bologna Conservatoire.

Possibly in Beethoven's assessment of Rossini and Italian music generally there was more than a little professional jealousy. After all, *Leonore-Fidelio* had not been exactly a *succès fou*. He consoled himself, according to Schindler, by saying: 'Well, they cannot rob me of my place in musical history!'[12] To Freudenberg, during a visit to Baden in 1824, Beethoven gave what was probably his most considered judgement of Rossini, whilst at the same time reflecting his deeper-seated dissatisfaction with the general climate of the times: 'Rossini is a talented and lyrical composer; his music suits the frivolous and sensuous spirit of the age, and his output is so great that he requires only as many weeks as the German composers need years to write an opera.' Given the compositional history of *Leonore-Fidelio*, that was certainly true.

Rossini's description of the actual visit doubtless became somewhat heightened in colour over the years, but in 1860 this is how he recounted it to Wagner:

> As I went up the staircase that led to the poor apartment where the great man lived, I had difficulty in controlling my emotions. When the door opened, I found myself in a kind of den as dirty as it was in a dreadful state of disorder. I remember above all that the ceiling, directly under the roof, was criss-crossed with cracks, through which the rain must have poured in.
>
> The portraits that we have of Beethoven convey his overall physiognomy quite well. But what no etcher's tool could express is the indefinable sadness that permeated all his features, whilst under thick eyebrows burned, as in the depth of caves, eyes which though small, seemed to burn right through one. His voice was soft, and ever so slightly veiled.

At first Beethoven gave no indication of being aware of the fact that he had visitors, and went on scrutinising some music proofs that he had just finished correcting. He then looked up and spoke to Rossini in fairly comprehensible Italian. He congratulated him on *Il barbiere di Siviglia*. He wished him success with *Zelmira*, but his last words were an exhortation to write more 'Barbers'. Prior to this, Rossini said that he had expressed his admiration of his genius to Beethoven, and his gratitude at having been allowed to express it in person. In response to this, Beethoven sighed deeply and said: 'O! un infelice!' As Rossini went back down the stairs, he could not help but weep, he said, at the thought of the painful impression the visit had made on him, and that great man abandoned and destitute. Carpani shrugged it off, saying that Beethoven wanted it that way, that he was a misanthrope, churlish, and unable to sustain any of his friendships. Even so, that evening, as Rossini attended a gala banquet given by Metternich, he could not forget the lugubrious visit earlier in the day, and he could still hear the words 'un infelice'.

He could not fail to note the contrast between the esteem in which he himself was held, especially in that brilliant assembly, and the condition of Beethoven. He even voiced his opinions there and then, about the way the Court and the aristocracy had treated the greatest genius of the age, but the response he elicited was the same as the one Carpani had given him: it was entirely Beethoven's fault. To a large extent that was true, though equally there were many people who simply did not know, and it would be true to say that there was more concern in London, towards the end of Beethoven's life, than there was in Vienna. The Philharmonic Society sent to Beethoven the sum of £100 'to be applied to his comforts and necessities during his illness'. Rossini mooted a pension, provided by the rich families of Vienna, though in fact since 1809 Beethoven had been in receipt of an annual pension of 4,000 florins, payable in half-yearly instalments, provided by Prince Lobkowitz, Prince Kinsky and Archduke Rudolph, and although at times payment was not always regular from all parties Beethoven was able to save money, which he invested for his nephew. There was a good deal of truth, then, in the assertion that Beethoven preferred things that way. More accurately, by now he was incapable of living any other way.

It must have been very galling to the 'serious' musicians to see the reception accorded Rossini, and one can well understand Beethoven's dismissal of his music as suiting the 'frivolous and sensuous spirit of the age'. Rossini was born of a tradition where music was still very much required to suit the spirit of the age. Indeed, it was a fairly recent phenomenon for music *not* to be suited to the spirit of the age, and it was one of the most striking results of the effect of Romanticism on music that from now on it was possible for music to exist in a kind of vacuum, which Beethoven illustrates supremely. Perhaps the last word on this encounter may be left to Schumann: 'The butterfly crossed the path of the eagle, but the latter turned aside so as not to crush it with the beating of his wings.'

Rossini's success in Vienna was no overnight phenomenon. *L'inganno felice* and *Tancredi* had been heard in 1816; *Ciro in Babilonia* and *L'italiana in Algeri* in 1817; *Demetrio e Polibio* and *Elisabetta, regina d'Inghilterra* in 1818; and *Il barbiere di Siviglia, Otello* (in German), *La gazza ladra* and *Ricciardo e Zoraide* (in German) in 1819. The following year, 1820, *Torvaldo e Dorliska* and *La cenerentola* (in German) were given there; and then in 1821 *Mosè in Egitto* and *Edoardo e Cristina* (in German). What was planned for Vienna now by Barbaia, in 1822, was virtually a Rossini festival from 13 April to 8 July, but his music came as no sudden dazzling revelation to the Viennese public, but was rather an affirmation of the popularity and success that had been growing for over five years. Not all the operas had been successes. *Elisabetta*, for example, failed to please in 1818, but the intensity of the attacks of some of the critics and the animosity of composers such as Weber point clearly to the fact that Rossini had a large enough following among the opera-going public to stimulate such a reaction.

Barbaia's programme was a mixture of operas already heard in Vienna – *La cenerentola*, *Elisabetta*, *La gazza ladra* and *Ricciardo e Zoraide* – with the addition of one or two new ones such as *Matilde di Shabran* and, to open the season, *Zelmira*, with Colbran in the title role. She sang, despite the fact that she was indisposed, but did justice neither to herself nor to the part. One of the problems for the company seems to have been that of accommodating to the somewhat restricted acoustic of the Kärnthnertortheater, when compared with the San Carlo. Nevertheless the opera was a success, and enthusiasm for it increased the more it was heard.

Although Rossini prepared and staged the opera, he left the conducting to Joseph Weigl (1766–1846), opera-composer and resident chief conductor, and possibly because Weigl, in company with Weber, had been branded as anti-Rossinian he gave it his best possible care and attention, which contributed in no small way to the eventual success of *Zelmira*. Indeed, it provoked Rossini himself to reflect to Ferdinand Hiller how unlike his own style it all was, and at the same time Rossini's reaction makes an interesting rider to the Donizetti letter referred to previously. As Rossini said:

> He was aware that he [Weigl] had been portrayed to me as one of my enemies. So as to persuade me of the opposite, he rehearsed the orchestra for *Zelmira* with such care as I have never encountered in myself or anyone else. On occasion I wanted to ask him not to take his precision to such lengths; but I have to confess that it went off magnificently.

The season progressed in a truly Rossinian crescendo of delight and praise, culminating in the climax of the final evening, 8 July, which was Rossini's benefit and Colbran's name-day.

Rossini had condensed *Ricciardo e Zoraide* into a single act, which seemed to turn it into a continuous ovation for the composer, his wife and the other singers. The performance was followed by supper in the Rossinis' rooms, where gradually a crowd began to gather outside because it was rumoured that Vienna's leading musicians would come and serenade the couple. When Rossini learned why the crowd had gathered, according to the Leipzig *Allgemeine musikalische Zeitung*, he declared that the people must not be left disappointed by the lack of a serenade, and therefore he and the cast obliged. Unfortunately this failed to satisfy the populace; and, although by now it was gone two o'clock in the morning, when the lights were extinguished upstairs, clearly indicating that it was high time everyone went home to bed, the atmosphere among the crowd began to turn unpleasant, and the police had to disperse them.

Rossini composed an 'Addio ai Viennesi', for tenor and piano, which he subsequently used elsewhere, so that it became known simply as the 'Addio di Rossini'. He had good reason to be grateful to the Viennese, for in addition to his benefit, the *Allgemeine musikalische Zeitung* reported, Rossini also received a gift of 3,500 ducats on a silver salver at the end of the banquet at which the 'Addio' was sung. Although the last night of the opera season was 8 July, Rossini and his wife did not leave the city until two weeks later. They then went south to Bologna, stopping at Udine on the way, where a performance of *Matilde di Shabran* was being given on the 25th. The Rossinis were recognised, and once again received what was by now becoming the statutory ovation, not to say rapturous reception.

For the enthusiasm, bordering on hysteria, that now surrounded Rossini, one draws parallels with the progress of Paganini around Europe. No doubt commercialism played its part. The souvenir trade, for example, became a lucrative source of income for dealers in Vienna both for Rossini's and Paganini's visits. Alongside this, however, is the fact that perfectly serious people were caught up in the 'hysteria', and were moved by what they heard and saw.

Towards the end of July, Rossini and his wife were installed in the villa at Castenaso, where they signed the contract for the Carnival season of 1822–3 at Teatro La Fenice in Venice, and where Rossini, almost certainly with his wife's assistance, wrote his *Gorgheggi e solfeggi per soprano*, subsequently published in Paris in 1827 by Antonio Pacini. As an indication of his married state and enhanced financial standing, he began negotiations for the purchase of what was effectively a *palazzo* in Bologna: 243 Strada Maggiore, now 26 Via Mazzini. He paid 4,150 Roman scudi for it that November (1822), and two years later began to alter and restore it, though it was not until the autumn of 1829 that he settled in.

By the autumn of 1822, Rossini was at work on a new opera for Venice, *Semiramide*, to a libretto by Gaetano Rossi, based on Voltaire's *Sémiramis* (1748). In the mean time, however, international political events were developing in a way that would extend even to the quiet world of Castenaso, and draw Rossini up on to the world stage even more than his recent visit to Vienna.

Before the Congress of Laibach was formally adjourned on 28 February 1821, it was agreed that the representatives of the allied powers would meet in Florence in September the following year. Metternich had been unwilling to let the congress disperse until it had become apparent what was going to happen in Italy, and in Naples especially. In fact the Russians and Austrians stayed in Laibach until May and, as we saw earlier, King Ferdinand only returned to Naples on the fifteenth of that month. As the time approached for the congress to convene in Florence in 1822, Metternich felt that it would be easier, and wiser, to keep things under Austrian control, so changed the venue to Verona. He and his party arrived there on 12 October, eight days before the congress was due to open. Superficially, at least, it was the most impressive gathering of heads of state since 1815. The Emperor of Austria, the Tsar of Russia, the King of Prussia, and all the rulers of Italy except the Pope were present.

Byron was suitably acerbic about the occasion. Precious little was said about Italy, which was the original *raison d'être* of the Congress of Verona, apart from the reduction of the size of the Austrian army in Naples and its phased withdrawal from Piedmont. There was much talk of Spain, but a deputation of Greek patriots was turned back at Ancona, having been intercepted by the Austrians, and so did not even reach Verona. So wrote Byron:

> Strange sight this Congress! destined to unite
> All that's incongruous, all that's opposite.
> I speak not of the sovereigns – they're alike,
> As common coins as ever mint could strike;
> But those who sway the puppets, pull the strings,
> Have more of motley than their heavy kings.
> Jews, authors, generals, charlatans, combine,
> While Europe wonders at the vast design. . . .[13]

As a social event, however, the congress was a great success. There was a banquet in the Roman amphitheatre, and there was Rossini. Two of his operas were given during the course of the congress: *L'inganno felice* and *La donna del lago*. He was not responsible for the production of either work, though he attended a performance of the first. He was not present for the second opera, however. He provided two cantatas, both with texts by Rossi: *Il vero omaggio*, which drew on *La riconoscenza* (Naples, 1821), and *La santa alleanza*. Unfortunately both works are lost, but we know that the first was scored for soprano (Velluti on this occasion), two tenors, bass, chorus and orchestra, and was given in the Teatro Filarmonico in Verona on 3 December 1822. The second had been given on 24 November in the amphitheatre, and was scored for two basses, chorus and orchestra. As Rossini observed to Hiller: 'In view of the fact that I was "*le dieu de l'harmonie*" [so Metternich had written] would I go there where harmony was so badly needed?'[14]

Rossini had a tussle with the Royal Chamber of Commerce in Verona, who had officially commissioned *Il vero omaggio* and arranged its performance in the Teatro Filarmonico. After the show, the representative of the Chamber of Commerce tried to obtain the autograph score of the work, regarding it as part of the commission. Luckily Rossini had foreseen the eventuality and given specific instructions that the score be returned to him. Matters dragged on into April 1823, but Rossini prevailed in the end.

By this time, of course, he had long since left Verona. He and Isabella were in Venice, in fact, by 9 December 1822 at the latest, and under the terms of his agreement with La Fenice he was to prepare a version of *Maometto II* and compose a new opera with a

Isabella Colbran (1785–1845), depicted by Heinrich Schmidt as Sappho in Mayr's first opera *Saffo* (1794). The portrait was painted in 1817, by which time Colbran and Rossini were presumably lovers. The soprano had created the role of Desdemona in *Otello* in December 1816, and went on to create the title role in *Armida* – one of her most dramatic – in November 1817. In all Rossini was to write ten operas for Colbran between *Elisabetta* (1815) and *Semiramide* (1823).

Left: Geltrude (or Gertrude) Righetti-Giorgi (1793–1862), who created the role of Rosina in *Il barbiere di Siviglia* in 1816, and the title role in *La cenerentola* in 1817. She and Rossini had known each other since childhood, and she left a detailed account of the opening night of *Il barbiere*.

Below: A French production of Beaumarchais' play, *Le Barbier de Séville*, from about 1822. Count Almaviva, disguised as a drunken soldier, asks Dr Bartolo which of the two is the doctor in question, while Rosina slips him the letter giving details for their planned elopement. Rossini's opera had been heard for the first time in Paris some three years previously, and may well have been responsible for giving new significance to a play that was by now almost fifty years old.

Above: A lithograph by Villain satirising Rossini's use of the drum, which in its day was seen as destructive of existing music. Apollo, for example, retreats to Mount Parnassus, his lyre on his back and his hands over his ears. Nevertheless, the Rossini opera festival that Barbaia organised in Vienna in 1822 was a huge success. The composer, newly married, was present in the city for its duration, and managed to obtain an interview with the increasingly reclusive Beethoven.

Right: Rossini in Paris in 1823, as portrayed by Boilly, in a lithograph by Villain. At this time the composer was in close negotiation with the French Royal Household to settle in Paris for a year and compose two operas, as well as staging one of his existing operas for the Théâtre-Italien. In the event he also took over the direction of the Italien for a period.

Above: Rossini's last opera for Italy was *Semiramide*, first heard at Teatro La Fenice, Venice, on 3 February 1823. Here is one of the sets by Alessandro Sanquirico (1777–1849), the interior of the Sanctuary for Act Two, scene four, when the opera was given the following year (1824) at both La Scala – where he worked for some fifteen years – and San Carlo, Naples.

Left: Costume design for Joséphine Fodor-Mainvielle (1789–1870) in the title role of *Semiramide*, when the opera was given in Paris at the Théâtre-Italien in December 1825.

Above: Lake Lucerne, which provided the setting for Rossini's last opera, *Guillaume Tell*, first heard at the Paris Opéra on 3 August 1829. Rossini's treatment creates in musical terms the atmosphere of the Swiss landscape in a Romantic vein that becomes an essential ingredient of *grand opéra*, but which Rossini declined to develop further.

Right: Costume designs for *Moïse et Pharaon* (1827), the Paris version of *Mosè in Egitto* (1818), which later became known in Italy as *Il nuovo Mosè*. The role of Moses was sung by Nicolas Levasseur (1791–1871), the star bass of the Paris Opéra.

Above left: The Salle Favart in Paris (later the Opéra-Comique), which housed the Théâtre-Italien from 1825 to 1838. After Rossini became director, he and his successors attracted a host of distinguished singers, including Grisi, Malibran and Lablache.

Below left: Maria Malibran (1808–36), whose interpretation of Desdemona in Rossini's *Otello* was especially admired.

Above right: Luigi Lablache (1794–1858), the half-French, half-Irish, Neapolitan-born bass whose fame was truly international. Schubert dedicated three *Lieder* to him, and Wagner praised his Leporello.

Right: Giulia Grisi (1811–69), who in 1831 was to create the role of Adalgisa in Bellini's *Norma*, and then went on to sing the title role in later life.

Rossini in the 1830s, in a Benjamin caricature from *Le Charivari*. The composer oozes prosperity, with a bag full of the proceeds from his operas, though the Opéra itself is in a state of collapse. The attitude of the more highbrow critics to Rossini's music is seen from the designation '*musique facile*' on the paper emerging from Rossini's coat pocket.

starring role for his wife. The revision of *Maometto* did not make it attractive to the Venetians. Basically he provided an overture and a happy ending, which was 'Tanti affetti' from *La donna del lago*. There was more borrowing – from *Ermione* and *Bianca e Falliero*. The first night was on 26 December 1822, with Colbran singing the role of Anna, which she had created in Naples. Unfortunately she was not on form, and for that and other reasons the complete opera was withdrawn, and in its place the first act only was given, with the one-act version of *Ricciardo e Zoraide*. It would seem that the combination had little success, either. What came next, namely *Semiramide* on 3 February 1823, was to be distinguished by several characteristics, not least the fact that it was the last opera Rossini composed for Italy.

The overture, long a war horse of Toscanini, incorporates several themes to be heard later in the opera, and Rossini developed the form in a way that is almost symphonic. The orchestration and the development of the material are deployed on an appropriately symphonic scale.

Semiramide, Queen of Babylon, has murdered her husband, King Ninus, aided and abetted by Prince Assur, as well as attempting to murder her son. He escaped, however, and now, under the name of Arsace, some fifteen years later, has become a successful soldier with a command on one of the kingdom's remotest frontiers. Neither Semiramide nor Assur knows, of course, who he really is when he is summoned to Babylon. He brings with him a casket in which is a sword and some scrolls which belonged to his father. The queen is soon to announce whom she will take as her consort, but when she meets Arsace she declares that she will marry him, and not her partner in crime, Assur. The voice of Ninus speaks from beyond the grave, charging Arsace to avenge his death.

From this central situation the plot devolves, allowing ample scope to the composer for interplay of character in what is a particularly highly charged emotional tale of love and duty in conflict. There is more than a passing similarity to the plot of *Hamlet* in the Semiramide–Arsace–Assur triangle and the ghostly voice of Ninus. Probably the most famous individual aria from the opera is Semiramide's *cavatina* from the first act, 'Bel raggio lusinghier', which is a love-song conveyed through vocal brilliance. There is also an impressive mad scene for Assur, before the finale to Act II. This was the last of the great parts that Rossini wrote for the bass Filippo

Galli, but it is no dying fall. Indeed, the opera as a whole seems to find an inspiration, as it proceeds to its conclusion, that Rossini did not always find, by any means. When *Semiramide* was revived in Paris in 1825–6, Rossini gave more music to the queen's death scene – and, indeed, he may well have felt that the original ending, with the death of Semiramide, Arsace's distress, attempt at suicide, and proclamation as king, was all too sudden.

Some time in mid-March the Rossinis left Venice, and on 1 April 1823 a bust to Canova was unveiled in nearby Treviso, with a Rossini cantata, *Omaggio pastorale*, for three female voices and orchestra, to celebrate the occasion. After that, however, for the rest of the year, the composer remained in Bologna and Castenaso. He did not return to Naples – and, indeed, he had no intention of doing so. He was preparing for yet another trip abroad, this time to London, via Paris.

CHAPTER SEVEN

Triumph and Farewell

During 1823, Rossini and his wife signed contracts with Benelli, impresario of the Italian Opera at the King's Theatre in London. Colbran, naturally, was to sing, and Rossini was to compose a new opera. It was even said that the title of the opera, *La figlia dell'aria*, had been decided, though it seems unlikely that Rossini ever worked on an opera with this title, and certainly he did not complete one. There was one eventually called *Ugo, re d'Italia*, which remained incomplete; and, according to Kobbé, when Garcia first gave *Semiramide* in New York (1845) it had as its subtitle *La figlia dell'aria.*[1]

On 20 October the Rossinis left Bologna for Paris and London, via Milan, where a week later the Duke of Devonshire gave them letters of introduction for the British capital. By 4 November they were in Geneva, where they spent the night, and reached Paris by the evening of 9 November. They stayed in rue Rameau, between rue Sainte Anne and rue de Richelieu, just opposite the Bibliothèque Nationale; there they were guests for a month of the Genoese writer Nicola Bagioli.

By this time no less than twelve of Rossini's operas had been staged at the Théâtre-Italien in Paris. Curiously, there was a rumour that its director, Ferdinando Paër, had deliberately tried to delay, and even prevent, the launching of Rossini's career in Paris. On 11 November 1823, *Il barbiere di Siviglia* was given at the Théâtre-Italien as a benefit performance for Garcia, with Rossini present. After the opera, the first clarinettist of the orchestra, Gambaro, led the band of the Garde Nationale to rue Rameau to serenade the composer. There was another benefit for Garcia at the theatre on 25 November, again attended by both Rossinis, when the opera was *Otello*. Pasta was also in the cast, and at the end Rossini took his place between the two stars on the stage and acknowledged the applause. Meanwhile he had appeared in some of the grandest salons in Paris, such as those of the duchesse de Berry and the comtesse Merlin;[2] but the social high point of Rossini's first visit to Paris was the banquet given by some of his admirers on Sunday, 16 November 1823, at the Restaurant du Veau qui tette, place du Châtelet.

Although *La Gazette de France* described it as a 'vast picnic', some 150 guests packed into a room decorated with medallions bearing the titles of Rossini's operas in gold, and surrounded with garlands of flowers. The composer's initials were inscribed over the seat of honour, to which he was escorted on his arrival, whilst an orchestra, led by Gambaro, played the overture to *La gazza ladra*. Rossini was seated between Pasta and the actress Mademoiselle Mars (Anne-Françoise Boutet), and opposite was Jean-François Lesueur, flanked by Madame Rossini and another actress, Mademoiselle George (Marguérite-Joséphine Weimer). Amongst those present were the composers Auber, Boïeldieu and Hérold; the singers Pasta, Laure Cinti (known as Cinti-Damoreau after her wedding in 1827) and Manuel Garcia; the actors Joseph de Lafont and François-Joseph Talma; and the painter Horace Vernet. By a curious quirk of fate, Venet's mistress at the time was Olympe Pélissier, later to become the second Madame Rossini.

During the meal excerpts from Rossini operas were played, and then there were various speeches and toasts. Nicola Bagioli recited his own poem 'La nascità del gran Rossini', which Talma then repeated in French. Lesueur gave the toast: 'To Rossini! His ardent genius has opened up a new path and inaugurated a new age in the art of music.' Rossini replied with: 'To the French school and the prosperity of the Conservatoire!' And so it went on: Gluck, Grétry, Mozart, Méhul, Paisiello and Cimarosa were all duly acknowledged, and the band attempted to play a piece by each composer. There was even a special medal struck for the occasion, handed to each guest, and before the guests' departure – to 'Buona sera' from *Il barbiere* – it was announced that receipts had covered costs and the surplus was to be donated to impoverished artists. Possibly Rossini recalled Metternich's banquet that he had attended in Vienna in 1822, and the plight of Beethoven.

Such an extraordinary outburst of adulation of Rossini could hardly have been allowed to pass without some sort of reaction, especially in a city so dedicated to literary and musical vendettas as Paris. Sure enough, on 29 November the Théâtre du Gymnase-Dramatique gave a one-act *vaudeville* entitled *Rossini à Paris ou Le grand dîner*. The authors were Auguste-Eugène Scribe (later to be Rossini's librettist for *Le Comte Ory*) and Edmond Mazères, who took the precaution of inviting Rossini to a rehearsal, thus giving him an opportunity to voice objections he might have to any of the proceedings. There was nothing that he found offensive, though when he heard a cancan chorus sung to the words 'Rossini! Rossini! Toi que j'implore aujourd'hui. Rossini! Pourquoi n'es-tu pas ici?' he is reputed to have said that if that was French national music he might as well pack his bags, because he would never succeed in that genre.

In Paris the mania for Rossini was every bit as evident as it had been in Vienna. It touched all sorts of people, and gave thinking persons – and musicians in particular – food for thought. There is a letter dated 16 December 1823 from Boïeldieu to Charles Maurice in which he set out under four heads his position with regard to Rossini.[3] His third and fourth points are remarkably frank and clear-sighted:

> Third: I believe one can make very good music by copying Mozart, Haydn, Cimarosa . . . one will never be other than an ape by copying Rossini. Why? Because Mozart, Haydn, Cimarosa . . . always speak to the heart, to the intelligence. They always speak the language of feeling and reason. But Rossini is full of effects and epigrams in his music. One cannot copy this style; one must either steal it in its entirety or keep silent when one is unable to devise new epigrams, which would be new creation.
> Fourth: I find it maladroit to risk achieving much less effect than Rossini when one uses the same means, the same orchestral effects, etc., etc. To do that is to invite defeat at his hands on his own ground, which is always humiliating.

That month, when it was suggested at the Académie des Beaux-Arts that Rossini be nominated, the musicians opposed the motion; the painters and architects, however, ensured by acclamation that he be voted a foreign associate. It seems that about this time the marquis de Lauriston, Minister of the Royal Household to Louis XVIII, made an approach to Rossini that would have kept him in Paris. At this particular moment, however, Rossini had designs on London – indeed, contractual obligations there – so on 7 December he temporarily said farewell to the French capital.

The Rossinis arrived in London on 13 December 1823, and took rooms at 90 Regent Street, in Nash's quadrant, which had a colonnade at ground level. The composer, in the company of a splendid parrot, was in the habit of sitting out on the top of the colonnade and watching the crowds go by. It took him a week to recover from the rough Channel crossing, and his weakness as a sailor became legendary. When, therefore, the Russian ambassador, Count Lieven, whose wife Dorothea had been in Verona during the congress and had met Rossini, came to call on the composer with an invitation from the king to present himself at Court, Rossini was obliged to make his excuses.

Several Rossini operas had already been heard in London, beginning with *Il barbiere di Siviglia* in March 1818, and twelve others had followed. During the 1823 season at the King's Theatre, six of the nine operas were by Rossini, and now, in 1824, the tally increased to eight out of twelve. Such an ambitious undertaking implied considerable expense, with equal concomitant risk. Another composer, Carlo Coccia, had been engaged in addition to Rossini, but the two together only received as much as Isabella Colbran, Pasta and Giuseppina Ronzi De Begnis individually, and Manuel Garcia was paid as much as Rossini, who directed all eight of his operas. Also in the company were Lucia Elizabeth Vestris, Maria Caradori-Allan, Alberico Curioni, Giuseppe De Begnis, Raniero Remorini and Matteo Porto. Small wonder, then, that the impresario Benelli, who was no Barbaia, ended the season £25,000 in debt.

On 29 December, Rossini went to the Royal Pavilion in Brighton to be presented to George IV. The overture to *La gazza ladra* was played by the court wind band in a special arrangement by its director, Franz Cramer (1772–1848), brother of the pianist Johann Baptist Cramer (1771–1858). The king asked Rossini to accompany himself at the piano in one of his *buffo* arias, and Desdemona's 'Assisa al piè d'un salice' from *Otello*, presumably in falsetto. This caused the *Quarterly Musical Magazine and Review* some indignation, because it seemed that Rossini had sounded like one of the *castrati* who had been 'banished from the stage for many years because they offended the humanity and modesty of the English'. The *Morning Post*, however, on 1 January 1824, declared that 'He has a clear and limpid tenor voice'. The king, at any rate, was pleased to have met Rossini and have been entertained by him, though there was always likely to be an undercurrent of jealousy among those who resented his relaxed manner with the monarch, and in the metropolis at large, reflected in certain sections of the press, at the adulation accorded to a foreigner. This was nothing new, however: in Handel's day the problems of introducing foreign musicians had been just the same.

Harriet, Countess Granville, wrote to Lady Morpeth from the Pavilion, dated 29 December:

> We had Rossini last night. He must have been much pleased with his reception; the King was quite enraptured at having him. The singing is delicious, such varied powers of expressing whatever he pleases. He is a fat, sallow squab of a man, but with large, languishing eyes and *des traits* which justify his thinking himself, as they say he does, something very irresistible. We gave him in return lots of Handel, the Coronation Anthem, etc.[4]

To the Duke of Devonshire, however, on 1 January 1824 she wrote:

> On Monday we had Rossini. The King all graciousness to him. He sang, which went to our musical hearts, 'Otello' and 'Figaro', etc., but the courtiers and the rest of the society were indignant at his familiarity. Being fat and lazy, and consequently adverse to standing, he took a chair and sat by the King, who, however, gave him the kindest reception, and, less *petit* than his suite, understood the man, and treated him as his enthusiasm for music disposed him to. I hope to hear more of him, for it is an unspeakable pleasure.[5]

The king insisted on accompanying Rossini, but kept putting him out because of his somewhat erratic rhythm. According to Gronow, the king 'at last offered an apology which Rossini accepted with civility and good-naturedly said, "There are few in your Royal Highness's position who could play so well"'. Rossini was reported subsequently as saying that he had met no other monarch – apart from Tsar Alexander I – nearly so amiable. It was, he said, 'scarcely possible to form an idea . . . of the charm of George IV's personal appearance and demeanour'.[6]

Once the royal interview was out of the way, Rossini devoted himself to the production of his operas, conducting at concerts, and appearing either as an accompanist or simply as a celebrity in the houses of the aristocracy and the rich, for which he was well remunerated. Rossini later told Ferdinand Hiller that he had never earned enough from his art to be able to save any money, except when he was in England, and even there it was not as a composer but as an accompanist: 'I may have been prejudiced, but in a way it went against the grain to allow myself to be paid as a piano accompanist; and I did it only in London. But they wanted a chance to see my nose and to hear my wife.' He said that he charged fifty pounds for their participation in a musical soirée, which he admitted was rather expensive. Nevertheless, he estimated that there were about sixty such occasions and that, after all, he conceded, made it worth all the trouble. On 7 March 1824, Thomas Moore recorded in his journal that he had been to call on Henry Luttrell: 'Lady Caroline Worsley and her son came soon afterwards; and we joined in the choruses of "Semiramide". Rossini, a fat, natural, jolly-looking person, with a sort of vague archness in his eye, but nothing further. His mastery over the pianoforte miraculous.'

From the *Quarterly Musical Magazine and Review* we have another – possibly somewhat chauvinistic – description of Rossini at this time: 'He certainly looks more like a sturdy beef-eating Englishman than a sensitive, fiery-spirited native of the soft climate of Italy. His countenance when at rest is intelligent yet serious, but bears no marks of the animation which pervades and indeed forms the principal feature of his compositions.'[7]

Not content with having Rossini at their soirées and salons, the aristocratic and wealthy ladies, and even some of their menfolk, pressed Rossini for singing lessons. He was said to have tried to keep down their numbers by asking large fees, and when he was asked how he dared ask so much he replied: 'Because not even £100 per lesson could compensate me for the tortures that I suffer while listening to those ladies, whose voices creak horribly.' It is no exaggeration to say that the money he amassed in London formed the foundation for his financial stability for the rest of his life. Had the affairs of the King's Theatre been his own responsibility, however, then the story might have been a very different one.

The first opera that Rossini conducted at the theatre was *Zelmira* on 24 January. Neither his wife nor Lucia Elizabeth Vestris was in particularly good voice, and the opera did not attract a large audience. *Il barbiere di Siviglia* was no more of a success; Vestris was again below standard, and Benelli, who sang Figaro, was incapable of doing justice to the part since he was now primarily an impresario, and not a singer. Colbran by now seems to have been *hors de combat*, for it was Pasta and Garcia who retrieved the situation with *Otello* and *Semiramide* as far as Rossini was concerned. This was Pasta's début as Semiramide. As far as Benelli and his finances were concerned, however, things did not improve, and he called in Angelica Catalani, whose name was a draw for the audiences. However, she demanded half the box-office receipts and a portion of the subscriptions for the boxes, so that Benelli only exacerbated his financial problems.

Rossini, however, went from strength to strength. Two benefit concerts were arranged at Almack's Assembly Rooms by a committee of admirers in order, so the *Harmonicon* asserted in May 1824, 'to compensate the Maestro for the sufferings borne and for the dangers undergone in crossing the execrable Straits of Dover'. The first concert was on 14 May, and for the second, on 9 June, Rossini produced a cantata on the death of Lord Byron, who had died at Missolonghi on 19 April. *Il pianto delle muse in morte di Lord Byron* was for tenor (Apollo), chorus and orchestra. Rossini himself took the solo part. The *Morning Post* described the cantata as 'Frenchified' and 'extravagant', and that it 'would have seemed ridiculous had not respect toward the dead suppressed the desire to laugh'.

This, however, seems to have been the reaction of only a section of the press, and was no doubt the voice of those musicians who were anti-Rossini. Others were clearly not. In July, Rossini went to Cambridge to take part in the University Music Festival, and what may have been the last social function the Rossinis attended in London, a rout at the Duke of Wellington's, attended by the king, and possibly organised at his suggestion. On 26 July the maestro and his wife left London and, it would seem, Rossini left behind an incomplete opera, *Ugo re d'Italia*, deposited at Ransom's bank, with a bond for £400 to be forfeit in the event of non-delivery. Needless to say, he never did complete the opera, nor did he return to London. He had, however, signed an agreement at the French embassy there on 27 February 1824, so that as one episode of his career ended another began.

As we saw earlier, just before Rossini left Paris in December 1823 he was in negotiations with the French royal household to compose a *grand opéra* for the Académie Royale de Musique, and either an *opera semiseria* or *buffa* for the Théâtre-Italien. He would also stage one of his existing operas, suitably adapted to the capabilities of the Théâtre-Italien's existing company. As remuneration, he asked for 40,000 francs and a benefit performance. The financial details had been the stumbling-block. However, when it seemed that Rossini might be disposed to stay in London, the French Ambassador, the prince de Polignac, was instructed to conclude a contract on the basis of what had been discussed prior to his departure for London. It was this contract, consisting of ten clauses, which was signed in London on 27 February 1824, and is now in the Bibliothèque Nationale. Technically, therefore, Rossini was under contract to the French royal household for one year from the date of his arrival in Paris, assumed to be some time in July that year; which is why he knew that he must leave London that month.

Rossini's return to Paris on 1 August brought a new element into the situation, however, for the vicomte de la Rochefoucauld, Director of Beaux-Arts to the king, asked him to accept the directorship of Théâtre-Italien. Effectively this meant co-directorship with Paër, for Rossini had no wish to see him dispossessed. Nevertheless it created a difficult situation, and Paër eventually resigned, but then withdrew his resignation when he was informed that if he gave up the theatre post he would also cease to be *maître de chapelle* to the king. None of this had been finalised, however, before Rossini and his wife left for a visit to Bologna, so that they could see family and friends and put their affairs in order in preparation for the stipulated year's residence in Paris. During their absence Louis XVIII died, on 26 September, but negotiations continued in the name of his successor, Charles X.

On their return, the Rossinis moved into 10 boulevard Montmartre: a new address marking the start of a new and final phase in Rossini's operatic career. It was not one that he plunged into without a considerable amount of preparation. He was well aware that Paris had different requirements now, and with his usual prudent, even astute, approach to matters of importance he was determined to take his time. From its inception, French opera had tended to be a thing apart, ever since its creator, Lulli, subsumed his Italian origin into the French composer Lully, and ensured that henceforth France always protected itself against foreign musical incursions, or if it accepted strangers, then it was usually on its own terms.

Rossini was well aware that he needed to improve his French, his ability to handle French prosody and the French declamatory style. That in turn would entail a certain amount of modification to his compositional style, irrespective of any changes that he might wish to make in any case. Then there were the singers, who needed help to respond to the new demands imposed on them by the performance of works in both the French and Italian traditions. He was lucky in that he could draw on a remarkable pool of talent at this time, which certainly facilitated productions of such operas as *La cenerentola*, *La donna del lago*, *Otello* and *Semiramide*. The trio of tenors, Donzelli, Nourrit and Rubini, were only outdone in number by the *prime donne*: Laure Cinti, Joséphine Fodor-Mainvielle, Maria Malibran, Giuditta Pasta, Benedetta Pisaroni and Henriette Sontag. Rossini also mounted other composers' operas, but from the outset it was always expected that he would produce a new *grand opéra* and a new *opera buffa* of his own, and it was here that he felt caution was necessary.

Even so, his hand was forced because of the coronation of Charles X, planned for June 1825 at Rheims, the cathedral traditionally used for the ceremony under the *ancien régime*. It was expected that Rossini would provide a suitable offering as his contribution to the celebrations. The critics, and those who were against him in any case, were on their guard; and they had a focal point for their discontent in a botched version, by Castil-Blaze and Sauvage, of Weber's *Der Freischütz*, known as *Robin des bois ou les trois balles*, which had opened at the Théâtre de l'Odéon on 7 December 1824 and ran for over three hundred performances. Although Berlioz described it as 'a great travesty, hacked and mutilated', *La Gazette de France* articulated what several people clearly felt:

> Undoubtedly the hearing of this opera will force the supporters of Rossini to consider seriously. One looks in vain in M. de Weber's music for that pitiful excess of deafening notes, that chattering of ritornellos, that same old succession of corrupt crescendos that so uselessly inflates the scores of the Italian Orpheus. The musical structure of the German master is always soundly based, and all its components, even those which evade the ears of the multitude, are painstakingly deployed.

And, in Italy, Rossini had been accused of being too Teutonic in his writing!

Wisely, then, Rossini stuck to an Italian text by Luigi Balocchi for his coronation offering, *Il viaggio a Reims ossia L'albergo del giglio d'oro* ('The journey to Rheims, or the Inn of the Golden Fleur-de-lys'), which had its first performance at the Salle Louvois on 19 June 1825. There was a star-studded cast, which included Giuditta Pasta, Laure Cinti, Ester Mombelli, Domenico Donzelli, Marco Bordogni, Carlo Zuchelli, Felice Pellegrini, Vincenzo Graziani and Nicholas-Prosper Levasseur. The work was a success, though because Rossini wished to withdraw it after only three performances it was often assumed that it had been a failure. In fact he was persuaded to allow a fourth performance for charity on 12 September 1825, but his intransigence seems to suggest that he had some very fixed ideas about the work. What precisely those ideas were one can only surmise. It was, after all, a *pièce de circonstance*, even if the *circonstance* itself was important in establishing more firmly Rossini's relationship to the French royal family. However, as a *pièce de circonstance* it could expect a distinctly limited life. As an opera on a different subject, however, it could be assured a much longer existence. But if it were heard too often in its original form it would become difficult for Rossini to redeploy the material. Too many performances, therefore, were not to be encouraged.

An attempt to prevent familiarity with the music may also have been the reason why Rossini vetoed the transferring of the work in September to the larger Salle Le Peletier, despite the fact that it held almost 2,000 people and therefore financial returns would be greater. On the other hand, he was also worried about the adverse effect on the opera created by a transfer to a larger theatre. He had already experienced such an effect on *La donna del lago*. Whatever the reason, Rossini found it desirable to adapt a good deal of material from *Il viaggio a Reims* for *Le Comte Ory* in 1828, and it is not inconceivable that even at an early stage in the composition of *Il viaggio* he saw the possibility of preserving for posterity what might otherwise have sunk without trace.

For all Rossini's care, the work had an eventful history, for it happened that the sections used in *Le Comte Ory* were sent to Troupenas and then lost, and the manuscript of the rest passed to Rossini's second wife, Olympe Pélissier, who left it to the composer's doctor, Vio Bonato, though it was not identified properly until 1977. An edition of *Il viaggio* has subsequently been published, and performances once again made possible, and a recording with a galaxy of stars has now been made under the direction of Claudio Abbado.[8]

The plot, drawing on a literary device as old as *The Decameron* or *The Canterbury Tales*, and more recently encountered in Garrick's Shakespeare Jubilee of 1764, is set in the Inn of the Golden Fleur-de-lys at Plombières. An international company of guests assembles at the inn, kept by Madame Cortese, on the way to Rheims for the coronation. Nothing more is needed to get things going, for the interplay of love-interest and national characteristics gives ample scope for varied musical numbers.

The most important guest is Corinna (a role for Pasta), a famous Roman *improvvisatrice*, attended by a Greek orphan girl and two gentlemen, Don Profundo (Pellegrini) and Lord Sidney (Zuchelli). There are two widows, the young Contessa di Folleville (Cinti) and the Marchesa Melibea (Schiassetti), the Polish widow of an Italian general. She is pursued by a Russian, Conte di Libenskof (Bordogni), and to increase the international coverage there is a Spanish naval officer, Don Alvaro (Levasseur), a French officer, Il Cavalier Belfiore (Donzelli), and a retired German officer, Barone di Trombonok (Graziani). The musical highlights of the work are the *sestetto* and the *gran pezzo concertato a 14 voci* – reused, in a reduced form, in *Le Comte Ory* – and fun is poked at Madame de Staël's *Corinne* in the course of the opera. After the various interchanges, amorous and otherwise, between the guests, a farewell entertainment is organised, with a ballet and a succession of national songs and anthems. As a grand finale, portraits of the French royal family appeared, with suitable effects of lighting, and at the first performance an aquatic display.

Castil-Blaze, who had been largely responsible for the distorted version of Weber's *Der Freischütz* given at the Odéon the previous December, reviewed *Il viaggio* for the *Journal des débats*. He acknowledged that Rossini knew voices, and the ways of combining them effectively, to the highest degree, and thereby produced 'the most splendid and picturesque results'. Having said that, however, Castil-Blaze somewhat diminished his praise by saying that one ought not to judge Rossini by this first offering for Paris, since it was, after all, an occasional piece, and had been written very quickly. Moreover, in his opinion, the opera lacked action and the libretto lacked interest. What the Parisian public was really waiting for, the critic went on, was Rossini's French *grand opéra*. *Il viaggio a Reims* consisted of only one act, but in view of the fact that it lasted three hours and there was no action it seemed even longer than it was. The king, for one, was certainly of that opinion, and took no pains to conceal his boredom.

The finale, however, was received with pleasure by the Parisian audience. Each of the chief guests sang a national song or anthem. Barone di Trombonok sings Haydn's 'Gott erhalte Franz den Kaiser', Marchesa Melibea a polonaise with a decidedly Italianate accent to it, and Lord Sidney, who does not claim to be at all musical, sings a suitably embellished version of 'God Save the King'. Corinna provides a second improvisation (her first has come earlier in the opera) – 'All ombra amena' – after which the portraits of the royal family and the aquatic display took place. One of the press accounts praised the fourteen-part *gran pezzo*, but declared that the rest was 'noise, crescendos, and the other cumulative musical forms that are now used, and abused, to satiety'.

Of course such a view ignores much that is excellent. The *gran pezzo*, justly praised by the critic above, is infinitely preferable in its original version when compared with the seven-part adaptation that Rossini made of it for *Le Comte Ory*, and the *sestetto* did not even find its way into the later opera. It has the quality of a Rossini Act I finale, begun by the first bass, Barone di Trombonok, who is then joined by the second bass, Don Alvaro, and the tenor Libenskof, both rivals for the affection of Marchesa Melibea, who now joins in, with Madama Cortese. The second movement, by contrast, gives time for reflection and asides. Rossini uses technical devices such as canon, and cross-rhythms (duple against triple time), but in doing so allows the melodic lines to lose nothing in elegance or allure, while the vocal texture retains a clarity and refinement throughout. Corinna now has her first improvisation, 'Arpa gentil, che fida'. Underneath the vocal display there is a tender, almost melancholy vein which is apparent elsewhere in the music of *Il viaggio*, even when Rossini and his librettist, Balocchi, are deliberately making fun of some of the excesses of Romantic language and sentiment.

There are other rewarding numbers which Rossini did not introduce into *Le Comte Ory*, such as Lord Sidney's praise of Corinna, with its flute obbligato, and the duet between Libenskof and Melibea, 'D'alma celeste, Oh Dio'; whereas one that was taken over, Don Profondo's strophic song on national characteristics in keys that descend in thirds for succeeding verses, is decidedly less successful in its second version, in which Raimbaud tells how he has found the wine-cellar of the castle. The same might be said for the aria in *Il viaggio* in which the Contessa di Folleville laments the overturning of the coach that was bringing her some new fashions from Paris, and then is delighted when a hat is retrieved from the wrecked vehicle. In *Le Comte Ory* Rossini used it for the Comtesse to express her love for her cousin, Isolier; and, although the melodic beauty remains, the delicious irony of its original application in *Il viaggio* has been lost.

After the fourth performance of *Il viaggio a Reims*, Paris saw the first night, on 22 September 1825, of Meyerbeer's *Il crociato in Egitto*, which had had its first performance in Venice, at La Fenice, on 7 March 1824. It was one of Rossini's most imaginative decisions to stage the opera at the Théâtre-Italien, and he invited the composer to come to Paris and direct the final rehearsals. It was not only the start of Meyerbeer's remarkable career in Paris, but also the affirmation of a friendship between the two composers that had begun in Venice in 1819, and which was to last until Meyerbeer's death in 1864.

It was a friendship that withstood several tests – both real and imagined – especially as far as their respective careers and compositions were concerned. The first performance of *Robert le diable* on 21 November 1831, for example, prompted Azevedo to assert that Meyerbeer's treatment of the voices in that opera had largely undone, if not actually destroyed, all the results of Rossini's patient efforts to bring an acceptable standard of singing to the Paris Opéra. It was not only the changes in vocal style that Rossini may have had reason to regret, but the fact that with the impact of *Robert le diable* and *Les Huguenots* (29 February 1836) Meyerbeer's operas were reducing representations of his own on the stage of the Opéra at this time more or less to Act II of *Guillaume Tell* and Act II of *Moïse*. Rossini is said to have met Charles Duponchel, Director of the Opéra, in the street one day, and the latter told him that he hoped the composer would have no grounds for complaints against the Opéra, since that evening they were giving Act II of *Guillaume Tell*, to which Rossini retorted: 'Really? All of it – the whole thing?'

That situation was to alter dramatically in 1837 when Duprez took the role of Arnold in *Guillaume Tell* and the opera took on a new lease of life. Moreover, when asked about Duprez, Rossini was reported by Charles de Boigne as having said: 'He doesn't sing my little music too badly, but I have no idea how he will sing the big.' By 'the big', de Boigne wrote, Rossini meant the music of Meyerbeer, and went on to say that Rossini had never forgiven his so-called rival the success of *Robert le diable*, which is what had driven Rossini from composing for the stage. By adding an otherwise undocumented anecdote, in which Rossini was supposed to have said that the reason he wrote no more operas was that he was waiting for the Jews to finish their Sabbath, de

Boigne compounded his concoction of misinformation about Meyerbeer and Rossini. The latter admired at least some of the music of *Robert le diable*, for when discussing the programme for the first performance of one of his occasional pieces for Bologna in 1848 he wanted the concert to open with 'a majestic piece', and for that he suggested the prelude to Meyerbeer's opera.

For his part, Meyerbeer admired Rossini almost to the point of idolatry. It was he who wrote to the Italian in 1843 with the news that he had been elected as an honorary member of the Royal Academy of Fine Arts in Berlin, and Meyerbeer contributed to the cost of the marble statue of Rossini by Antoine Étex erected at the Paris Opéra in 1846 but destroyed in the fire of 1873. In the closing weeks of his life, as we shall see, Meyerbeer was deeply moved by the first performance of Rossini's *Petite Messe solennelle*, and referred to himself as Rossini's 'constant admirer and old friend'.

There now followed a succession of Rossini's own operas at the Théâtre-Italien, beginning with *La cenerentola* on 6 October, in which Giovanni Battista Rubini made his Parisian début. Next came *La donna del lago*, with Rubini and Amalia Schütz-Oldosi. There was also a French version of the opera, as *La Dame au lac*, arranged by Lemière de Corvey, at the Odéon on 31 October 1825. Rubini appeared again, in the title role of *Otello*, which Donzelli had sung for his Parisian début on 26 April that year; then came *Semiramide* on 6 December, which was the only one of these operas that had not already been given in Paris.

Although Colbran was in the French capital, she did not sing the title role. Instead it was given to Joséphine Fodor-Mainvielle, who had sung the part some sixty times in the 1824–5 season in Vienna but had seriously damaged her voice and, although she began the evening well, had to withdraw during the performance, and the opera could not be given until 2 January 1826, by which time Pasta had learned the role and sang it with great success. It remained very popular with the audiences in Paris, and in 1853 Eugène Delacroix wrote about it in glowing terms in his journal on 1 April that year. Although he had been critical of the work in performance, it was the after-effect that remained with him and continued to give pleasure. He also felt that the critics had ignored the romantic content of Rossini's music. In Delacroix' opinion, that was the one feature of the composer's talent that was inimitable.

Rossini introduced *Zelmira* on 14 March 1826; but, although it had

Pasta and Rubini, it took a while to catch on before it achieved popularity. Criticism of Rossini's failure to produce the long-awaited new operas for Paris began to increase, and Weber's visit, referred to earlier, *en route* for London towards the end of February that year, was the occasion for yet more criticism of Rossini in the press. He was not slow, however, to support the cause of Greek Independence from Turkey, and conducted a charity concert on 3 April which raised some 30,000 francs. For all this, complaints were again voiced in the press on 13 June about the latitude given by the authorities to Rossini, deploring his laziness, his presumption and his wilful disregarding of the rules imposed on other theatre directors. Had the critics but known, Rossini would soon cease to make himself such a focus for this kind of obloquy.

The section of Rossini's contract with the royal household relating to the Théâtre-Italien was terminated by mutual agreement and a new one negotiated dated 17 October 1826 by which the composer was to receive an annual salary of 25,000 francs from the Civil List with the titles of Premier Compositeur du Roi and Inspecteur Général du Chant en France. Cherubini, for one, objected to the second part of the appointment, which he saw as a potential threat to the professors of singing at the Conservatoire, and that despite Rossini's imaginative appointment of Hérold as a coach at the Théâtre-Italien. In a letter La Rochefoucauld sought to convince Cherubini that Rossini had no such designs; indeed, he was sometimes reported to have been seen on the streets of Paris listening to itinerant vocalists and, when asked what he was doing, said that he was carrying out his official duties. At least in this way, he said, he had something to report, for he had no other means of gathering information.

About a month prior to the confirmation of the new appointment, a *pasticcio* of Rossini's music followed at the Odéon where *La Dame au lac* had been given the previous October. The opera was entitled *Ivanhoé*, and the libretto, based on Scott's novel, was by Émile Deschamps, later to collaborate with Scribe on Meyerbeer's *Les Huguenots*, and Wailly. The man responsible for stringing together Rossini's music – from *La cenerentola*, *La gazza ladra*, *Mosè in Egitto*, *Semiramide*, *Tancredi* and *Zelmira* – was Antonio Pacini. *Ivanhoé* was repeated in Strasbourg that same year, and in Coburg in 1833, and was but one of the many *pasticcios* to include music by Rossini produced at this time. Inevitably, eyebrows were raised in certain quarters at the composer's condoning such a practice.

In response Rossini might have observed that at least it kept his music before the public at a time when, as we saw earlier, audiences were not exactly overwhelmed with performances of Rossini operas. In *La Fausse Agnès*, arranged by Castil-Blaze (13 June 1826), Rossini's music rubbed shoulders with that of Cimarosa and Meyerbeer, and in another Castil-Blaze arrangement, *Monsieur de Pourceaugnac* (24 February 1827), the music was by Rossini and Weber. Because of the inadequate legal protection of composers' copyright at this time, it would have been a lengthy and costly – if not impossible – undertaking for Rossini to have prevented such use of his music, had he so desired. Nevertheless, as the Romantic movement gathered pace, such *pasticcios* were condemned by the critics and composers as totally contrary to the concept of an opera as an integral act of creation; and a 'serious' composer would have been expected to make some sort of protest, which Rossini failed to do in 1826, though he did much later, in 1859.

By now, however, Rossini was ready to offer himself as a composer of opera to a French text; and, although the work in question was not new, it was such an important reworking of the Italian original – *Maometto II*, itself already reworked for Venice – that it ought to be considered as a separate work. Luigi Balocchi and Alexandre Soumet collaborated on the new libretto. The siege of Negroponte, which occurred in 1470, was changed to that of Corinth, which had taken place in 1459, and the besieged were changed from Venetians into Greeks, which gave the story much more current interest in view of the struggle for Greek independence – a cause espoused by many in sentiment and in reality by Byron, and enhanced by his death.

Le Siège de Corinthe, as the new work was called, had its first night at the Salle Le Peletier on 9 October 1826, and was an immediate success. For Paris, Rossini provided an overture which borrows from both Mayr's *Atalia*, which he had conducted in Naples in 1822, and the 'Gloria' from his *Messa di Gloria*. More fundamentally, he turned the original two-act Naples opera into a three-act work, and in so doing broke down into shorter and more succinct units the long architectural blocks which represented much of the originality of the opera in its earlier form. The orchestra and chorus were given more prominent roles in the Paris version; and this factor, combined with the shorter musical episodes, made the work more easy to stage, though it became a more conventional Paris opera in the process.

There was one fairly long set-piece for Paris, the *hymne* 'Divin prophète' that precedes the finale to Act II; and another substantial new section was the Act III episode in which the Greek banners are blessed. The sack of Corinth which ends the opera was a reworking of the original finale, but done with telling effect by Rossini. Of course, the issue of Greek independence enhanced the work's success at this time, but from a purely dramatic point of view the new version certainly made its own impact. Perhaps more questionable is the musical revision, in so far as the original opera had more grandeur than the Paris version.

Nevertheless, one should not underestimate the effect of the work on the musical establishment in Paris. A professor from the Conservatoire, Pitet, who attended the first performance at the Opéra, wrote:

> A man has arrived who has so abused all the means of effect that he has put his successors in great danger of not being able to find any new ones, even when they possess genius; and he has taken harmonic effects to such a degree of complication that one is fully entitled to ask if he has not made any further innovation impossible.[9]

There was no doubt that this was a popular triumph for Rossini. According to *La Quotidienne*, he was applauded for almost half an hour at the end of the performance, and after that several of the musicians went to play the finale of Act II under his windows in boulevard Montmartre. Unfortunately Henri-Étienne Dérivis, who sang Mahomet, fell and hurt himself in the final moments of the opera, so that the second performance had to be postponed until he was well enough to return to the stage. By 24 February 1839, however, it had been given one hundred times, and it remained in the repertoire until 1844. *Le Siège de Corinthe* became the first opera that Rossini sold to a publisher, to Eugène Troupenas for 6,000 francs.

Of course not everyone greeted the work with such rapture. Berlioz, for one, laid fairly and squarely at Rossini's door the responsibility for first having introduced noisy orchestration into France.[10] Yet, he complained, the critics never even mentioned his name in that context, nor did they blame Auber, Halévy or Adam for having taken up Rossini's ideas and exaggerated them. Instead, Berlioz maintained, they blamed Weber and himself, and he cited the occasion in Vienna when Prince Metternich asked him if he were the composer who wrote for five hundred players. With what was, in the circumstances, a certain amount of sang-froid, Berlioz replied: 'Not always, your highness. Sometimes I only use four hundred and fifty.' For a person with Berlioz' acute sensitivity to orchestral effect, such a wholesale and often indiscriminate use of instruments purely to increase the volume was indeed painful, and for this he held Rossini ultimately responsible, even when privately acknowledging that he was only partly to blame. His aversion to Rossini was something even more fundamental, however, than orchestral volume.

Writing in his *Mémoires* of this period (1827), Berlioz accused Rossini of melodic cynicism, and contempt for dramatic expression and good sense, which, together with endless repetition of a single form of cadence, the eternal crescendo (which he found puerile), and the use of the bass drum, irritated him to such an extent that, as Berlioz admitted, he was completely immune to whatever qualities of genius Rossini possessed, even in his exquisitely scored masterpiece *Il barbiere di Siviglia*. He maintained that on more than one occasion he had contemplated blowing up the Théâtre-Italien. He put himself firmly with Ingres, who had described some of Rossini's music as that of a dishonest man.

But, whatever Berlioz and others of his opinion might say, the authorities were pleased with Rossini's contribution, and it was announced in *Le Moniteur* on 14 October 1826, five days after the first performance of *Le Siège de Corinthe*, that Rossini was to be made a *chevalier* of the Légion d'honneur. The composer was not – as some had it – totally insensitive, however, and he went to La Rochefoucauld and said that he did not want the accolade in recognition of an old opera that he had revised; nor did he, as a foreigner, wish to accept it when French composers such as Hérold had not yet received the recognition its conferral implied. As we have seen, his appointments as First Composer to the King and Inspector-General for Singing were gazetted on 17 October, and soon after that *Le Moniteur* announced that the information about the Légion d'honneur had been incorrect. Hérold did in fact receive the honour on 3 November 1828.

Another element in Rossini's assessment of his future at this time seems to have been a proposal from John Ebers in London. In his *Seven Years of the King's Theatre*, Ebers recalled that he had gone to Paris in the autumn of 1826 to engage artists for his future productions, and that he saw a good deal of Rossini at that time.[11] It was even mooted, according to Ebers, that Rossini, Barbaia and himself should jointly assume the management of the King's Theatre in London. Such a triumvirate would indeed have been a force to be reckoned with, but although Rossini wrote to Ebers on 24 November and told him that he was taking steps to seek leave from his Parisian obligations, he never returned to London. Certainly the city offered seductive financial opportunities to Rossini; but he had no doubt reflected on the extent to which his carefully planned *entrée* into French opera had succeeded, and was continuing to do so. In fact he was planning another step along that road with another adaptation, this time of *Mosè in Egitto*, which he was going to turn into a four-act opera entitled *Moïse et Pharaon ou Le Passage de la Mer Rouge*, with a libretto by Luigi Balocchi and Étienne de Jouy. Its first performance, on 26 March 1827, aroused even more enthusiasm than *Le Siège de Corinthe*; and by 6 August 1838 the opera had received a hundred performances.

As with the change from *Maometto II* to *Le Siège de Corinthe* for Paris, the change from *Mosè in Egitto* to *Moïse et Pharaon* is not always for the better. The very opening, the 'Scene of the Shadows' in C minor, much admired by Wagner, which made such a striking start to the opera in the Italian original, is moved to the beginning of Act II, where its effect is diminished considerably, partly because Act I has just closed in the same key of C minor. Indeed, it is the disruption of Rossini's harmonic scheme as it existed in *Mosè in Egitto* that is one of the more regrettable casualties of the Paris version. Of course, some critics have questioned whether Rossini ever gave much thought to overall harmonic schemes in his operas, and up to a point they may be right; but such a view totally ignores Rossini's innate flair for the appropriateness of certain keys to certain situations, and their juxtaposing. One of Rossini's hallmarks is his use of keys in succession a third apart. We saw an application of this in Don Profondo's strophic aria in *Il viaggio a Reims*, where the keys descend by a succession of major or minor thirds. Sometimes successive movements of Rossini's operas are related in this way, too, but it is more the exception for Rossini to plan any extended overall key scheme to embrace a whole act, let alone a whole opera, as Benjamin Britten was to do to such dramatic effect in *The Turn of the Screw*, for example. This is not to say that carefully planned key schemes necessarily make for a better opera, but at the very least, when a number of sections or movements are to follow each other, the listener is helped if the keys fit together, even if he or she is not aware of how this is achieved. In such a situation, however, one must concede that Rossini often seems to have relied largely on his instinct.

In an Italian version, entitled *Il nuovo Mosè*, the revised version had considerable success in Italy; and in Milan, for example, had 160 performances over nine seasons between 1835 and 1869.[12] Again, one must not underestimate the effect that the opera had on the Parisian opera-goers – in particular the style of singing, heard for the first time at the Opéra, though of course it had been standard at the Théâtre-Italien for some time. As *La Gazette de France* put it: 'This is no less than a lyric revolution brought about in four hours by M. Rossini. From henceforth French "shouting" is banished irrevocably, and at the Opéra they are going to sing in the way that they sing at the Salle Favart. Vive Rossini!' Without Rossini, it is no exaggeration to say that the establishment and flourishing of *grand opéra* in Paris for almost forty years between Auber's *La Muette de Portici* (1828) and Meyerbeer's *L'Africaine* (1863) would not have happened.

While *Moïse* was in rehearsal in Paris, it had become clear that the composer's mother was mortally ill with a heart condition. Dr Gaetano Conti had arrived from Bologna with the news, and Rossini's initial reaction was to leave at once. However, Dr Conti reminded him that on a previous occasion he had arrived home unexpectedly and so alarmed his mother that she had had to spend a fortnight in bed. If he were to appear now, he could well be responsible for hastening her death. Giuseppe Rossini felt bound to explain this to his wife's brother, Francesco Maria Guidarini, in a letter of 26 February, six days after his wife finally succumbed to her malady at the age of fifty-five: 'Gioachino [sic] . . . would have been here some time ago, but he was advised not to do so because if he came, she would surely die in his arms. Two years ago, when he came to Italy . . . just seeing him, from happiness, she remained ill in bed for more than two weeks.'

When the composer received the news of his mother's death he was understandably moved, and arranged for Masses to be said. It was not practical for him to go to Bologna, so he tried to persuade his father, now sixty-eight, to come to Paris. Unfortunately we no longer have the originals of any of Rossini's letters to his father (or to either of his wives, for that matter), and we have to rely on published extracts or, in some cases, facsimiles. We have to read between the lines of his father's reply, dated 20 March, to know how he presented his invitation. His age was one of the factors that made Giuseppe Rossini reluctant to accept the invitation – that and his constipation, and the weather, and the difficulty of the journey. Also, he wanted an assurance that his son would stay in Paris for some time if he agreed to come, which makes one wonder whether his son had not already told him in previous letters that he was contemplating leaving Paris. Eventually Francisco Fernándes, Isabella's Spanish servant, was sent to Italy to fetch him, and they set out towards the end of March 1827.

Once he reached Paris, however, Giuseppe Rossini became a useful supplementary source of information about his son's life there. On 24 July, for example, he wrote to his late wife's brother, Francesco Maria Guidarini, giving details of a cantata that his son had written in the space of six days for the baptism of the son of Alexandre-Marie Aguado. For six solo voices and piano, the cantata was sung at the banker's country home on 16 July, with Rossini himself playing the accompaniment. This letter is also of interest – indeed, perhaps primarily so – for the light that it sheds on the enigma of why Rossini gave up composing opera when he did. His father wrote: 'Gioachino [sic] has sworn to me that he wants to retire back home from everything in 1830, wishing to enjoy being a gentleman and being able to write what he wants, since he is quite exhausted (may Heaven want it as I want it in my heart).' By a strange coincidence, Rossini himself was writing to Italy on the very same day, 24 July 1827, to Dr Conti: 'Embrace all our friends on my behalf and tell them that your departure [from Paris] has revived in me all the more the need to repatriate myself; and I will do it sooner than you think.' More and more, then, it seems that Rossini's eventual decision to 'retire' was no caprice, but a long-planned aim. Indeed, there is a letter from Stendhal to Baron Adolphe de Mareste eight years previously, when he was in Milan, in which he said: 'I saw Rossini when he arrived yesterday. Next April he will be twenty-eight, and he is keen to stop working at thirty. This man, who did not have a penny four years ago, has just invested 100,000 francs with Barbaia at seven-and-a-half per cent.'

Barbaia happened to be in Paris during the summer of 1827, on a mission which could well have ended his long-standing friendship with Rossini, or at the least caused friction between them. The reason for the visit was the position of the singer Domenico Donzelli, whom Rossini had advised in fairly precise detail how to set about breaking his contract with Barbaia in February 1826. Matters then dragged on into the following year, so that Barbaia felt impelled to try to resolve them in person. When he failed to do so to his personal satisfaction, he contemplated a return to Italy, having suffered a tactical defeat. Rossini's letter to Barbaia on this occasion is, to say the least, a masterpiece of legerdemain. He manages both to uphold Donzelli's right to support himself and his family – whilst working for Rossini in Paris – and at the same time make Barbaia seem slightly incompetent and somewhat heartless; but, even more ironic, Rossini casts himself in the role of the anxious mediator, when he had been in great part responsible for the altercation:

> Has my amicable and disinterested mediation, then, not affected your heart in any way? . . . He [Donzelli] has certainly been guilty of an oversight, but what he did was for the good of his family. . . . I don't intend by this letter of mine to be the advocate of anyone, but I do intend to address a friend of fifteen years [i.e., Barbaia] in the language of probity and of the heart.[13]

That autumn (1827) found Rossini in a rather more relaxed state of mind. He prepared his *Gorgheggi e solfeggi* for publication by Pacini by the end of the year, and on 21 November wrote to Dr Conti in Bologna, telling the latter that he and Isabella had been to Dieppe, where they were horribly bored. Again, the letter is interesting for the fact that we see Rossini fretting about the lack of progress on the decoration of his *palazzo* in Bologna, with the inference that he was anxious to know that it would be completed by the time that he would live there.

The following April (1828), *La Revue musicale* asserted quite categorically that Rossini had promised to write *Guillaume Tell*, and that this would be his last opera. Once again, then, his desire to abandon the operatic stage was no sudden decision; but before he reached his operatic finale there was to be one more work.

The libretto of *Le Comte Ory* had been initially a one-act *vaudeville* written in 1817 by Scribe and Delestre-Poirson, whose source had been a Picard Crusaders' ballad collected by De la Place in 1785. Scribe then expanded it to a two-act libretto for Rossini. In fact the original play is the basis for the second act of the opera, in which Count Ory disguises himself as the Mother Superior of a group of nuns (his followers) and gains admittance to the castle of Formoutiers to try to win the countess's affections whilst her brother is absent on a crusade. In the first act the characters are introduced and Count Ory attempts a similar exploit, this time disguised as a hermit who succours those in need of spiritual counsel. The opera works well in the theatre because the second act is dramatically much stronger than the first act – and in its overall effect musically stronger, too – so that there is a feeling of continuous development sustained from the beginning right to the end of the whole opera. There is a very amusing scene when the nuns, having discovered the wine-cellar of the absent count, go on a drinking spree but revert to suitably reverent prayer when the countess appears. There is also a much noted trio, 'A la faveur de cette nuit obscure', which even Berlioz came to admire in time, and declared it Rossini's masterpiece, in the *Journal des débats* of 28 May 1839.

Most of the borrowing from *Il viaggio a Reims* comes in the first act of *Le Comte Ory*, and in general Rossini compressed the material. There is no overture as such, but a 'Prélude' which uses what was a very traditional Italian scheme for opera overtures of ABA. There is also some delightful orchestration, both here and throughout the opera, that shows Rossini's mastery of technique and sensitive ear. Given the fact that so much of the music for *Le Comte Ory* is borrowed from *Il viaggio*, it is difficult to claim that Rossini provided the opera as a whole with any unique musical qualities. Apart from the duet for Ory and Isolier, all the music of Act I is from *Il viaggio*, though admittedly only two pieces from the latter were used in Act II. It is Rossini's skill at adapting the borrowed material that is perhaps most to be admired in Act I. From the start of Act II, however, he creates an impressive extended sequence that opens with the countess, Ragonde and the female chorus, followed by the storm, and the 'nuns'' prayer, which is at first off-stage and unaccompanied, and then integrated into the storm. Musical integration is also evident between the duet for Comte Ory and Isolier, which is in the same key as, and has close thematic links with, the Trio already mentioned.

Adolphe Adam maintained that it took over a year from the first night of *Le Comte Ory* on 20 August 1828, and sixty performances, before it caught on with the Parisian public. Nevertheless Troupenas paid Rossini 16,000 francs for the publication rights, and the Opéra was said to have taken 7,000 francs for every performance given of the work.

Once the second performance was over, Rossini retired to Aguado's country home at Petit-Bourg on the way to Fontainebleau, where he worked in earnest on *Guillaume Tell*. He had already turned down two librettos submitted by Scribe. One became Auber's *Gustave III* and Verdi's *Un ballo in maschera*, and the other Halévy's *La Juive*. Rossini then took up Étienne de Jouy's adaptation of Schiller's *Wilhelm Tell* in four acts. Hippolyte-Louis-Florent Bis was then called in to rework the second act, Rossini himself made some changes, and Aguado's secretary, Armand Marrast, also made a contribution. In his interview with Wagner, Rossini also mentioned Crémieux as having had a hand in the libretto. Certainly in September it was reported in the press that Rossini was hard at work on his new opera, and on 15 October it was stated with confidence that he had returned to Paris and was to begin rehearsals on 1 November. In the middle of the month it was asserted that at least some of the music had gone to the copyist. Even at this point, however, there was speculation that Rossini's *grand opéra* written specifically for the French stage might well turn out to be his last, since he had declared his intention of retiring to Bologna 'to enjoy his glory and his well-earned fortune in peace'.

Be that as it may, everything was far from settled, either for the first performance or for Rossini's own future. He had envisaged the role of Mathilde in the opera for Laure Cinti, recently married to the singer Damoreau and now pregnant. The Austrian soprano Annetta Maraffa-Fischer was brought in to replace her at the Opéra, but when it became clear that the audiences did not take to her the first night of *Guillaume Tell* was postponed until Cinti-Damoreau (as she now became known) returned to the stage.

Rossini took the opportunity to finish the score with less pressure on him, and also to regularise his situation *vis-à-vis* the Court. For two years he had left the matter unresolved, ever since his letter of 13 April 1827 to La Rochefoucauld in which he requested an annuity of 6,000 francs, amongst other things. In principle the king had always been willing to agree to this stipulation, and Rossini had been careful to dissociate the annuity from any other working contract. He had also foreseen that the personnel might not always retain their posts, in which case he wanted the terms clearly and legally set down. However, now that Rossini had let it be known that he wanted to retire – in which case the annuity would be in respect of services already rendered, and Rossini may even have intended this in 1827 – the court officials assumed that he was bluffing. He was not, of course, and when the annuity and other conditions had still not been confirmed after two years Rossini wrote again to La Rochefoucauld on 10 April 1829.

In this new letter he pointed out that he had continued to commit himself to France, despite the more advantageous offers he had had from England, Germany, Russia and Italy, which he had refused. Moreover, he no longer needed to prolong his musical career, but a sense of gratitude to Charles X required him to continue. He proposed writing a further four operas after *Guillaume Tell* over a period of ten years, for a fee, with five benefit nights, and of course the annuity. Behind the courtly language of Rossini's letter to La Rochefoucauld, however, was a very pragmatic course of action. He told Émile-Timothée Lubbert, Director of the Opéra, that if the contract were not approved he would cancel the rehearsals of *Guillaume Tell* and decline to deliver the third and fourth acts of the score to the copyist. Lubbert in turn wrote to La Rochefoucauld. Everything was ready, but now Rossini was threatening to withdraw the opera completely. In the circumstances, La Rochefoucauld was forced to act, and on 14 April presented the matter to the monarch. Early in May, Charles X signed the contract personally – a vitally important factor when Rossini had to fight to ensure that his annuity was paid in future years.

By 5 July full rehearsals of *Guillaume Tell* were taking place, with the first night scheduled for 24 July, but then postponed until 27 July. Then Cinti-Damoreau was indisposed, so it was not until 3 August 1829 that the first performance, conducted by François-Antoine Habeneck, finally got under way. On 5 August, *Le Globe*, describing the first night, declared that from that evening a new era had begun, not only as far as French music was concerned, but throughout the musical world, and in *La Revue musicale* Fétis wrote:

> *Guillaume Tell* continues on its successful way, or rather embarks upon it; for the public now understands this music, which at first was too much for it. As for those of us who have had rather more experience, at each performance we find a hundred beautiful things that had evaded us, even in numbers that do not especially stand out. There is sufficient in this opera to make ten very fine operas, full of ideas.

The overture is a marked departure from any preceding Rossini overture. It falls into four distinct sections which announce the action and seem to synthesise the most important moments of it. There is a remarkable opening passage for five cellos which suggests, as Berlioz pointed out, 'the . . . silence of nature when the elements and the human passions are at rest'.[14] Indeed, it prefigures the peace for which the whole drama is enacted, uniting human passions, the elements and nature itself and transfiguring them in a hymn to freedom which is not only Switzerland's freedom, but that of a human spirit in its highest aspiration.

The second (*allegro*) section depicts a storm, with a swift and economic crescendo, then section three is an *andante* which employs a *ranz des vaches*, announced by the cor anglais, with flute answering, and delicate use of the triangle to produce one of Rossini's most exquisite effects of orchestral colour. The *ranz des vaches* will appear in many guises throughout the opera. The fourth section opens with a rather unexpected fanfare, and then the famous *cavalcata* which for many people is an archetypal Rossini climax.

The spaciousness of the layout of the overture is a foretaste of the spaciousness of Rossini's first act, which lasts rather more than an hour. There is a good deal of work for the chorus, and there are dances, since preparations are in hand for a wedding. Rossini thus deftly fulfilled a requirement of the Opéra that ballet be included. He did not assign the role of Tell himself to a tenor, as generally became the tradition for the hero in subsequent nineteenth-century operas, but to a baritone. The tenor role is given to Arnold, whose father, Melcthal, is a revered elder of the Swiss community, whereas Arnold himself has fought in the army of the occupying Austrians and has fallen in love with Mathilde, an Austrian princess. From the outset, then, Rossini firmly establishes the contrast in musical, vocal and dramatic terms between the mature character of the patriot Tell, loving husband and father, and the young Arnold, torn between his love for Mathilde and that of his father and fatherland. The most memorable aria from the act is Arnold's 'O Mathilde, idole de mon âme', whose opening phrase uses a very basic form of augmentation with rising intervals, the first of a fourth for the first two syllables, the second of a sixth for the word 'idole', thus giving the tenor ample scope, on open vowels, to convey the intensity of his affection. His dilemma will become more pronounced as the events of the plot unfold, up to the point where he is forced into action, whereas Tell's stability as a character goes from strength to strength. Rossini underpins the conflict of loyalties, and that between Swiss and Austrians, throughout the first two acts by using a horn fanfare at various points to denote the all-pervasive influence of the governor, Gesler, and the Austrian presence in general, though we do not meet Gesler in person until Act III.

In Act II, Mathilde, who has been out hunting with the Austrians, lingers behind when the others return home, since she has glimpsed Arnold. She sings of her love in a *scène et aria*, 'Sombre forêt', in which Rossini uses the magical effect of a gentle drum-roll to introduce each of the stanzas: 'There is poetry, there is music, there is art, fine, noble and pure,' wrote Berlioz. In the following 'Oui, vous l'arrachez à mon âme', the pronounced chromaticism in the music, coloured by the use of flute, oboe and clarinet, heightens the poignancy and tension of the situation. Mathilde then exhorts Arnold to rejoin the Austrian army so that he can make himself worthy in her eyes and in the eyes of those around her. Rossini now uses the brass, and suitably martial rhythms, to convey this resolve, but the atmosphere quickly evaporates as the lovers become aware that someone is coming, and they part in recitative, which is more appropriate to the situation than a fiery *cabaletta* or final duet would have been.

Tell and Walter Furst have seen the two together, and when they inform Arnold that Gesler has had his father murdered he now resolves to fight for his country and avenge his death. The trio, 'Quand l'Helvétie est un champ de supplices', then leads on to the assembling of the men of the cantons of Unterwalden, Uri and Schwyz, each group characterised individually by Rossini. In Schiller's play Tell was not present at the oath-taking which follows, but Rossini's musico-dramatic sense, and Tell's role in his conception of the opera as a whole, demanded it. After the oath-taking, accompanied by trumpets, the act does not end with a *stretta*, as one might have expected. The dawn is greeted with a gentle drum-roll, there is a threefold call 'Aux armes!', and then in a brief tempestuous orchestral coda – only sixteen bars long – Rossini brings down the curtain. It was Donizetti who said that, though the first and last acts were written by Rossini, it was God who wrote the second, and Berlioz found the conclusion of it 'sublime'.

Such an achievement is indeed hard to follow, and some critics have pronounced that the opera loses its impetus after Act II. The third act opens with the farewell scene between Arnold and Mathilde, to which she responds with her 'Sur la rive étrangère', in which the closing section is one of the few moments in the opera where one feels that the embellishment of the vocal line is excessive, for in general Rossini kept a restraining hand on ornamentation throughout the opera. The scene then switches to the square at Altdorf, with the homage-paying to Gesler's hat and Tell's shooting of the arrow at the apple on his son Jemmy's head. Tell's words to his son, 'Sois immobile', constitute a powerful and moving aria with cello solo, which Rossini told Wagner had been influenced by the loss of his mother. Indeed, it ends with the cry 'Jemmy, Jemmy, songe à ta mère'. For Wagner, however, the interest lay more in the way in which Rossini set the words according to their innate speech rhythm and sense, rather than subject them to a regular rhythm, and in so doing – in Wagner's opinion – Rossini reached 'the highest degrees of lyric expression'.

Act IV opens rather like the previous act, with a scene for Arnold in which he visits his father's house – 'Asile héréditaire' – and in one of the most taxing arias in the tenor repertoire (which Berlioz thought the best number in the opera) realises that he must take the place of Tell, who has been imprisoned by Gesler, and lead the revolt against the Austrians. Rossini uses the fiery *cabaletta* to convey his new resolve and sense of purpose. In Berlioz' opinion the aria as a whole was too subtle for the audience, but he especially singled out Rossini's use of harmony and modulation to reinforce the expression of the vocal line, and never simply for 'musical caprice', for which Berlioz had reproached Rossini only two years before. The scene now moves to Lake Lucerne again, where a storm is lowering. Tell's wife, Hedwige, is overwrought, then Mathilde arrives with Jemmy, whom she has taken under her protection, and offers herself as a hostage against Tell's safety. There follows a trio, 'Je rends à votre amour', in which the somewhat academic device of false canon is used by Rossini to brilliant effect in what comes across as a luxuriously harmonic and melodious number. Jemmy then lights the beacon that is the signal for the revolt to begin.

The storm approaches, and the women pray for Tell's safety, 'Toi qui du faible es l'espérance', which begins as a solo for his wife, then becomes a duet, and finally a chorus. Tell arrives in an Austrian boat, driven across the lake by the storm, and pursued by Gesler. Jemmy hands his father a crossbow, with which he kills the oppressive governor. Furst and his men arrive, then Arnold, who has liberated Altdorf from the Austrians. The storm recedes, and the majestic mountains reappear in their sublime purity. Harps and horns begin the closing hymn which brings to an end not only one of the most important grand operas, but also Rossini's operatic career in a transfiguration that is exhilarating in its effect.

The first Tell was Dabadie, and Arnold was Nourrit (Gilbert-Louis Duprez did not sing the role until April 1837). Mathilde was Laure Cinti-Damoreau, Hedwige Mademoiselle Mori, and Jemmy Madame Dabadie. After the first or second performance, Arnold's aria in Act IV, 'Asile héréditaire', and the *cabaletta* that follows, 'Amis, amis, secondez ma vengeance', had to be omitted because Nourrit was apparently unable to cope. It was not until Duprez took over the role that it was heard as intended, and it was his singing more than anything else that helped to re-establish the opera's popularity in Paris. He sang the top C in a chest voice, and the E above in falsetto, or head voice. Auguste Laget, whilst describing *Guillaume Tell* as an immortal masterpiece, went on to call it a 'destructive opera that has exterminated three generations of tenors in twenty years'. What he and many others overlooked was the fact that Rossini had no desire to launch himself into this new operatic world, even if he had played an important part in creating it. His own operatic world had, in many respects, ceased to exist by 1829.

Romanticism was now in full flow; and, although *Guillaume Tell* has many of the marks of a Romantic *grand opéra*, for Rossini it was not the threshold of a new stage in his career but, rather, the closing of a door on an operatic style with strong roots in the eighteenth century, for which he had an innate talent. It is true that in his Italian operas revised for Paris and, especially, in *Guillaume Tell* he had introduced new elements; but he had no wish to go further and compete with Meyerbeer or, later, Verdi, who detected in *Tell* a lack of the 'sincerity' that he found in *Il barbiere di Siviglia*, and which he attributed to the 'fatal atmosphere' of the Paris Opéra.

Troupenas paid Rossini 24,000 francs for the publication rights of *Guillaume Tell*, and as an indication that the royal household recognised Rossini's talent and achievement, and had no ill-feelings over his contract, he was awarded the Légion d'honneur on 7 August. That evening, when he returned home after dining with friends, he was serenaded with the overture to the opera, and Levasseur, Nourrit and Dabadie sang the oath-swearing trio. On 13 August, Rossini and his wife left Paris for Bologna. For Isabella it was to be the last time she saw the city. The fact that they were giving up the apartment in boulevard Montmartre would seem to imply that neither of them envisaged spending any prolonged periods in Paris in the future. In Rossini's own case, however, events would decide otherwise.

CHAPTER EIGHT

The Return to Italy

The change from the bustling cosmopolitan world of Paris to the much more parochial one of Bologna in the late summer of 1829 in no way made Rossini feel bored or *dépaysé*. After all, it was something he had longed and waited for. Initially he went to Castenaso on 6 September and only moved into his *palazzo* in Bologna itself with the onset of winter. During the opera season three of his operas – *Tancredi*, *Otello* and *Semiramide* – were given at the Teatro Comunale, with Pasta heading the cast. There is no evidence that Rossini was in any way involved in the productions, or even that he attended any of the performances; but it would have been strange if he had not had contact with Pasta, for one, at some point during the season.

In the wake of Rossini's departure from Paris, the Théâtre-Italien now had Édouard Robert and Carlo Severini as co-directors from 1 October 1829. Robert was in Bologna in March 1830, and found Rossini extremely difficult to corner, as he explained in his letters back to Paris:

> I am unable to retain the Maestro's attention for more than a moment at any one time, and it is much more difficult to talk to him about matters here than in Paris, since he amuses himself too much here with these accursed Bolognese idlers. . . . They come and pester him at his home from noon onwards, when he is scarcely awake, and they never take their leave until one o'clock in the morning. . . . When I go out with him in the hope of having his company for at least a short time, more often than not he ends up slipping away behind the pillars of an arcade, and once he has started gossiping with his friends, it is no longer possible to agree on anything with him.

As spring returned, Rossini moved out to Castenaso, and began to feel the urge to compose, despite all his protestations that his career was over. On 4 May he wrote to La Rochefoucauld to ask about a libretto, which he said he had been waiting for since he left Paris, though one must also allow for the fact that Rossini was simply keeping in touch with court officials:

> Above all, I should have liked to take advantage of the beautiful spring days and my time in the country, where I have been installed for a short time, to move the opera on speedily; for I would like my industry and my keenness to prove to you my wish to please you. But I cannot work without a poem.[1]

The following month Rossini went to Florence for about ten days, where he paid visits to the Teatro della Pergola on 12 and 13 June, and sat for the sculptor Lorenzo Bartolini. On his return to Bologna, he wrote to Severini in Paris on 7 July and again complained about the failure of the Parisian authorities – this time Lubbert, Director of the Opéra – to send him a libretto. He was not devoid of ideas of his own, and had sketched a scenario based on his own reading of Goethe's *Faust* in Italian. He told Doussault, the French architect, as much in 1854, and the following year he revealed to Hiller that it had been a cherished project for a long time, and that he had collaborated on it with Étienne de Jouy. There were various reasons why he had not taken the idea further, according to the Hiller record, though the sequence, as recalled in 1855, is somewhat telescoped. Rossini said that Paris was suffering from *Faust*-mania, which rather dampened his enthusiasm; then came the July Revolution of 1830, and the Opéra ceased to be a royal establishment. He then went on to recall the death of his mother, and the fact that his father was uncomfortable in Paris because he did not speak French. Clearly this happened well before the 1830 Revolution; but what is interesting is that, though Rossini stated categorically that he dissolved his contract – certainly as far as the obligation to compose four more operas was concerned – there is no record of his having done so.

It would be interesting to know precisely what manifestations of *Faust*-mania in Paris had impressed Rossini. Although the first part of Goethe's drama had been completed in 1807, it was not until some twenty years later, when Gérard de Nerval's French translation appeared, that *Faust* gained wide popularity in France. Spohr, it is true, had composed an opera on the theme for Prague in 1816, but it does not seem likely that Rossini was familiar with it. Certainly French interest dates from about 1827, the year in which Berlioz read the translation; and, although he composed his *Huit Scènes de Faust* the following year, and published it as his opus 1, he subsequently withdrew it. His *La Damnation de Faust*, incorporating the *Huit Scènes* in revised form, did not appear until 1846. Apart from a ballet by Adam of 1833, which also postdates the time of which Rossini was speaking, it is hard to see what he had in mind. He may have known that Berlioz was using Goethe's *Faust* in 1828–9, of course, and being well aware of the opinions that Berlioz had expressed about him Rossini did not wish to compete with him, either on purely musical grounds – and now that he had renounced opera composition he would have been even less likely to want to do so – or because Berlioz had begun to publish musical criticism in April 1829 and so had a large public to whom he would now make known his views.

At the end of July 1830, Charles X was forced to abdicate, and Louis-Philippe, the citizen-king, came to the throne in his place. The Civil List, from which Rossini's annuity was drawn, was reduced from 40 million francs to 12 million a year. Rossini continued to enjoy his relaxed social life during August; then, on 4 September, set out for Paris with a manservant, but left his wife at home. No doubt he imagined – or hoped – that the matter of ensuring the continuing payment of his annuity would be of relatively short duration, and that he would soon be back in Bologna, but in the event husband and wife did not meet again for almost four years, and it was more than five years before Rossini finally secured the payment of the pension. The fact that Charles X himself had signed the contract was said to have played a crucial part in deciding matters in Rossini's favour, and when he was ultimately successful he was paid retrospectively from the moment in 1830 at which payment had been suspended.

In Rossini's absence, his father found himself in the somewhat invidious situation of looking after his son's affairs whilst trying to reconcile those interests with the demands of his daughter-in-law. In any case, husband and wife were no longer in amity. He was now thirty-eight; she was forty-five. She found it extremely difficult to accept that her career as an opera star was ended, although she still sang on occasions at parties. She was bored, and her boredom was expressed in extravagance and a taste for gambling. Because the allowance made to her by Rossini was insufficient to indulge her tastes, she began to give lessons secretly. She told Rossini that she did so purely out of friendship and concern for her students. Gossip, however, had it that it was Rossini's meanness that had forced her into the situation, and when he heard the stories he was upset and confronted his wife with the whole business. Rossini left for Paris with no improvement in the conjugal relationship, and Christmas that year was a sad affair, as Giuseppe wrote to his son on 31 December 1830: 'On Christmas Day our table consisted of your wife, me and her two maids. You may imagine how happy that was!'

Meanwhile Rossini had found himself staying first with Aguado at Petit-Bourg and then, since he had given up the boulevard Montmartre apartment on his departure from Paris in August 1829, he went to stay in the Théâtre-Italien. As a result of the change of regime the Opéra administration had been taken out of the domain of the royal household and transferred to the Ministry of the Interior, who in turn had assigned it to a private consortium. So Rossini had nothing to do with the Opéra at this time, but a good deal to do with the Théâtre-Italien, which derived great benefit from his presence. Among the singers in Paris at this time – the majority of them Italian – were Giulia Grisi, Giuditta Pasta, Luigi Lablache, Maria Malibran, Giovanni Battista Rubini and Antonio Tamburini. Under Rossini's care and attention, the operas of Bellini, Donizetti and Mercadante were performed. Rossini still hoped to return to Bologna, as he told Emilio [Émile?] Loup in a letter of 8 November 1830. He was indeed to leave Paris in three months' time, and travel south; but it was to Spain, and not to Italy.

On 4 February 1831, Rossini left with Aguado for Madrid, which they reached on 13 February. That same evening Rossini conducted a performance of *Il barbiere de Siviglia*, which was attended by King Ferdinand VII, and was subsequently received by the royal family, as he recounted to Hiller in 1855. If Rossini had ceased composing opera, however, he had not renounced composition entirely, and while he was in Madrid he accepted a commission from a friend of Aguado's, Manuel Fernández Varela, Archdeacon of Madrid, and a state counsellor. The work in question was a setting of the *Stabat Mater*, made all the more challenging for Rossini because of his admiration for Pergolesi's setting. He made the stipulation – wisely, as it turned out – that once he had completed it the manuscript should not pass out of the possession of the man who had commissioned it, nor be published. Rossini may have begun the composition in Madrid, or left it until he returned to Paris, which seems more likely;

for, in spite of repeated requests from Madrid, Rossini still had not completed it a year later. The date of the dedication on the autograph is 26 March 1852. As subsequently became apparent, Rossini had not even been able to complete the work himself, and had had to ask Giovanni Tadolini to help him out.[2] A far cry from the days when he composed three operas a year, and an indication that Rossini's health was beginning to deteriorate. Indeed, on his return from Spain, he had a bad attack of lumbago, which kept him in bed for six weeks, though it is also possible that he was suffering from the effects of gonorrhoea, too, which he had contracted some years before.

The year 1831 saw a considerable amount of change for Rossini, some of which was apparent at the time, some only perceived subsequently, and much of the change in the political and social spheres, of course, was beyond his control. We have little or no indication as to what he thought of things – or, indeed, what he was doing for much of the year after his return from Spain. It was as if he had retired not only from opera composition, but from society, too, apart from a small circle of intimates.

Musically, the event of the season was the first performance of Meyerbeer's *Robert le diable* at the Opéra on 21 November. Chopin, writing from Paris on 12 December, by which time he had met Rossini and seen *Il barbiere di Siviglia*, *Otello* and *L'italiana in Algeri*, also saw a performance of *Robert le diable*, which he found an overwhelming experience, both aurally and visually. Certainly it was the sort of *grand opéra* for which Paris quickly became famous, but is clearly a move away from Rossini's early *bel canto* which had been current at the Théâtre-Italien almost since his operas began to be performed there in 1817 with *L'italiana in Algeri*, and on a more regular basis from 1819 onwards. By the time of *Guillaume Tell*, therefore, Paris had had a decade of Rossini *bel canto* at the Théâtre-Italien, though it had only reached the Opéra itself in 1827 with *Moïse et Pharaon*. Inevitably, however, the demands of the larger house and the scale of its production drew Rossini into the realm of *grand opéra*, which tended to militate against *bel canto* and which, it must be said, his own Parisian operas had played a crucial part in accelerating. This, then, was one of the changes that Rossini was witnessing; and, although initially Meyerbeer's approach to the voice was basically little different from Rossini's, because of the requirement that the singers compete with a much larger orchestra, inevitably vocal technique would have to adjust. It is interesting that when Édouard Robert was in Italy in 1830 he had passed through Milan on his way to Bologna, and had experienced the *urlo francese*, or French shouting, of which, he said, Rossini had rid the Opéra, but which now seemed to have taken over in Italy.[3] From several points of view, therefore, the signposts were now pointing away from Mozart, Cimarosa, Paisiello and Rossini to Rossini, Meyerbeer and Wagner.

The new year of 1832 saw a cholera epidemic in Paris, starting in February, when Bellini's *Il pirata* was being given, and the theatres began to empty. In March, as we saw earlier, Rossini put together the *Stabat Mater* and sent it off to Madrid; and, since the epidemic began to reach new proportions in May, Aguado suggested that Rossini should go away from the capital and head south. On 9 June the composer wrote from Bayonne to a friend in Bordeaux, saying that he was bored to desperation, but on 17 June he was in Pau, from where he wrote to the same correspondent in a rather more buoyant mood.[4] On 12 September, Boïeldieu told a correspondent that he was expecting to find Rossini in Toulouse, and on the same day Édouard Robert wrote to Rossini to tell him that the cholera epidemic was abating in Paris and that it was safe to go back. Rossini did return, but if Paris itself was now more healthy Rossini was not. He was back in Petit-Bourg by 7 October, but his health was giving cause for considerable alarm.

It was extremely fortunate for Rossini that by this time he had established a relationship with a woman who was destined to be his companion for the rest of his life. Olympe Pélissier was born on 9 May 1797. Her mother was unmarried, and her father seems to have shown no interest in her impending birth. She was known at first as Olympe-Louise Alexandrine Descuilliers. When her mother married Joseph Pélissier, he adopted the girl and she took her step-father's name. Olympe became a courtesan, and at some point the mistress of Horace Vernet, who is supposed to have used her as the model for Judith in his painting 'Judith et Holopherne'. We do not know when she and Rossini met, or where the meeting took place, but by the beginning of 1832 she knew him well enough to invite him to dinner, as we learn from a letter she wrote to Balzac, dated 2 January that year: 'May I count on you for Monday next at nine o'clock? Rossini is coming to dinner, and it will make a good start to the New Year. You must be your most charming self; a period of repose ought to have made you more sparkling than ever.' A dinner

Cara Marietta

Sono venuto a Casa tua per
sedurti, e condurti a pranzo
da Dubragne che ha improvisato
un eccellente pranzetto, ma oh Dio!
Al ritorno del tuo domestico (dopo
una lunga aspettativa) ho tutto
rovinato, avendomi annunziato
che pranzavi in Città.

Altro argomento

Il Barone Delmar, vorrebbe averti
domani sera alla sua Società per
cantare un Pajo di pezzo, ti pre=
vengo che non è un Concerto
però lo sarà per il tuo pregio
se potessi deciderti mi obligheresti
oltremodo non vi sarà che Rubini,
La Blache, e tu che sei fatta
per ornare tutti i Giardini.
Come vedi ho bisogno di una
risposta questa sera stessa per
spiegare in caso tu mi rifiu-
tassi, addunque al ricevere
della presente mandami al
Teatro una risposta, e cerca
sii questa favorevole.

Io t'abbraccio colle solite lagrime
ed auguro a tè ed all'altra successione
tutte quelle felicità che desideri
il

tuo Aff.° amico
G. Rossini

Da Casa tua li 14 Genn.° 1832

P.S. Ho aspettato Charles ma non
si vede ed io parto addio

Con Espressione

Addio addio

A Mad.ma

Mad.e Malibran
Celebre Compositrice, Cantatrice, Suonatrice,
Pittrice, [illegible], Sartrice, Declamatrice,
Danzatrice etc, etc, etc. ecc.

Facsimile of a letter from Rossini to Maria Malibran dating from 1832.

invitation to meet Rossini was not necessarily in itself a sign of an established relationship, but the fact that also in 1832 Rossini composed a cantata for soprano and piano entitled *Giovanna d'Arco* ('Joan of Arc'), which he inscribed himself on the autograph as having been composed especially for Olympe Pélissier, indicates that he had more cause than a good dinner to record his gratitude to her.

In fact the gratitude was largely in recognition of Olympe's skill as a nurse; and, although Édouard Robert dubbed her 'Madame Rabatjoie numéro deux' ('Mrs Killjoy the Second') because she intruded on the relationship the two men had hitherto enjoyed, Rossini's health and general comfort were of far more importance in the long run. As to the nature of his illness, he seems to have suffered from chronic urethritis at this period, and used a catheter almost every day to prevent the urethral canal from becoming blocked. He also suffered from haemorrhoids. In a more general way, he had manic-depressive tendencies, which became even more pronounced later. And one can appreciate that Olympe Pélissier was a far more suitable companion than Isabella Colbran could ever have been, now that Rossini had retired from composing operas and she from singing in them.

Apart from a *cantatina* for soprano, alto, tenor and three-part male chorus with piano accompaniment, dating from July 1832, and presumably some of the *Soirées musicales* (*c.*1830–5), there was precious little music composed that year after the sections contributed by Rossini himself to the *Stabat Mater*. The first performance took place in the Chapel of San Felipe el Real, Madrid, on 5 April 1833, during the Easter celebrations. This was essentially a fallow period for Rossini, then, as far as composition was concerned, though he continued to give the Théâtre-Italien his attention, and early in 1834 tried to get Donizetti to go to Paris and compose for the theatre, though it was 1835 before an opera of his was produced there, when *Mario Faliero* was given on 12 March. In June 1833, Rossini was still pursuing the matter of the annuity, but it was not until 12 March 1834 that the Seine Tribunal found in his favour, whereupon the Government appealed against the decision on 21 May, thus effectively ensuring that the affair dragged on into the following year (1835). However, the decision of March 1834 seems to have helped a good deal to assuage some of Rossini's anxiety, and when the season at the Théâtre-Italien ended that summer he set off for Italy with Robert and Severini, who were looking for operas to produce and singers to engage for their forthcoming season. By 11 June they reached Milan, where Rossini was given a rapturous reception, and four days later he was in Bologna.

He spent the best part of the next two months recuperating at Castenaso. Such a long absence from the public eye in Paris gave rise to rumours that he was dead. On 19 July, Édouard Robert wrote to his brother Joseph in Paris to say that he and Severini would return, with Rossini, whom they would meet in Milan, round about 25 August. 'Rossini is feeling very well,' he wrote, 'and by his presence will of necessity formally confound the good souls who kill him off with such confidence and ease.' The very next day (20 July) Rossini wrote from Castenaso to a friend in Milan, extolling the delights of country living. It was little wonder, therefore, that he returned to Paris in late August refreshed and invigorated, and on 1 September was entertained to dinner with Olympe Pélissier by Balzac.

Olympe's acquaintance with Balzac has been the subject of a great deal of speculation. Certainly she moved in a circle that included Balzac, the painter Horace Vernet and by now, of course, Rossini. In his *Prométhée ou La Vie de Balzac*, André Maurois maintained that, although Olympe was not the model for Foedora in Balzac's *La Peau de chagrin* (1831), the famous bedroom scene in that novel was supposed to have taken place between Olympe and Balzac in real life, and that the latter had often visited her at Ville d'Avray. There is, however, no documentary evidence for this, and all that one may say with certainty is that during the period 1832–5, through Olympe, Rossini met Balzac socially, possibly on several occasions; but by 1855, when Rossini returned to Paris, Balzac was dead.

On 4 September 1834, Bellini wrote to Francesco Florimo in Naples, informing him of Rossini's return to Paris, and his reception of the younger man, who was working on *I puritani* [*di Scozia*]. Bellini was naturally very keen to enjoy Rossini's friendship and esteem, especially in view of the authority he wielded in the world of Italian opera in Paris, and was even making himself 'useful' in Rossini's financial affairs in a letter of 24 November 1834 to their mutual friend Filippo Santocanale in Palermo. Since the business matters were in Sicily, presumably they concerned Isabella's estate and assets there, and one wonders why Bellini was making such a heartfelt plea to Santocanale, unless it was that Rossini had made reference to the business first, and Bellini had pounced on what was his apparent concern and used it as a means of ingratiating himself. For, as he told Santocanale, if Rossini took him under his wing, then his reputation and career would be considerably enhanced, for 'in Paris, he is the musical oracle'.

Bellini's hopes were amply fulfilled. *I puritani* had its first performance at the Théâtre-Italien on 24 January 1835, and two days later Rossini wrote to Santocanale, telling him how singers and composers were called for twice, which in Paris was a true accolade. With Giulia Grisi as Elvira, Rubini as Arturo, Tamburini as Riccardo and Lablache as Giorgio, Bellini had a truly star-studded cast for his opera. Rossini then went on to comment on Bellini's progress in orchestration, whilst at the same time issuing a warning that he ought not to be seduced by 'German' harmonies. Simple melodies, Rossini maintained, were the best. Since Bellini also added words of his own to the letter, he must have been fully aware of what Rossini had written.

On 12 March, Donizetti's *Marino Faliero* was heard for the first time at the Théâtre-Italien, with the same quartet of soloists as Bellini had had for *I puritani*. These were great days for the theatre, and the fruits of Rossini's encouragement and persistence were now available for all to enjoy. At the Opéra, however, only *Guillaume Tell*, and that in a cut version, kept Rossini's name in the limelight. On 17 September 1834 it had its official hundredth performance, and enjoyed renewed interest and vitality because of Duprez' performance as Arnold – first heard on 17 April 1837.

Bellini died on 23 September 1835. He had been kept in isolation from all his friends throughout the month at Puteaux since he had fallen ill at the end of August with what was suspected to be cholera but turned out to be a sudden flare-up of an illness akin to dysentery from which he had suffered five years earlier. On 3 October, Rossini wrote to Filippo Santocanale to tell him about the funeral at the Invalides and the subsequent interment at Père-Lachaise. Habeneck conducted a choir of 350, and the soloists in an arrangement of 'Credeasi misera', the finale of *Il puritani*, were Nicholas Ivanoff (a Russian tenor, Rossini's protégé), Lablache, Rubini and Tamburini. Rossini himself was one of the pallbearers, along with Carafa, Paër and Cherubini (now seventy-five years old), and insisted on going to the cemetery despite the fact that it rained all day. Not surprisingly, he told Santocanale that he was in bed, half-dead from having spent three hours in the mud and drenched with rain.

On 24 December 1835 the Committee of Finance finally upheld Rossini's claim to his annuity, and the Ministry of Finance agreed to pay the money from Treasury funds, making it retroactive from 1 July 1830. From now on, his financial worries were much less; and when, in April 1836, Carlo Balochino, one of the co-impresarios of the Kärnthnertortheater in Vienna, wrote to Rossini to try to commission an opera from him for the spring of 1837 he did so without success. The composer was in fact planning to return to Bologna, but Lionel de Rothschild invited him to join him on a tour in June 1836 which included Brussels, Antwerp, Aix-la-Chapelle, Cologne, Coblenz, Mainz and Frankfurt, where Lionel was to marry his cousin Charlotte.

Rossini was given a warm welcome in Brussels, Antwerp and Liège. He was made an honorary member of the Académie Philharmonique in Brussels, presented to the king and given a decoration, though the experience of the return train journey from Antwerp to Brussels had been so shattering for Rossini that he could never be persuaded to travel by train again. There is an amusing piano piece in the *Album pour les enfants dégourdis*, which is Volume 6 of the *Péchés de vieillesse*, which depicts a train disaster, probably composed some twenty-five to thirty years later, but still vivid in the composer's memory.

Rossini's week in Frankfurt involved no such discomfort, and again he was given a warm welcome. At Ferdinand Hiller's home he met Mendelssohn, who wrote to his mother and sister Rebecka on 14 July 1836: 'Yesterday morning I went to Hiller's, and can you guess whom I found there? Rossini, big and fat, in his most friendly and relaxed mood! Really, I know few men who can be as lively and as amusing as Rossini when he feels like it. And we did nothing but laugh.' In fact Hiller wrote: 'Rossini had lost the enormous corpulence of former years [he was now forty-four years old]: his figure was still full but not disproportioned, and his splendid countenance, which displayed both the power of the thinker and the wit of the humorist, beamed with health and happiness.'[5] Certainly Rossini seems to have been on top form at this time, and Mendelssohn found him very amusing about musical life in Paris, as he told his mother and sister in the letter of 14 July:

> About Paris and all the musicians there, about himself and his music, he relates the funniest and most amusing things, and he

> evinces almost limitless respect for everyone present, so that one would really believe him if one had not eyes to watch his sly face. But [there is] intelligence, vivacity and elegance always, and in each word; whoever does not believe him to be a genius ought to hear him holding forth only once, and he will change his mind immediately.

Hiller's recollection was much the same, and he recounted that when Rossini met Mendelssohn it was after the twenty-seven-year-old composer had spent the night travelling in a diligence, so Rossini, full of concern, suggested that they wait until the following day before hearing Mendelssohn play the piano. It was a characteristically generous act of consideration on Rossini's part. However, when they finally got down to the serious business, Rossini told Mendelssohn that one of his pieces had the smell of Scarlatti – or so the German composer complained to Hiller when they were taking a swim together. Luckily Hiller persuaded Mendelssohn to meet Rossini again, for it became clear that there was much in Mendelssohn's music that the Italian admired; and Mendelssohn, for his part, was delighted that he was able to share Rossini's devotion to the music of J. S. Bach.

Hiller recorded an incident that took place at Trouville in 1855, eight years after Mendelssohn's death, when he and a Madame Pfeiffer played Mendelssohn's A minor symphony in a duet arrangement for Rossini. Recalling a performance of the Octet which he had heard in Florence, Rossini observed that 'Mendelssohn knew how to treat the smallest motif with so much sensitivity and with such spirit'. That led him to speculate as to why Mendelssohn had never written opera: surely all the German theatres would want to commission operas from him. Hiller told him that no German theatre director would dream of commissioning a new opera. To Rossini this seemed a gross failure to encourage young talent. However, as Hiller explained, German composers tended to prefer instrumental music in any case. Rossini observed that they usually began with instrumental music, and that that may have made it difficult later on to adjust to the restrictions imposed by vocal music: 'It is difficult for them to become simple, whereas it is difficult for Italians not to be trivial.' In fact, Mendelssohn had composed several stage works, including a youthful opera, *Die Hochzeit des Camacho*, which had had one performance in Berlin on 29 April 1827, and a *Liederspiel*, *Die*

Heimkehr aus dem Fremde, which was performed privately in 1829, and then publicly in Leipzig on 10 April 1851, as well as other works for the stage.

Rossini went from Frankfurt to Kissingen in Bavaria, possibly for a short cure, where he was on 16 August, then returned to Paris, and on 24 October set off for Bologna – via Turin, Milan and Mantua – which he reached on 23 November. Five days later, in a letter to Carlo Severini at the Théâtre-Italien, he told his friend that his father was well and delighted to see his son again, and that Isabella, too, was well and 'very reasonable'. It would seem, then, that Rossini had made the suggestion of a formal separation, and that his wife had not objected. Indeed, from the constant references in this correspondence to Olympe Pélissier, it is clear that she was now the woman in Rossini's life, and that whether his original relationship with Isabella had ever been a love-match, or was merely a mutual decision to share their lives together, it was now over.

During the night of 12–13 December 1836, the Teatro La Fenice in Venice burned down, and on 26 February 1837 the impresario Alessandro Lanari, who was in Florence at the time, wrote to Rossini to suggest that to celebrate the reopening of the theatre they should put on *Guillaume Tell*. In his reply Rossini pronounced himself flattered by the invitation, but clearly had no great desire to travel to Venice, let alone find himself involved in the production of an opera – even one of his own. His initial reason for refusing was that he did not know where he was likely to be, so could not commit himself, and then he went on to say that he felt that the choice of *Guillaume Tell*, with its 'melancholy' music, peasants, mountains and miseries, was hardly a suitable choice for such an occasion. In the event the chosen opera was Donizetti's *Lucia di Lammermoor*, which was hardly festive, and really no better suited for what was essentially a joyous occasion than *Guillaume Tell*. Since it took almost ten months from Lanari's letter to the opening night, Rossini could claim that his doubts about where he would be turned out to be justified. He was, in fact, on the threshold of yet another phase of his life.

At some point after Rossini's return to Bologna and discussion with Isabella (therefore between 23 and 28 November 1836) it was decided that it was 'safe' for Olympe to leave Paris and take up residence in Bologna, in the same city as the composer, though not, of course, under the same roof. So she, too, found herself on the threshold of a new phase in her life. It was much more of a risk for her, and the implication of what she was doing is not too far removed from the worlds of *La traviata* and *La Bohème*. That she felt so is reflected in the fact that she made her will, dated 26 January 1837, in which Rossini was named her sole heir – 'légataire universel'. She had also decided, if the worst came to the worst, what she wished to be done with her mortal remains: 'Rossini will decide whether, by my conduct, I have deserved to repose near him eventually. My last wish will be to be buried near his mother; if Rossini does not deem that fitting, a plot will be purchased in perpetuity so that my mother may repose near me.' Such specific directions were the source of considerable problems later, when Rossini's remains were taken from Paris to Florence.

By 5 February, however, when Rossini again wrote to Severini, one of the chief reasons for the delay in writing was the fact that he had been finalising the details of his separation from Isabella. He derived satisfaction from the fact that he had behaved so magnanimously, whereas in the eyes of Bolognese society her conduct seemed wayward, even unbalanced. At all events, they were to have separate but contiguous establishments. Olympe might now arrive in Bologna with impunity. Édouard Robert, writing to Rossini, said that she set off from Paris in a rather dilapidated carriage, taking a great deal of luggage, including table linen, which was the heaviest stuff in the world. In her situation, Olympe had had to assemble her effects around her as and when she could, and she would not dispose of them lightly. At that moment she was, as far as she knew, leaving Paris for good, and all her worldly possessions would therefore go with her. When she reached Turin, Olympe wrote to her friend Hector Couvert, with whom she had deposited her will, and who was in control of her financial affairs. She had experienced a blizzard in the Mont Cenis Pass, so that the journey from Chambéry to Turin had been alarming. Nevertheless she reached Bologna at the end of February, and on 8 March 1837 wrote to Couvert again, chiefly about financial matters, but – inevitably – about her situation *vis-à-vis* Rossini and the woman who would remain his wife as long as she lived.

Clearly Rossini did not want Olympe to be put in a situation any more compromising than was necessary in the circumstances. There was no question, therefore, of there being a common home: Olympe would have to reconcile herself to setting up house on her own in Bologna. That would have been a relatively small achievement, however, if in addition Isabella had effectively denied Olympe's existence – at least, socially – in the city. But, according to Olympe's letter to Couvert, Isabella's friends convinced her that it was far better for her to accept the situation, and that she had more to gain by receiving Olympe in her home than by denying her existence. So it was, then, that, although Olympe would rather have left Bologna there and then, she found herself calling on Isabella, whom she described as 'pretty and unaffected'. Isabella was, after all, a woman of the theatre and a woman of the world, and by this late stage was unlikely to be heartbroken at the loss of her husband's affections.

It was typical of Rossini's sensitivity and tact that he managed to uphold his wife's place in society and at the same time install his lover (in spirit, if not in physical reality) in a way which offended only the most conservative members of society. As Olympe expressed it to Couvert in the same letter: 'God gave me strength, a long time ago, to see Rossini as simply a friend.' She may, of course, have been consoling herself, since she could never be Rossini's wife as long as Isabella lived, or she may have been totally honest, by accepting that she would not enjoy a physical relationship with the composer, especially in view of his illness. She took comfort from the strength of their relationship, which nothing could alter, and which Isabella could not deny. It was the very stuff of a future Verdi or Puccini opera, though with the crucial difference of a happy outcome. Isabella invited Olympe to lunch, and behaved very well in what Rossini acknowledged to Severini, in a letter of 29 March, was a delicate situation.

It would have been unreal, however, not to say sinister, if Isabella had formed a deep liking for Olympe and they had settled down without further ado into what was a classic triangular situation. Moreover, in these early days, living in a foreign country, Olympe did not have the self-control and determination that she evinced in later years. Her letters to Couvert in these first weeks and months indicate that it was no simple adjustment to make, and her relationship with Rossini was considerably tested. Because of her life hitherto, she had lived very much in the world of men, and she was – in common with other women in her situation – never friendly with women, so she lacked a confidante who might have helped her through this difficult period.

She told Couvert, for example, that Rossini indulged her caprices, but had had to tell her quite plainly that if she were to leave Bologna that would be the end of their relationship. He had, however, foreseen that she might be unable to settle there, so had promised when they were still in Paris together that if that turned out to be the case, then he would set her up in Milan or Florence, or anywhere else in Italy for that matter. What Rossini genuinely wanted, and what Olympe herself was well aware of, was her happiness, for without that the whole venture was worthless. At the same time, there was Rossini's own situation to think of, and that of his aged father, too. By openly acknowledging that his marriage had failed, and by choosing the most decorous solution possible, Rossini needed to demonstrate that the person for whom he had risked so much was truly worthy of his affection. With the benefit of hindsight, however, one may see this awkward and uncomfortable initial period as one of adjustment, on several fronts, by the principal players exposed to the harsh light of the public gaze. Olympe was to triumph in the end, though in the early days she was the most vulnerable, and probably had the most to lose.

Meanwhile, behind the scenes, negotiations were being conducted over the details of the legal separation between Rossini and Isabella, and by September 1837 agreement was reached. Under the terms of their marriage contract, Isabella had made over to her husband the entire income from her inheritance, and made him joint owner with herself. As well as the villa and land at Castenaso, there was property in Sicily. Rossini now made her a monthly allowance, gave Castenaso over to her, and made provision for the rental of winter accommodation in Bologna. Once all of this had been arranged, Rossini and Olympe left for Milan at the beginning of November 1837 where they settled for almost the next five months. They took rooms in Palazzo Cantù at Ponte San Damiano; and, on 28 November, Rossini wrote to Severini:

> I am here in Milan, enjoying quite a brilliant existence. I hold musicales or musical gatherings in my home each Friday. I have a fine apartment, and everyone is eager to be present at my gatherings. We pass the time of day, eat well, and often talk about you. I shall spend all of the winter here and return to Bologna at the end of March.

In Milan, Rossini found little to tempt him at La Scala, but he was not merely being chauvinistic, since the regular audience was not very receptive, either, to what was on offer – Mercadante's *I briganti* and *Il giuramento* before the close of 1837, and Carlo Conti's *Gli Aragonesi a Napoli* in the new year. Besides, Rossini's own musical evenings attracted almost all the best musicians in Milan at the time. He even tempted Pasta from her villa on Lake Como, where he and Olympe had stayed with her for five days at the end of November, after a disastrous summer season in London. Already Olympe was organising her side of these occasions with the unobtrusive efficiency that was to become legendary when the Rossinis subsequently instituted their *samedi soirs* in Paris.

Olympe, too, wrote about the visit to Milan, and there is a letter to Antonio Zoboli in Bologna, dated 29 November, telling him that they were going to perform Haydn's *Die Schöpfung* at the next Friday *soirée*, and that Liszt would make his second appearance for them.[6] One hopes that the reception given in Rossini's home to Liszt was better than that which he experienced on 10 December during a solo recital at La Scala, when one member of the audience shouted out that he went to the theatre to enjoy himself, not to study ('Vengo al teatro per divertirmi e non per studiare').[7] Still, Beethoven had experienced a similar reaction during the first public performance of the 'Eroica' Symphony in Vienna, when (according to Czerny) a man shouted: 'I will give another *kreutzer* if only it will stop!' Beethoven is supposed to have retorted to Christoph Kuffner: 'If I write an hour-long symphony they will find it short enough.' Liszt did not have quite the same Beethovenian response to such situations, but in his own way he pursued his individual artistic path in the face of lack of comprehension, especially in the late piano music, with a single-mindedness worthy of Beethoven.

Liszt's relationship with comtesse Marie d'Agoult at this time was little different from Rossini's with Olympe Pélissier, except that Marie d'Agoult had already borne Liszt one daughter; and on Christmas Eve, two weeks after Liszt's Milan recital, she bore him a second girl, named Cosima after Lake Como, who would later become the wife of Wagner. There was a vast difference between the characters of the two women, and Marie d'Agoult's aristocratic *hauteur* made her unpalatable to many people. She certainly regarded Olympe as her social inferior, and in her memoirs declared that no unmarried woman of any standing would frequent the Rossini *soirées* in Milan. Perhaps Liszt had made a great mistake in telling Marie d'Agoult that he liked Olympe, thus inciting her jealousy. It is interesting that in the painting by Joseph Danhauser, 'An Evening at Liszt's', in which Liszt plays the piano to a group of friends, Marie d'Agoult is the only woman included, apart from George Sand, who is in any case *en travesti*, and Rossini is depicted with his arm around Paganini's shoulder. Somewhat perversely, on her return to Milan from Como after the birth of Cosima, Marie d'Agoult expected to be introduced to Olympe by Rossini; instead of which he alone made a call of only ten minutes' duration and that was the end of the matter. In Liszt's opinion, given in a report published in *La Revue et gazette musicale* dated 10 March 1838, Rossini had now become 'rich, idle and illustrious'. However, Liszt made piano transcriptions of Rossini's *Soirées musicales* (*c.*1830–5), and Rossini gently parodied Liszt's style in Volume 8 of the *Péchés de vieillesse* (*Album de château*), number 12, 'Spécimen de l'avenir', so it was evident that they did not fall out.

A dark shadow suddenly fell across this glittering social scene in Milan in January 1838 when Rossini read in the newspapers that in the night of 14th–15th the home of the Théâtre-Italien in Paris, the Salle Favart, had been gutted by fire. He had stayed in the building during his last visit to the city, and he had left a considerable amount of music there, all of which was destroyed. Much more devastating to him than the loss of the music, however, was the loss of his friend Carlo Severini, who perished whilst attempting to escape the conflagration. Jumping fifteen feet to the ground, he landed on a pile of stones, broke his spine and died instantly. Severini had been planning to retire to Bologna, and had bought a property nearby, but Édouard Robert, his co-manager at the Théâtre-Italien, had persuaded him to return to Paris. With the demise of Severini, Rossini lost not only a close friend, but also his chief point of contact in the French capital.

Robert, who had sustained considerable burns in the fire, was in a difficult situation. Not only was he without a theatre; he was effectively without working capital, too, since the theatre's bank account was in Severini's name, and until his estate was settled could not be drawn upon. In addition to his theatrical venture, Severini had also been looking after Rossini's financial affairs in Paris, and fortuitously Rossini owed Severini a considerable amount of money, which he was able to transfer to Robert. On 23 January, Rossini wrote a long letter to the latter, with suggestions and practical advice about the way ahead.[8] By 24 February 1838, Robert was able to tell Rossini that the repertoire (including two operas by Donizetti, *Lucia di Lammermoor* and *Parisina*) in their temporary home at the Salle

Ventadour was successful. However, he had tried to do too much too soon, so that the wounds on his legs, caused by his burns, opened up, and he had to return to bed for a further two weeks. If only Rossini had been there! But at least he had the benefit of his advice by letter. The company had to move yet again, from the Salle Ventadour to the Odéon, and at the end of the 1839 season Robert gave up the directorship of the company.

So closed, in a particularly regrettable way, a chapter of Rossini's association with the Théâtre-Italien that had lasted some twenty years; though, of course, his works were presented there later, under different managements. Moreover he himself was about to enter a depressing period marred by ill-health, which the death of friends and family was to exacerbate further. He was perhaps for the first time to look down into the Valley of the Shadow of Death, and perceive it as an eventual pathway for himself.

CHAPTER NINE

Bologna and the End of an Era

Despite its climate in winter, Milan clearly pleased Rossini, and he would no doubt have been happy to remain there. However, his father, now almost eighty, was unhappy with his prolonged absence; and, at the end of March 1838, Rossini and Olympe returned to Bologna. In truth Giuseppe Rossini's health was giving cause for concern, though he was to survive into the spring of 1839. In the September of 1838, Rossini returned to Milan, however, at the invitation of Prince Metternich, and he appeared at a musical party along with Pasta, but in general he tended to shun society from now on, as he explained to his friend Principessa Maria Hercolani who had reproached him for having deserted her: 'I must tell you that my poor father was ill all summer and autumn, and part of the winter. I, too, am in poor health, weighed down in spirit as I am. I see no one, I go nowhere, and I live sadly, always waiting for a better future. I hope that is sufficient to excuse me.'[1] Certainly a physician's report, made in 1842 and sent by Olympe to Hector Couvert in Paris, dates a marked deterioration in Rossini's health to this winter of 1838–9.

One positive step in this somewhat negative period was an offer from the Liceo Musicale in Bologna, made in January 1839, that Rossini should become perpetual honorary consultant. In this way they hoped that they might take advantage of Rossini's prolonged presence in Bologna to improve the standing of their conservatoire. Rossini did not accept with alacrity, partly because of his own ill health at the time, as well as that of his father, and the depression that he was suffering. Finally, however, on 28 April, he replied in the affirmative. The very next day his father died. A letter to an unidentified friend in the Raccolta Piancastelli at Forlì leaves no room for doubt as to what this meant to Rossini:

I have lost everything that was most precious to me on earth, without illusions, without a future, imagine how I spend the days! My doctor wants me to go to Naples to take mud baths, sea baths, and another medicinal cure. I spent such a hard winter that I shall have to decide to make the journey. In different circumstances it would have been delightful, but in the sorrow in which I live at present, it will be a matter of total indifference to me.[2]

Aguado invited him to come and stay with him in France, but Rossini declined. He paid one visit to the Liceo Musicale, and then on 20 June set out with Olympe for Naples. He had not been there for ten years. After a stop in Rome on 23 June, they went on to stay with Barbaia in his villa at Posillipo. Rossini had only been there two days when he went into Naples, to the Conservatory of San Pietro a Maiella, where a concert was given in his honour, and he was given an enthusiastic welcome by teaching staff and students.

Olympe, writing to Antonio Zoboli in Bologna on 11 August 1839, found Barbaia a great 'original' – no education but lots of heart. It is hard to think that Rossini did not enjoy the company of his old colleague, either, though the cures and the change of environment did little or nothing, either for his health or for his state of mind. He and Olympe left Posillipo in early September, reaching Rome on the 11th, but for two days Rossini accepted no invitation. There was a performance of *Semiramide* at the Teatro Valle, and the Società Filarmonica wanted to receive their honorary president at a special session. Rossini declined both invitations. He dined with the Duca di Bracciano (Torlonia), and then left for Bologna, which he and Olympe reached four days later.

Rossini now intended to devote himself to the affairs of the Liceo Musicale in Bologna. He tried to attract Mercadante as Professor of Counterpoint and Composition, which would also have made him executive director. Mercadante accepted, and then made off to Naples, where he became Director of the Conservatoire the following year (1840). Rossini still tried to find a suitable candidate, and approached both Pacini and Donizetti with this in view. He himself attended the examinations for admission to the Liceo and conducted the orchestra during the course of January 1840, but his illness only grew worse.

The change that had come over Olympe since she had arrived in Bologna three years before is quite remarkable, as evinced in her letters to Hector Couvert. Unable to be a blushing bride in April 1837, she had instead been a rather nervous mistress. At the beginning of March 1840, still writing to Couvert, she has achieved an almost matronly serenity and urbanity: 'We are not well . . . it is from eating too much . . . the Maestro and I live for food . . . and we perform this duty religiously.' There is still the *cocotte*, when she tells Couvert that Rossini has provided her with a 'very elegant small carriage' and a pair of horses, and that she felt positively Parisian as she drove out. Even so, there was a decidedly realistic element, too: 'I am neither proud nor gracious; I am a fat woman engaged from morn till night with digestion.'

In the autumn of 1840, *Guillaume Tell* was put on in Bologna, under the title *Rodolfo di Sterlinga*, with Rossini's protégé the tenor Nicholas Ivanoff as Arnoldo. Rossini gave no opinion that has come down to us about the adaptation, but it seemed to him an excellent part in which Ivanoff might make his début at La Fenice in Venice. To this end Rossini had already been in correspondence with Caresana, secretary to the board of the theatre, as he relayed to a Venetian friend, Giuseppe Ancillo, in an attempt to get him to mediate, intrigue, lobby – in short, do everything possible to persuade the authorities to mount *Rodolfo di Sterlinga*. The attempt failed, though in February 1841 Rossini and Olympe went to Venice in an act of solidarity with the Bolognese composer Vincenzo Gabussi (1800–46), whose *Clemenza di Valois* had its first performance at La Fenice on 20 February that year.

Rossini was suffering from diarrhoea when he left for Venice, and his condition was no better when he returned in early March. By now the diarrhoea had persisted for several weeks. The following month Carl Gustav Carus, a famous doctor from Dresden, was in Bologna, and Rossini decided to consult him. The doctor established a connection between the composer's inflammation of the urethra and his haemorrhoids, and prescribed flowers of sulphur mixed with cream of tartar, with the application of leeches to the haemorrhoids. He also recommended castor oil instead of salts, and extolled the virtues of a cure at Marienbad for similar complaints.

The composer declined to go to Marienbad, and instead took the trouble to try to implement his ongoing programme for improving standards at the Liceo in Bologna by writing to Domenico Donzelli in Vienna on 9 May 1841, commissioning him to look for and purchase music by Mendelssohn, Weber and others. He particularly wanted chamber music for wind and stringed instruments, and solo songs in Italian or French with piano accompaniment, which shows the extent to which Rossini had identified specific needs in the Liceo. He thought Donzelli a particularly good person to carry out the commission because he knew that he exercised care in the amount of money he laid out when selecting music for himself.

Still Rossini's health did not improve, however, and in June he and Olympe went to Porretta, in the Reno Valley near Pistoia, where a cure of the waters was available. Despite spending some three weeks there, Rossini's urethritis was no better; in fact the secretions increased, and he lost a great deal of weight. The diarrhoea only got worse, as Olympe told Couvert, but it was the moral change in Rossini that gave her even more concern than his physical weakness. He seemed to lack even the energy to move. He had returned to Bologna by 21 June no better for the experience of Porretta.

It was during the summer of 1841 that the Belgian musicologist François-Joseph Fétis visited Rossini in Bologna. Fétis was working on the second edition of his *Biographie universelle des musiciens et bibliographie générale de la musique*, and contributed what one might regard as an interim report to *La Revue et gazette musicale* in Paris.[3] In it Fétis drew his readers' attention to Rossini's labours in improving conditions at the Liceo Musicale in Bologna, which he contrasted with the composer's somewhat lax administration of the Théâtre-Italien in 1824. On 25 July this year (1841) *Le Temps* in Paris told its readers that the Duca di Modena had tried to commission Rossini to compose an opera for the inauguration of the new opera house in Modena, but that the composer had declined. Fétis now asked Rossini whether he did not feel the need to compose, not for the theatre, because of his health, but perhaps for the Church. 'For the Church?' asked Rossini. 'Am I, then, perhaps, an academic musician? Thank God I no longer occupy myself with music.' Fétis then expressed the opinion that the desire would surely return to Rossini. With his characteristic realism and bluntness, the composer retorted: 'How can it return to me, seeing that it has never come to me?'

Fétis was not to be deflected, however, and returned to the subject before his departure from Bologna. He felt that if Rossini approached church music in the belief that it required an academic formation – which in any case the composer had never had – then he would only put restraints on his creative spirit. Fétis felt that, because of the increasingly dramatic style of music for the Church, there was no one better suited than Rossini to provide such music. It would indeed, Fétis concluded, give him a noble aim for the autumn of his career. For the fruits of this noble aim one has to look ahead some twenty-five years to the *Petite Messe solennelle*, but if Rossini remembered Fétis' remark he would surely have reflected, in his wry way, that it had indeed been a long autumn. What Fétis must soon have discovered, of course, was that on 22 September of this year (1841) Rossini signed an agreement with Troupenas about the *Stabat Mater*, though it was somewhat unrealistic of Fétis to imagine that he had been responsible for Rossini's 'conversion' to the cause of church music so soon after his visit. As we shall see, it was sheer necessity that forced Rossini's hand.

Before leaving Fétis, however, it is interesting to consider his summing-up of Rossini's 'case' as a contemporary view, and one which is generally more sympathetic than many others at this time. In Fétis' opinion, Rossini's education had been neglected, he had led a nomadic life, meeting many people but having no time to form true friendships (which was not strictly true), and in general had existed in a virtual state of delirium. On top of this, Rossini was by disposition inclined to make jokes about everything, so that his apparent indifference to things made him seem egotistical. If Rossini's true character had hitherto been concealed from the general public, then it was his own fault, because he had continually misrepresented himself, saying things that did not truly reflect his own opinion, and failing to deny falsehoods about himself when he had the chance to do so. One may compare this with the attitude of Paganini, who positively relished the more extreme claims about his character by way of a public relations exercise. Fétis looked forward to a time in the not too distant future when Rossini would let people see the real person; and then the world would be amazed to discover how a great man had gone to such lengths to diminish his own stature.

Be that as it may, Rossini was soon galvanised into activity, with the eventual result that his stature was enhanced in no uncertain way. On the death, in 1837, of the Spanish cleric who had commissioned the *Stabat Mater*, his heirs sold the manuscript of the Rossini–Tadolini version – in the belief that it was all Rossini's work – to Oller Chetard on 1 December that year. Chetard in turn sold the manuscript to the Parisian publisher Antoine Aulagnier for 2,000 francs on 1 September 1841. Aulagnier then wrote to Rossini to find out whether he had

had any private restrictions on its publication when he sent the manuscript to Manuel Fernández Varela. Rossini's reply to Aulagnier made quite clear that he had merely dedicated the work to Varela, and that he had reserved the publication rights to himself. He threatened legal action against anyone who presumed to publish, and then proffered the information that only six of the numbers had been composed by himself, and that because of illness he had had to ask a friend (Tadolini) to help him out. If Aulagnier examined the work, Rossini suggested, he would easily determine which numbers were by him and which were not.

In the circumstances, this was by far the best course of action for Rossini to have pursued. It is only the next section of the letter that is open to question. Rossini went on to tell Aulagnier that 'shortly afterwards', when his health was better, he completed the work, and that he had in his possession the only version of the new numbers. The question is simply when Rossini composed them. It seems out of character for Rossini to have sent the composite version to Varela and then immediately begun composing the sections taken by Tadolini. He is much more likely to have felt the need to do so, however, after the death of Varela and the sale of the manuscript, and yet one suspects that it required Aulagnier's letter to spur Rossini into composition. In the event he sold the rights to Eugène Troupenas for 6,000 francs, in a contract signed in Bologna on 22 September 1841. Two days later, he wrote to Troupenas, telling him that Aulagnier now maintained that the gift of the diamond-encrusted gold snuff-box that Rossini had received from Varela for the *Stabat Mater* constituted payment, and that he was planning to perform the work at a public concert. In fact Aulagnier had already entered into collaboration with another publisher, Maurice Schlésinger, and had plates made of the Rossini–Tadolini *Stabat Mater* in Hamburg.[4] Troupenas had the plates seized, and brought an action against Aulagnier and Schlésinger for theft and falsification. Since Schlésinger was the owner of *La Revue et gazette musicale*, Rossini's reputation was henceforth damned as far as that publication was concerned. One might add in parenthesis that Schlésinger had many dealings with Beethoven, whose handling of his publishers was, at times, little short of dishonest, and tendentious at the very least.

When the Troupenas action was heard, the court decided that the Rossini dedication of the *Stabat Mater* to Varela and acceptance of a gift did not constitute a sale, and that Rossini was therefore perfectly within his rights to dispose of his property as he wished. Troupenas' action against Aulagnier and Schlésinger was dismissed, however. Aulagnier eventually published the six Tadolini numbers, and Troupenas the complete Rossini version.

In his letter of 24 September, Rossini told Troupenas that he was sending three numbers fully scored, and that he was putting in the metronome markings, as requested by the publisher. All that remained for Rossini to do, therefore, was to send the final chorus. This means that Rossini now had a ten-part work, rather than the previous twelve-part version:

(1) 'Stabat Mater dolorosa' – chorus and tenor solo
(2) 'Cuius animam gementem' – tenor aria
(3) 'Quis est homo qui non fleret' – soprano duet
(4) 'Pro peccatis suae gentis' – bass solo
(5) 'Eia, Mater, fons amoris' – *a cappella* chorus and bass solo
(6) 'Sancta Mater, istud agas' – quartet, two sopranos, tenor and bass
(7) 'Fac ut portem Christi mortem' – *cavatina* for second soprano
(8) 'Inflammatus et accensus' – aria for first soprano and chorus
(9) 'Quando corpus morietur' – *a cappella* quartet
(10) 'In sempiterna saecula. Amen' – four-part fugue for vocal quartet

The 'new' numbers provided by Rossini were 2, 3, 4 and 10.

The following month (October 1841) some sections of the work were performed privately in the Parisian home of the pianist-composer Pierre-Joseph-Guillaume Zimmerman, and then there was a formal performance of six numbers, organised by Troupenas, in the salon of the Austrian pianist Henri Herz on 31 October, attended by the press. The soloists were Pauline Viardot-Garcia, Madame Théodore Labarre, Alexis Dupont and Jean-Antoine-Just Géraldy. Théodore Labarre was the pianist. Adolphe Adam reported for *La France musicale*, founded by the brothers Marie and Léon Escudier, which was firmly on the side of Rossini and Troupenas, in opposition to *La Revue et gazette musicale* and the Aulagnier–Schlésinger faction.

The first complete public performance took place in the afternoon of 7 January 1842 in the Salle Ventadour in Paris. The soloists were Giulia Grisi, Emma Albertazzi, Mario and Tamburini, who, according to the Escudiers, overcame the reluctance of the others to take part after having twice read through his aria 'Pro peccatis'. It was a critical and commercial success, and bolstered up the hitherto flagging finances of the Théâtre-Italien, as well as having enriched the Escudiers, to whom Troupenas had ceded the rights for three months.

There were fourteen performances in all, which elicited a wide gamut of reactions, as one might expect. It cut right across the traditional divides. Of the Germans, for example, Heine was enraptured, whereas Wagner was dismissive in a letter of 5 February 1842 (probably) to Robert Schumann.[5] He had in any case written a fairly malicious article against Rossini in the *Neue Zeitschrift für Musik* of 28 December 1841, dwelling on the legal struggle, prior to the first performance, concerning the *Stabat Mater*. It must have been infuriating for Wagner, but the essence of his complaint in the letter to Schumann is that in Paris anything Italian is fashionable, and Italian sentimentalism is pernicious, and ultimately responsible for the decline in the standard of Parisian musical life.

Even today, the work is difficult to come to terms with, since it combines two very distinct traditions: that of the more traditional style of church music that goes back to Palestrina – as seen in the unaccompanied sections, the 'Eia, Mater' and the 'Quando corpus' – as well as Bach and Handel in the double fugue with which he completed the work in 1841. Then the other tradition is of course the operatic one. Here Fétis had hoped that Rossini would contribute something of value that would help to revive church music. He did not, but he cannot be said to have failed, since he had no desire to take on the task. This is not to imply that Rossini did not approach the act of composition with reverence and dedication, but the fact remains that the overall impression of the *Stabat Mater* is that it has always been more suited to the concert platform than to the church. Viewed as non-liturgical music, it is an accomplished and often appealing work, with some moving and occasionally thrilling moments. Whether it assists devotion, however, must remain a matter for the individual.

In all the controversy surrounding the *Stabat Mater*, and amidst the critical reactions – both favourable and unfavourable – to his music, Rossini had never even heard a performance of the work, and for March 1842 he planned to have one in Bologna, which he asked Donizetti to direct. As Donizetti told Antonio Dolci in a letter of 2 March, it was indeed an honour for him, bestowed by Rossini. There may have been more than a gesture of recognition to Donizetti in

Rossini's offer; for, although the older man had by now secured certain important figures for the Liceo Musicale in Bologna – Manetti for violin, Golinelli for piano and Liverani for clarinet – he still had no Director and Professor of Composition. Mercadante, as we saw earlier, had accepted the post, and then on the day that he was due to take it up (1 October 1840) had turned it down and gone to Naples. Pacini also turned it down, and so did Donizetti in October 1841. But Rossini was nothing if not persistent in his long-term plans, and invited Donizetti to Bologna.

On this occasion only two of the soloists, Clara Novello and Nicholas Ivanoff, were professionals; the other soprano was Clementina degli Antoni and the bass Conte Pompeo Belgiojoso. Rossini decided that he wanted the proceeds of the performances (there were three eventually, on 18, 19 and 20 March) to go to the setting-up of a home for retired musicians. The rehearsals took place in the Liceo, but the performances were in the Archiginnasio, which had a good auditorium. When Donizetti arrived in Bologna from Milan, where he had just attended the first performance of Verdi's *Nabucco* at La Scala, he found everything well prepared. The performances were a brilliant success, and Rossini gave Donizetti four diamond studs. By 4 April the latter was in Vienna, from where he wrote to his brother-in-law, Antonio Vasselli, who had asserted that Donizetti would reap small financial reward from having conducted the *Stabat Mater*. Well, if the diamond studs were regarded purely at face value, Vasselli was no doubt right, Donizetti acknowledged. However, in terms of Rossini's affection for him, then his reward had been infinitely more; and Rossini persisted in his efforts to lure the younger man to Bologna. He wrote to him in Vienna on 12 April, indicating that they had had detailed discussions, whilst Donizetti was in Bologna, about terms of remuneration and conditions of service, including leave of absence.[6] It was also Rossini's intention to have Donizetti appointed *maestro di cappella* at San Petronio. In the event, however, they failed to agree terms, even if Donizetti were at all seriously considering the offer, and he accepted court appointments in Vienna. It was ironic that he made his début there on 4 May with a performance of the *Stabat Mater*.

The sudden death of Aguado in April 1842 was a heavy blow for Rossini, for the banker, only fifty-eight, had been far more than a financial adviser and patron. His estate was put at some 60 millon francs, but Rossini was greatly concerned that he had still owed

Aguado 50,000 francs at his demise, so he asked for the sum to be credited to the family from his account at Rothschild's bank. Thereafter that bank took care of all Rossini's financial affairs in France, and Hector Couvert transferred all Olympe's assets to Rothschild also.

Resigned now to the fact that Donizetti had eluded him, Rossini had to accept Antonio Fabbri as Professor of Counterpoint, and so Director, of the Liceo Musicale. He still kept a close watch on its affairs, however, and on 15 June 1842 a chorus from Rossini's beloved *Die Schöpfung* was performed, along with the rather more 'advanced' Beethoven 'Egmont' Overture. In Bologna now Rossini merited a civic festival on his name-day, observed with a hot-air balloon, fireworks and an arrangement of the *Stabat Mater* for fourteen wind instruments by Giovanni André. He was also honoured abroad, and King Friedrich Wilhelm IV of Prussia made him a member of his recently created Order of Merit in the Sciences and Arts. Verdi wrote to Emilia Morosini:

> I have been in Bologna for five or six days. I went to visit Rossini, who greeted me very politely, and his welcome seemed to me to be sincere. Whatever it was, I was very pleased. When I consider that the one living reputation all over the world is that of Rossini, I could kill myself, and all the fools along with me. It is a splendid thing to be Rossini.

In a letter to Michele (Sir Michael) Costa of 12 September 1842, Rossini confessed that the unforeseen success of the *Stabat Mater* had rather gone to his head, and the wave of success carried him into the following year.[7] In January the Consiglio Comunale of Bologna approved a motion for the installation of a bust of the composer in the Liceo Musicale, and the next month Pesaro fixed a plaque on the house in which he had been born, and struck a medal to commemorate two performances of the *Stabat Mater* in the Teatro Nuovo on 16 and 17 February. On 15 March, King Otto of Greece awarded him the cross of a Knight of the Royal Order of the Saviour. Rossini remained constant in his efforts at fund-raising for the Liceo, and on 4 May conducted a semi-professional performance of his *Otello* in the Teatro Contavalli.

Almost the only thing which did not flourish at this time was Rossini's health; but the ever-attentive Olympe had matters in hand. As far back as 15 December 1841, she had asked Hector Couvert in

Paris to arrange for Rossini to have a consultation with a specialist in diseases of the urinary tract, since Rossini's doctor in Bologna was compiling a report on the composer's condition, going back to 1836. By 6 February 1842, Olympe had the report in her hands, and sent it to Couvert, clearly intending that she would set out with Rossini for Paris.[8] It was more than a year, however, before this happened, and it may well have been that the somewhat euphoric state induced by the success of the *Stabat Mater* gave him the moral courage and physical energy required to undertake the journey and face the consultations that Couvert had arranged with doctors in Paris, and especially with the famous urologist Jean Civiale.

Rossini paid his last visit to the Liceo for the time being on 11 May 1843, and early on the morning of the 14th, a Monday, he and Olympe departed for Paris. They passed through Parma, where Verdi called on them, then Turin and the Mont Cenis Pass, reaching Lyons on 20 May, and eventually Paris a week later, where they took rented accommodation in place de la Madeleine. They were to remain in the French capital for almost four months, and it is estimated that some 2,000 people paid their respects at the beginning and end of their stay. For the middle three months Dr Civiale ordered a complete rest, and very limited activity, even extending to a ban on writing and long conversations. Some visitors managed to gain admission, one of whom was Duprez, who wanted to try to persuade Rossini to write an opera for him. 'I came on the scene too early, and you too late,' was the reply.

At first the cure seemed to be having little effect, but by the end of July Rossini began to feel much better, and was beginning to contemplate a return to Bologna – and good *tortellini* – towards the end of September. In the event he was able to set out from Paris on 20 September, and was back in Bologna on 4 October 1843. He renewed his relations with the Liceo Musicale, attended the first performance of Verdi's *Nabucco* in Bologna, and even did some composition by adapting the 'Chorus of the Bards' from *La donna del lago* and turning it into the cantata *Santo genio dell'Italia terra* for chorus and orchestra, to verses by Giovanni Marchetti, in celebration of the tercentenary of the birth of Tasso. It was performed in March 1844 in the Palazzo Carignano in Turin.

Another small composition of this period was a chorus which Rossini composed to complement two others which he had written prior to 1817 as part of the incidental music to a translation of

Sophocles' *Oedipus at Colonus* by Giambattista Giusti. He had long since consigned the music to decent oblivion, it would seem, when his friend the Bolognese composer Vincenzo Gabussi unearthed the score and took it to a publisher, Masset – possibly a former assistant of Troupenas. In a signed authorisation dated 28 June 1843, in Paris, Rossini made over the publication rights to Masset, but the latter failed to do anything about them, and Troupenas acquired them. He then made the journey to Bologna in the spring of 1844 and persuaded Rossini to write a third chorus, which the composer completed and sent off on 22 June 1844. Troupenas provided suitable French texts, and they were designated *Trois Chœurs religieux*, 'La Foi', 'L'Espérance' and 'La Charité' ('Faith', 'Hope' and 'Charity'), for female voices and piano. They were first heard in public at the Salle Troupenas in Paris on 20 November 1844.

As might have been expected, Adam was enthusiastic, but Berlioz, writing in *Le Journal des débats* of 6 December that year, was dismissive, especially of the last and most recently composed of the three, 'La Charité': '. . . it cannot have interfered greatly with the increase of his musical fortune, and . . . his alms-giving will not ruin him.' Liszt, however, was sufficiently impressed to make a transcription of it for voice and organ, which was published as one of his *Deux Transcriptions* in 1848. The other was the 'Cuius animam', for trombone and organ, from the *Stabat Mater*.

Rossini continued to support his friends – singers and composers especially – and in May 1844 made the journey to Ferrara to hear Domenico Donzelli sing in Mercadante's opera *Il bravo*. He also commissioned an aria from Verdi for Ivanoff to sing in Act II of *Ernani*, and on 28 January 1845 Rossini sent the money with a covering letter to Verdi, who was in Milan for the first performance of his *Giovanna d'Arco* at La Scala on 15 February.

One of the reasons that Rossini gave for the delay in writing to thank Verdi was that he had been suffering acute pain from boils. He would, however, survive. His estranged wife would not. News reached him later that year that Isabella was seriously ill at Castenaso, and on 7 September Rossini and Olympe drove out to visit her. He was said to have been alone with Isabella for about half an hour, and when he came out of her bedroom he was weeping. He thereafter reeived daily reports on her condition until 7 October, when he was informed that she had died, after repeating his name several times. She was sixty years old. They had seen little of each other over the last eight years, but her death was nevertheless a watershed in his life. With his parents and Isabella now all gone, the close ties with Italy were dissolved. He did not choose to live at Castenaso, but rented it out, and then sold it in March 1851. After a respectable period of waiting, Rossini and Olympe married on 16 August 1846.

Such was Rossini's reputation that busts and statues were now being erected not only in cities such as Bologna, but also in Milan (May 1846) and Paris (June 1846, destroyed by fire in 1873). The same year he was made a foreign associate of the Belgian Académie Royale des Sciences, des Lettres, et des Beaux-Arts. The coronation of the new pope, Pius IX, on 21 June 1846, inspired yet another version of the 'Chorus of the Bards' from *La donna del lago*, this time as 'Su fratelli, letizia si canti', which was given its first performance on 23 July that year in Bologna. Rossini was prevailed upon to produce a second work to honour the occasion in Rome, though he made it clear in a letter of 6 August 1846 to Giuseppe Spada that he had no intention of producing anything new: 'I laid down my lyre in 1828 and . . . it will be impossible for me to take it up again.' What he did produce was a *pasticcio*-cantata for four soloists, chorus and orchestra, which was performed in the Senate on 1 January 1847, though it had an unofficial first hearing in Bologna on 16 August 1846.

His propensity for *pasticcio* at this time did Rossini's reputation no good at all among the critics and 'serious' composers. Times had changed, and it was no longer an acceptable practice, and certainly not in the opera house, where Rossini made a considerable error of judgement. During his 'cure' in Paris in 1843, he was approached by Léon Pillet for a new work for the Opéra, the direction of which Pillet was about to take up. Rossini declined, but expressed the opinion that if Pillet was looking for an opera suited to the French stage, then *La donna del lago* was by far the best, giving ample scope to the chorus, the orchestra and the Parisian kind of staging. In fact Rossini had wanted to make his own début at the Théâtre-Italien with it, he said, but had not done so, and in his opinion it had never been given a satisfactory production. For one thing, it lacked a suitable Malcolm, but now that Pillet could call on the services of Rosine Stolz it was a strong possibility.

It was not until June 1846 that Pillet pursued the idea in detail, and visited Rossini in Bologna, taking with him the composer Louis-Abraham Niedermeyer and the librettist Gustave Vaëz. Pillet left his

Olympe Pélissier (1797–1878), the redoubtable Frenchwoman who became Rossini's second wife after the death of Isabella Colbran in 1845, though she had been his mistress for twelve or thirteen years while Isabella and Rossini were estranged.

Rossini's place in the musical pantheon, *c.*1840, is depicted at the far right as that of a god basking in his glory, whilst 'little' composers draw from the river of harmony that cascades from the pitcher he is holding. On the far left, Meyerbeer, as Robert le diable, keeps the as yet unfinished *Le prophète* and *L'africaine* in a cage, whilst Halévy beneath him takes a pinch of snuff from his music box. Next are shown Niedermeyer and Labarre, with Rossini's friend Prince Carafa, a carafe-shaped figure on horseback. Boïeldieu is behind the horse's head, and above him Berlioz leans out of a coach, penning articles for *Le Journal des Débats*. Next come Crisar, Adam as *Le postillon de Longjumeau* (1836), Donizetti (who makes his music by steam power), and Auber on his *Cheval de bronze* (1835). Next are Clapisson and Montfort, Thomas and Spontini who, dissatisfied with the Opéra, is going off to see dawn break.

associates to get on with what he imagined was the fitting of *La donna del lago* to a French text on the theme of Robert the Bruce. However, what emerged was a *pasticcio* entitled *Robert Bruce*, which drew on *La donna del lago*, but also on *Armida*, *Zelmira*, *Bianca e Falliero*, *Torvaldo e Dorliska* and *Moïse*.

After various delays the work had its first performance at the Opéra on 30 December 1846, to a mixed reception from the audience, though it ran for thirty performances and was revived in 1848. The critics, however, were not so tolerant, and Berlioz in *Le Journal des débats* and Stephen Heller in the *Musical World* of London (subsequently published in *La Critique musicale* in Paris) both expressed their reservations in no uncertain terms. This inspired Olympe to put her pen to paper to Pillet and announce that she was sending a pair of ass's ears to Bertin, the editor of *Le Journal des débats*, and to Berlioz. The most regrettable aspect of the whole affair was that, as Rossini's reputation began to fade amongst the more informed members of the musical fraternity, it gave ammunition to those who were only too ready to denigrate Rossini's artistic and personal integrity. Once such a juggernaut begins to move, it is almost impossible to stop it, let alone send it into reverse.

What Rossini's reputation suffered in a purely musical context it also suffered – at least temporarily – in the political and social sphere. The death of Pope Gregory XVI in 1846 had been the signal for a group of distinguished members of Bolognese society to draw up a petition, addressed to Cardinal Tommaso Riario Sforza, requesting political reform in the Papal States. Rossini was one of the signatories; and the election of Pius IX, who had a reputation for being a liberal, gave reason to hope that the petition would not be in vain. There had been nothing inconsistent, therefore, in Rossini's having composed or arranged some of his music in honour of the new pontiff.

By 1848, however, matters had taken on a rather different complexion. Starting with the revolt in Sicily on 12 January that year, a wave of revolutionary uprisings spread through Italy and Europe in general. Although Rossini had openly supported the petition and the cause for reform, he was against anarchy. There had been assassinations in and around Bologna, and it may well have been for this reason that he placed his will in the keeping of Cesare Stagni on 26 April, naming the Liceo Musicale as his principal heir. Possibly he had had advance warning of what was about to happen, or he had even sensed it himself. On 27 April a band of volunteers was about to leave Bologna to take part in the struggle for independence in Lombardy. They gathered outside Rossini's house to honour him before their departure, so Rossini went out on to the balcony to acknowledge their gesture; but mingled with the applause were cat-calls and shouts of condemnation of Rossini as a rich reactionary. After all, he had only contributed 500 scudi and a pair of horses to the independence fund, when it was assumed that he was able to afford far more.

Those who knew Rossini were well aware that it would have been totally foreign to his nature to take part in any sort of direct action, or even lend positive support to any kind of active political movement. That was not his brand of courage. He was shaken, Olympe was not well, so the following morning they left for Florence. The majority of the citizens of Bologna were shocked and dismayed. Padre Ugo Bassi, who was a well-known patriot, and may have done something – deliberately or not – to arouse feelings against Rossini, preached in San Petronio the following day (29 April) and that evening led a demonstration by torchlight, during the course of which he defended Rossini, and then sent an account of the event to the composer in Florence, inviting him to return.

Rossini was not to be so easily persuaded, and in his reply of 1 May, while being highly complimentary to Bologna and its citizens, made it clear that he was in no hurry to return. His wife's health was the immediate pretext for remaining in Florence, and by way of a sop to the Bolognese he agreed to set to music the text of an Italian hymn to be supplied by Bassi. In the event Bassi left for the North and was wounded near Treviso, so Filippo Martinelli sent the words. On 19 May, Rossini sent a sketch of a chorus in march time, which he sent to Liverani in Bologna, asking him to orchestrate it for him. By 3 June, Liverani had complied, and Rossini wrote and thanked him. It also fell to Liverani's lot to conduct the first performance in Piazza Maggiore on 21 June 1848, the anniversary of Pius IX's coronation. 'Segna Iddio ne' suoi confini' was repeated in Florence on 29 June, probably in the presence of the composer.

It is hardly surprising that, in the circumstances, Rossini remained in Florence until September 1850. Not only was the general standard of cultural and social life higher than in Bologna; it was also a safer place to be. On 26 June, Rossini's *Inno alla pace*, *'E foriera la pace ai mortali'*, for baritone, male voices and piano was given in Florence.

Apart from a hymn to Napoléon III, written in the penultimate year of his life, this was to be the last of Rossini's cantatas, choruses and hymns. As a group these occasional pieces hardly represent him at his most distinguished.

Whilst he was living in Florence, Rossini wrote an enormous number of letters to friends in Bologna who were looking after his interests there. He was obsessed with detail – a condition exacerbated by the distance, the events in Italy, and his state of health. By the middle of September 1850, therefore, he decided that he ought to visit Bologna, though he asked for a police escort for the last stage of the journey into the city. By the end of the year it was fairly clear that, notwithstanding all that he had professed in his letter of 1 May 1848, to Bassi and, by extension, to the people of Bologna, he had lost his affection for the city. The more valuable contents of his home were packed up, and he began telling friends in Florence that he would be with them in early May. On 12 February 1851 he requested permission from the Austrian governor, Count Nobili, to have his goods escorted to Florence. On 1 May a most embarrassing incident took place in his home. Count Nobili called on him in person, whereupon Rossini's visitors deliberately left. Four days later he himself left Bologna, never to return. The villa at Castenaso had been sold in March that year, but he still had possessions in Bologna as late as 9 November 1852, when he sent a servant to assist in disposing of what remained and authorised one of his Bolognese agents to reduce the price as much as he liked in order to close what by now he regarded as a sad chapter in his existence. After that, nothing could redeem Bologna for him; and ten years later, almost to the day, it was still clear from a letter to Ivanoff that he regarded the citizens as thieves and liars, and the city itself a sewer.[9] He regretted ever having encouraged Ivanoff to establish himself there, he wrote.

Rossini now settled in Florence for the next four years, and his health – mental, though physical, too, at times – entered a new period of decline. It worried Ivanoff to the point where he spoke to Giuseppina Strepponi about it, and she in turn wrote to Verdi from Livorno on 17 January 1853: 'Rossini is not – as he might have been – happy. That man thought that he could obliterate his heart with his head; now his heart is taking its revenge.' Despite continuing honours – he passed from the grade of *chevalier* directly to *commandeur* of the Légion d'honneur on 12 April 1853, for example – and continuing performances of his works – *Guillaume Tell* was given that same month, by command of the Granduca della Toscana, in the Palazzo Pitti in Florence – Rossini had long periods of acute depression, and even talked of suicide at times. Occasionally he found his old form and sense of humour, as when he wrote to Giuseppe Bellentani on 28 December 1853 to thank him for the sausages and pasta he had received from him. More often than not, however, he was sunk in deep despondency, to the point where Filippo Mordani, on 27 May 1854, not only commented on Rossini's unhappiness, but also pronounced: 'The light of his great intelligence seems about to grow dim . . . he heaves great groans and sighs . . . breaks into violent sobbing . . . accuses himself of cowardice and says: ". . . what will people say when they see me reduced to having to be led about by a woman, like a little boy?"'

How Rossini himself felt about his condition is indicated in a letter of 3 February 1855 to Filippo Santocanale:

> You wish me to write to you in my own hand, and here I am obeying you; tortured as I have been for thirteen months by nervous crises which have denied me sleep, food, affected my hearing and sight, and debilitated me to such an extent that I am unable to dress or undress unaided. The doctors are unable to help me other than offering me words of comfort. . . .
>
> It is so long since I picked up a pen that I don't really know what I am writing, be indulgent towards a man who has become an object of compassion; patience![10]

The latent emotionalism, even sentimentality, evident here was also apparent on the occasions when Rossini could be persuaded to make music, which often reduced him to tears.

It seems, however, from another passage in his letter, that plans were already fairly well advanced to forsake Florence, and indeed Italy itself, for Paris. In view of Rossini's emotional and mental state, the decision may well have been Olympe's alone, and she persuaded the demoralised Rossini without much difficulty. No amount of visits to take the waters at Montecatini or Bagni di Lucca, or the dubious magnetic cure administered to Rossini's nightcap by a probably spurious 'Conte' Ginnasi, had achieved any improvement in his condition. Paris at least had different doctors and different methods, and Rossini seemed to have exhausted the medical possibilities in Italy. Then there was the fact that, having abandoned Bologna, Florence was for both of them an adopted home town, and perhaps

I. R. TEATRO ALLA SCALA.

In questa sera di Sabbato 24 Maggio 1834 si darà L'ULTIMA RECITA DI MAD. MALIBRAN coll' Opera

OSSIA

IL MORO DI VENEZIA

Musica del Maestro Cavaliere sig. GIOACCHINO ROSSINI.

PERSONAGGI

DESDÉMONA . . .	Signore	MALIBRAN MARIA.
EMILIA	„	BAYLLOU FELICITA.
RODRIGO	„	GARCIA RUEZ.
OTELLO	Signori	REINA DOMENICO.
ELMIRO	„	MARINI IGNAZIO.
JAGO	„	BALFE GUGLIELMO.
DOGE	„	MARCONI NAPOLEONE.

Dopo il primo atto, essendo indisposto tuttora il sig. *Priora*, avrà luogo un PASSO A QUATTRO **fra le allieve dell' I. R. Accademia, signore *Ancement*, *Ciocca*, *Romagnoli* e *Zambelli*.**

Prezzo del Biglietto { **Al Teatro . . . lir. 6** / **Al Loggione . . . „ 2** } **austriache.**
Per una Sedia chiusa „ 15

Daranno accesso alle File chiuse due ingressi a dritta e sinistra nell' atrio del suddetto Teatro. – Ciascun concorrente conserva il Biglietto a garanzia del posto.
Al Camerino si affittano Palchi di quinta Fila.

Lo Spettacolo incomincierà alle ore otto e mezzo.

Milano il 24 Maggio 1834. *Tipografia Pirola.*

Playbill for *Otello* at La Scala in 1834 – Malibran's last appearance in the opera on this occasion in Milan.

Olympe was simply homesick for Paris. Whatever the reason, or combination of reasons, it seemed as if there was nothing to lose, and at the very least a change of environment might act as a beneficial stimulus for Rossini. In the event it was an inspired decision, and on 26 April 1855, accompanied by their two servants, Tonino and Ninetta, the Rossinis set out on the long journey of almost a month, via Nice, to Paris. The composer never set foot in Italy again.

CHAPTER TEN

Paris and the Sins of Old Age

When they first arrived in Paris in late May 1855, the Rossinis took lodgings in rue Basse-du-Rempart, which no longer exists but was not far from the present Opéra. Initially few of the aspiring visitors were admitted, partly through lack of space, but also because Rossini's weak health had been further undermined by the journey. Olympe was also careful to ensure that he was not overburdened, and Rossini himself realised, as he looked back on those days, that she had provided a threefold defensive mechanism: first, there was the concierge; then the servant Tonino; and finally Olympe herself. One had to be hardy indeed to get past her.

Gradually, however, the change of environment began to have its effect, and there was a perceptible improvement in Rossini's general state of mind and body, and even glimmers of the old wit. He felt that he would like some sea air, and in July visited Trouville on the coast of Normandy, where he met Ferdinand Hiller once more, spending a good deal of time in his company over the course of the next two or three weeks. As we have seen, Hiller recorded a good deal of their conversation in the second volume of his survey of the current musical scene.[1]

When Rossini returned to Paris towards the end of September, the Théâtre-Italien was just about to mount a season in which his music featured, though he felt no urge to attend, as the management – with an eye on the box-office – had hoped. This first opera was *Mosè*, the Italian version of *Moïse* but lacking the ballet. Rossini seemed no more enthusiastic when the *Stabat Mater* was given on 20 and 21 March 1856 in the same theatre. In order to escape the heat of summer in Paris this year, in May he rented a villa from the music publisher Heugel at Passy near the Bois de Boulogne, and by now he seemed so improved that the doctors suggested that he go to the spa at Wildblad in Württemberg. He set out the next month, stopping at Strasbourg on the way; and from Wildblad went on to Kissingen and Baden, before returning to Paris in late September. It had been a successful trip, and he seemed to enjoy playing the role that he himself described as that of 'un vieux rococo'. There was also a resurgence of the old realist, too, for on his return to Paris he received a portrait of Mozart from the Frankfurt publisher Karl August André, who compared Rossini to Mozart in his accompanying letter. In his reply of 13 October, Rossini thanked André, describing Mozart as 'the master of us all' and yet a composer 'whom one cannot imitate'.[2] He then went on: 'Nothing could be . . . more pleasing to me than the point of comparison that you establish between him and me, but here I must assert to you that the intention cannot be accepted as fact.' In a postscript he asked André if he owned the manuscript of *Die Zauberflöte* and, if so, how much he would sell it for. One wonders whether Rossini had been inspired by the example of Pauline Viardot-Garcia, who had purchased the manuscript of *Don Giovanni* in London the previous year, selling her diamonds in order to do so.

With such a gratifying return of his old spirits, it is not surprising that Rossini began to feel the urge to compose once more; and in April 1857 he handed Olympe for her name-day a manuscript entitled *Musique anodine*. It consisted of a prelude for piano, and six settings of the same text by Metastasio, beginning with the words: 'Mi lagnerò tacendo della mia sorte amara' ('I shall complain silently my bitter lot'). Two of the songs are for soprano, one each for mezzo-soprano and contralto, and two for baritone. The dedication is touchingly simple: 'I offer these modest songs to my dear wife Olympe as a simple testimony of gratitude for the affectionate, intelligent care of which she was prodigal during my too long and terrible illness (Shame of the [medical] faculty).' This volume now constitutes number thirteen of the *Péchés de vieillesse* (1857–68), Rossini's 'Sins of old age'. It was a glimpse of the sun after a period of darkness and despair.

His renewed zest for life made Rossini much more eager to receive friends and visitors, and it became increasingly important for him to find a larger apartment. Eventually he and Olympe settled in a second-floor apartment on the corner of rue de la Chaussée d'Antin and boulevard des Italiens, so named because of the proximity of the Théâtre-Italien. It had a large entrance-hall and salon, a dining-room, a large bedroom with adjacent bathroom, a small sitting-room for

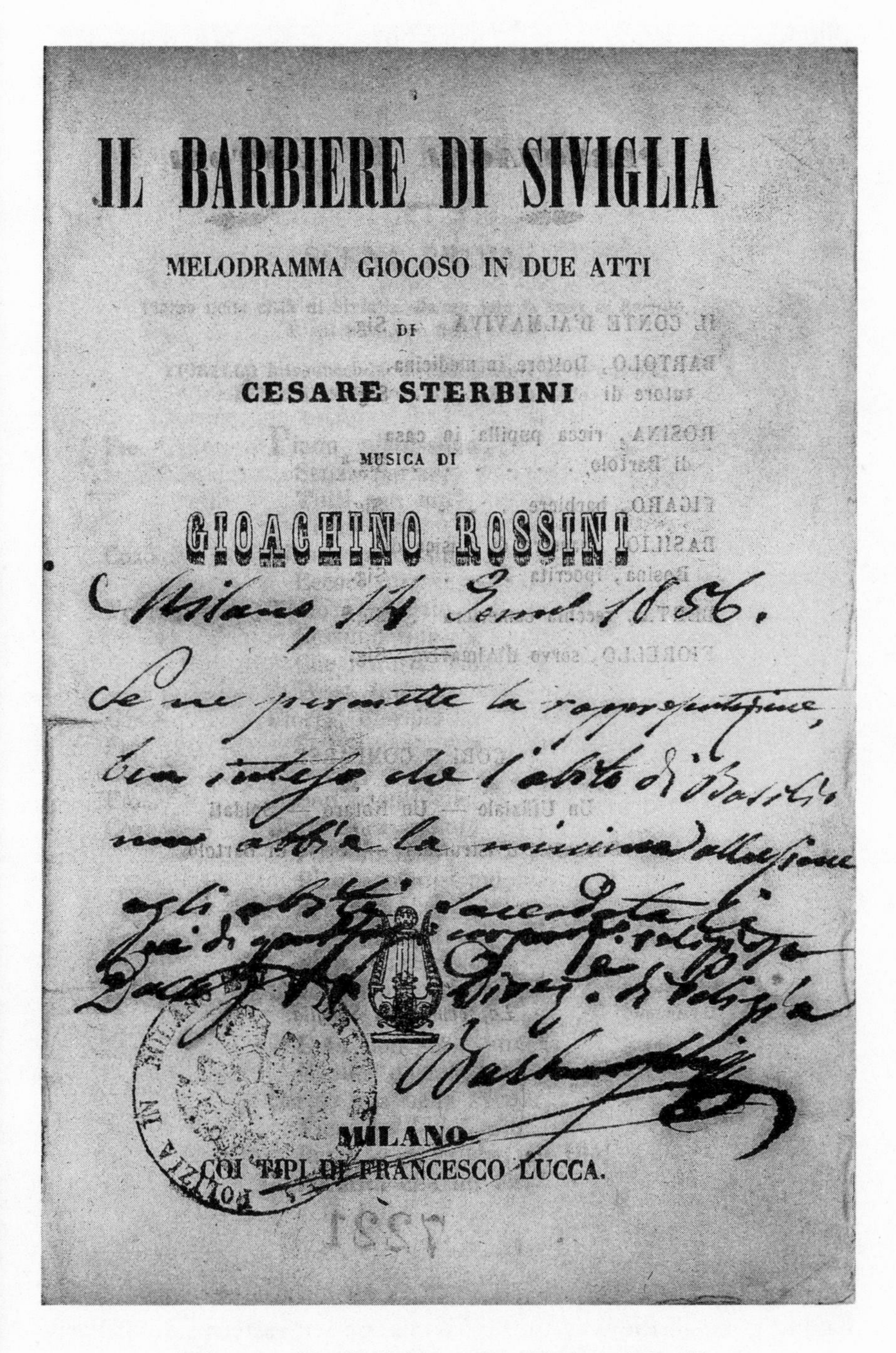

IL BARBIERE DI SIVIGLIA

MELODRAMMA GIOCOSO IN DUE ATTI

DI

CESARE STERBINI

MUSICA DI

GIOACHINO ROSSINI

MILANO

COI TIPI DI FRANCESCO LUCCA.

Title page of Sterbini's libretto for *Il barbiere di Siviglia*.

Olympe, the master bedroom for Rossini, a study and a large kitchen. There were also quarters for the servants. In time Rossini evolved the habit of receiving people in his bedroom, which he also used as a study, since the bed had a canopy and curtains. One or more of his wigs was on display, and in time an alluvial deposit of memorabilia and bric-à-brac accumulated here, including Isabella's jewellery, the decorations conferred on the composer, and a motley assortment of objets d'art.

Rossini rose relatively early, and for breakfast had a roll and a large glass of coffee, though in his last years he took two boiled eggs and a glass of Bordeaux wine. There was usually mail to be dealt with, at times so much that the postal service made special deliveries; Olympe would open it and give him a digest of the contents. If there was a particularly large batch, then friends helped out. Rossini for his part was always generous in providing letters of introduction. In one of these, dated 15 December 1857, he wrote to Felice Romani in Rome about a nineteen-year-old student from France:

> Signor Bizet, first prize in composition at the Imperial Conservatoire in Paris, will bring this letter to you. He is travelling so as to complete his practical musical education. He has done very well in his studies; he has had great success with an operetta performed here. He is a good pianist. He is an excellent person, deserving of both your and my solicitude. I recommend him to you, and I ask you to recommend him to the Ronzi brothers, for which I heartily thank you. . . .

In April of that year Bizet had had a great success with his operetta *Le Docteur miracle* at the Bouffes-Parisiens, for which he shared with Lecocq the first prize donated by Offenbach. A pupil of Halévy (whose daughter he subsequently married), Bizet won the Prix de Rome that year and was about to go and spend three years in Rome at the Villa Medici.

After dealing with the mail Rossini would then receive callers until about half-past ten, when he would put on a cloak, secure his cravat with a pin decorated with a portrait of Handel, and go out. In clement conditions he would walk along the boulevards for an hour or so, or take a cab and visit friends. He would also go shopping for Olympe, and especially to buy food. Edmond Michotte recalled his having gone all the way to the Marais, on the eastern side of Paris, to track down a shop which supposedly sold Neapolitan macaroni.

Unfortunately, when it was produced, Rossini pronounced it to be Genoese. The somewhat surprised shopkeeper observed to Michotte that if the man knew as much about music as he knew about pasta, then he must certainly be a good composer.

Rossini usually returned home at about one o'clock, when he drank a glass of wine or cordial, but tended not to eat until six o'clock. On Saturday evenings there might be as many as sixteen round the dinner table, though twelve was the preferred number. After dinner, more guests arrived, either to make music or simply to listen to it, and so evolved the famous *samedi soirs*, inaugurated on 18 December 1858 and continuing until 26 September 1868. Oddly enough, Rossini rarely dined out; in fact no more than twice a year – once before he moved to Passy for the summer and then when he returned to Paris for the winter. Passy appealed to him so much that on 18 September 1858 he brought some ground from the City of Paris for the very reasonable sum of 90,000 francs. He only half-jokingly explained that he chose the site because it was in the shape of a grand piano. Later, when the house was built and the garden was created, Rossini had flowerbeds made in the shape of musical instruments. The agreement with the civic authorities was that after the death of Rossini and his wife the City of Paris might repurchase the property from the heirs to the estate for the sum paid for the site, plus the value of the house built on it, at a price to be decided by a property valuer at the appropriate time.

On 10 March 1859 the foundation stone of the Villa Rossini, designed by the architect Doussault, was laid. Rossini buried a small casket containing a medal struck to commemorate the *Stabat Mater* (though he had suggested that he include a recently discovered coin of Caracalla, just to confuse any eventual excavator). He then laid the stone, and Olympe planted a rosebush. As the building began to take shape, Rossini would visit the site daily. When the interior decoration was being planned, Rossini chose to include portraits of composers in the ceilings of the drawing-room and dining-room. Visitors recalled seeing in the first Cimarosa, Haydn, Padre Mattei, Mozart and Palestrina, and in the second Beethoven, Boïeldieu and Grétry, among others.

Apart from Saturdays, Rossini's evenings followed a calm, orderly routine. He took a short nap after dinner, smoked a cigar, then later returned to the dining-room, where Olympe read to him from the newspapers. After eight-thirty friends might call, so beginning the

A canon for four sopranos, one of many album leaves composed by Rossini in later years.

collection of memorable – if not always accurate – anecdotes about this last decade of Rossini's life. Often they were grounded in fact. It was well known, for example, that Rossini disliked intensely the current fashion for what he regarded as shouting rather than singing in France. He referred to it as 'urlo francese'. When his servant Tonino announced Enrico Tamberlik, whose top C sharp in chest voice was then the object of great acclaim in the theatre and beyond, Rossini is supposed to have said: 'Let him come in, but tell him to leave his C sharp on the coat rack. He may retrieve it when he leaves.' This is one version of the story, but there are variants, and in such a situation it becomes difficult to establish exactly what were the *ipsissima verba* and, indeed, whether they were spoken at all. Sometimes Rossini would play the piano, and on one occasion played and sang from memory Haydn's cantata *Arianna a Naxos* (1789). At ten o'clock, however, everyone knew that it was time to leave.

For the Saturday evenings, engraved invitations were issued, to which a reply was expected, and which were to be handed in on arrival. Olympe would receive the guests in the salon. Only a select few enjoyed the food, which often consisted of specialities from Italy. Contrary to popular belief there was no groaning board or succession of gastronomic delicacies. Much more prized was the conversation, the celebrities one might encounter, the music – for which a programme was often printed – and Rossini's own comments, which were usually witty and sometimes acerbic.

It would be otiose simply to present a list of those who attended one or more of the *samedi soirs*, even if it were possible to establish a complete one, but in addition to the many musicians living and working in Paris, who paid their respects almost as a matter of course, Eugène Delacroix, Ernest and Gustave Doré, Alexandre Dumas *père*, Eduard Hanslick, Joseph Joachim, Franz Liszt, Anton Rubinstein, Pablo de Sarasate, Marie Taglioni and Verdi all were present at one time or another, whilst Saint-Saëns regarded himself as domestic pianist. Louis Diémer (1843–1919) also fulfilled this function. According to him, Liszt played his *Légendes* for the first time at Rossini's.

Diémer's recollections, found among his papers after his death in 1919, constitute an interesting source for these occasions.[3] It was the publisher Huegel who had effected the introduction, when Diémer was still a very young man. He was a brilliant pianist, and had carried off the first prize at the Conservatoire when only thirteen years old.

But, although he was frequently called upon to perform at the *samedi soirs*, Diémer was never allowed by Rossini to take the manuscripts away for study purposes. He had to go to the composer's apartment, and even then the music was usually kept under lock and key. Luckily, Diémer was usually able to memorise them after two or three readings. He was to meet many famous musicians there, including the nineteen-year-old Adelina Patti, shortly after she had made her début at the Théâtre-Italien in *La sonnambula* in 1862.

It was Patti's teacher and brother-in-law, Maurice Strakosch, who brought her to Rossini, but the composer had to take her to task because of the way in which she decorated 'Una voce poco fa'. According to Saint-Saëns (who was not actually present), Rossini paid her compliments about her voice, but then asked her who was the composer of the aria she had just sung.[4] As Rossini told Saint-Saëns a few days later: 'I know very well that my arias have to be decorated; they were written for that. But not to retain a note of what I wrote, even in the recitatives – really, it is too much.' He is also supposed to have punned on Strakosch's name to Patti, laying the blame at his door: 'I did not recognise the finale; no doubt it was altered by your teacher, who has Strakoschonized it.' As Louis Engel recorded it, in French this may also become a pun on *cochonnée* – made a piggish mess of – so ex-Strakoschonnée = *extra-cochonnée*.[5] Saint-Saëns recorded that Patti, who had already made a name for herself despite her extreme youth, was somewhat angry at Rossini's treatment, but on reflection decided that she did not want to incur his wrath, because he was still regarded as a power in Parisian musical circles, and so sought his advice. Two months later, she was singing arias from *La gazza ladra* and *Semiramide*, accompanied by Rossini himself. It is interesting, however, that despite his affection for Patti, and recognition of her talent, the composer never ranked her among the very greatest singers he had known.[6]

Rossini still found himself the frequent recipient of honours. One that fell to him in 1858 was the presidency of the twelve-man commission set up by the French government to establish a standard musical pitch. There were four civil servants, two physicists and six composers: Auber, Berlioz, Halévy, Meyerbeer, Rossini and Thomas. The following year they decided on A at 435 vibrations per second. When Verdi later told Rossini that, although he thought standard pitch useful, in his opinion it had been set too low Rossini replied that it was no good discussing the matter with him because he had never attended a single meeting. It was such comments that added to the charge that Rossini was insouciant, even irresponsible, in such matters.

Verdi subsequently recounted all of this with a certain amount of righteous indignation in a letter to Ricordi, written from Madrid in 1863. Berlioz, who also sat on the commission, had similar difficulty in coming to terms with the Rossini phenomenon. He found it hard to accept the reputation that the latter enjoyed in Paris, whilst at the same time appreciating some of his music and enjoying his wit; even though he, too, suffered the edge of Rossini's tongue on occasion. Berlioz had no hesitation, however, in speaking out against Rossini when he felt it to be necessary; but he must also have realised that by now Rossini had become rather a victim of his own success. It was said that when confronted with a score of the *Symphonie fantastique* Rossini commented: 'What a good thing it isn't music.' It was very unusual, however, for Rossini to be quite so direct about someone as established as Berlioz, especially when he knew how quickly such stories got about, or were so readily attributed to him when he had not even uttered the words in the first place.

Berlioz supervised the rehearsals of the opera *Esmeralda* by the crippled Louise Bertin (1805–77), whose father, Louis-François Bertin, had founded *Le Journal des débats* and was a patron of Berlioz. When it came to the dress rehearsal of *Esmeralda*, conducted by Habeneck, Rossini attended, sitting in an easy chair by the side of the stage. He was impassive throughout the first act, but during the second was seen to get up and go towards Habeneck. The house was electrified: 'Rossini va parler' ('Rossini is going to speak'). His words, however, were something of an anticlimax: 'Monsieur Habeneck, can't you see? One of the lamps is smoking.'[7] It is not the fault of the oracle, however, if the words spoken are not always those that the listener is anticipating.

Rossini did not attend many musical occasions, though there were certain composers or works whose attraction was strong enough to draw him out. One such was Carafa's *Le Valet de chambre* (1823) for which Rossini attended a rehearsal in 1858. The Neapolitan composer, who was also a prince, was an old friend of Rossini, and had supplied arias for *Adelaide di Borgogna* (1817) and *Mosè in Egitto* (1819). In this same year (1858), Rossini also attended the dress rehearsal of *Don Desiderio* (1840) by Giuseppe Poniatowski (another prince). After a sextet in the first act, Rossini said to the composer:

'One can see very clearly that you must have studied the great masters intently. Cimarosa must have been delighted!' The two knew each other well enough, however, for this well-placed remark not to have caused friction.

On 17 April 1859, Rossini attended a concert given by the Société des Concerts du Conservatoire at which the Empress Eugénie was also present. Rossini's music had featured in their very first programme, given on 9 March 1828 and conducted by Habeneck. Now, more than thirty years later, Rossini's music again appeared – part of the *Stabat Mater* and the finale of *Moïse* – after which Rossini was applauded for fifteen minutes. He was cheered as he left, leaning on the arm of Auber, Director of the Conservatoire.

Not all the events of Parisian musical life were so pleasurable for Rossini. Later the same year, on 11 November, he was obliged to write to Torribio Calzado, the Cuban-born Director of the Théâtre-Italien, who had announced, in both 1857 and 1858, a 'new Rossini opera' entitled *Un curioso accidente,* which had not materialised. This year, however, the work did appear; and it turned out to be a *pasticcio* in two acts to a libretto by Arcangelo Berettoni. The music was drawn from *La cambiale di matrimonio, La pietra del paragone, L'occasione fa il ladro* and *Aureliano in Palmira.* Rossini requested Calzado to alter the wording of his posters to 'Opera arranged on pieces by M. Rossini by M. Berrettoni [sic]'. If Calzado failed to comply, then Rossini threatened legal action. In the circumstances it was the least he could do. Calzado removed the posters but did not produce a rectification, as specified by Rossini. Despite Marietta Alboni and Cesare Badiali in the cast, there was only one performance of *Un curioso accidente,* on 27 November 1859. There would, however, be a proper production of a Rossini opera – *Semiramide* – the following year, and one to which the composer would feel able to give his wholehearted support. The critics do not seem to have pounced on Calzado's *pasticcio,* though Pierre Scudo recorded it in *L'Année musicale* for 1859 and noted some of the borrowings. For those who disapproved of Rossini, however, this was yet another nail in his coffin. It is all the more remarkable, then, that, as Edmond Michotte recorded, Wagner sought out Rossini the following year.

Wagner, who was in Paris trying to arrange performances of *Tannhaüser,* gave three concerts of his own music in the Salle Ventadour of the Théâtre-Italien on 25 January and 1 and 8 February 1860. He did not invite the press, who nevertheless reviewed the concerts savagely. Berlioz, however, in *Le Journal des débats*, was enthusiastic about the excerpts from *Der fliegende Holländer*, *Tannhaüser* and *Lohengrin*, though even he confessed that he found it hard to get to grips with *Tristan und Isolde*. Whatever the artistic merit of the concerts, they were financial failures, losing in the region of 10,000 or 11,000 francs.[8]

The following month Wagner made his visit to Rossini, through the intermediary of Michotte.[9] Possibly there was apprehension on the part of both men, for when Michotte asked Rossini if he would receive Wagner the composer said that he hoped that Michotte had made it quite clear to Wagner that he was in no way responsible for the stupid stories that circulated about him and his opinion of Wagner. To mention only two, as told by Michotte, Rossini is supposed to have served *Turbot à l'allemande* at one of his weekly dinners, but when the fish course was due to be served all that arrived at table was a sauce. 'Isn't it just like Wagner's music?' asked the host. 'A good sauce, but no turbot . . . no melody!' On another occasion, a visitor was supposed to have found Rossini wrestling with a huge score, which turned out to be that of *Tannhaüser*. 'Now I'm beginning to understand something,' Rossini announced. 'It was open upside down and back to front.' At that there was a loud crash from another room. 'It sounds just like the Venusberg music,' said Rossini. Then the valet came to announce that the maid had just dropped a trayful of crockery. Unfortunately such stories all too soon gained currency, though those who knew the real Rossini would know that it was uncharacteristic of him to be quite so blunt or crass. His noted acerbity was usually occasioned by a bad performance of his own music, and he was, in any case, rarely gratuitously insulting. Wagner, on the other hand, had gone into print with some fairly uncomplimentary things about Rossini.

After a generous preamble on Rossini's part, they soon got down to specifics, passing from Rossini's early experiences of cabals at the first performances of *Il barbiere di Siviglia* in Rome and Paris, and *Zelmira* in Vienna, to his memories of Weber, Salieri, Beethoven, Rossini's own compositions, Mendelssohn, Wagner's compositions, and general theories about opera. Rossini told Wagner that his method of responding to cabals and, by implication, malicious criticism too, was through silence and inertia rather than irate riposte. For his part, Wagner now cited three examples of what he considered to be Rossini's best music, namely the Plague of Darkness from

Moïse, the Oath-swearing from *Guillaume Tell* and 'Quando corpus morietur' from the *Stabat Mater* – no doubt the chromaticism of the last had a special attraction for him. Rossini conceded that they did indeed constitute some 'happy quarters of an hour' in his career, though what did that represent, he added, in the face of the output of Mozart or Haydn? Of course he was also supposed to have said that Wagner had 'some fine moments, but some bad quarters of an hour'. Possibly the composers' quarters of an hour, both good and bad, had now cancelled each other out. At all events, Rossini probably felt some need to praise German music, and singled out Bach and Beethoven: 'If Beethoven is a prodigy amongst humanity,' he said, 'then Bach is a miracle of God.'

A determination to be urbane was not Rossini's only motivation, however, for one of the strong tendencies of his later years was to extend his knowledge of Classical and Baroque composers. Rossini's position in music history is often thought of as being on the threshold of Romanticism, but he is a Janus figure, looking both ways, and the Classical tradition produced him and played a large part in his formation as a composer. Indeed, one might well claim that one of his greatest achievements was to renew serious opera through a finely balanced combination of Classical form and Romantic content.

The conversation got into much deeper waters when Rossini asked Wagner how he was getting on in his attempts to have *Tannhaüser* performed in Paris. At that point Wagner was still wrestling with the French translation. Well, proposed the pragmatic Rossini, he could always compose directly to a French libretto. He pointed to his own example when he settled in Paris. Wagner, however, had moved on from *Tannhaüser* to *Lohengrin*, and then *Tristan und Isolde*, and there was no possible going back. As reported by Michotte, he told Rossini:

> These three operas, from both the literary and musical point of view, constitute a logical development in my conception of the definitive and absolute form of lyric drama. My compositional technique has experienced the inevitable effects of this development. And if it is true that I still feel capable of writing other works in the style of *Tannhaüser*, I am totally incapable of returning to my compositional technique of *Tannhaüser*.

If he had to write an opera to a French text for Paris, then it would have to be in the manner of *Tristan*, and because it would cause great perturbation it would certainly not be understood, and therefore in the present state of opera in France it would never gain acceptance. Wagner no doubt felt that Rossini had played a vital role in bringing opera in France to its present state.

Rossini, however, did not evade the issue, or had decided to be diplomatic. Either way, he met the matter head-on, and invited Wagner to expound his theory of operatic reform. Once he began, it was hard to stop him, even when Rossini confessed that certain elements of opera, even in his early days, had seemed to him ridiculous. However, the public knew what it wanted, and if a composer failed to provide it, then . . . Wagner did not even deign to acknowledge such a mundane observation, but swept on to cast his baleful regard over orchestration as well. This time Rossini managed to break in and point out that opera is essentially bound by convention. For one thing, people do not habitually sing as they go about their daily lives, so opera inevitably implies the constraint of convention. Wagner agreed, and then went on to seek Rossini's sympathy for being wrongly accused of having denigrated Mozart, and from that for being misunderstood for his vision of opera as an organism, a perfect union of its constituent parts – poetry, music, painting and sculpture – which inevitably puts the composer on to a very different plane from the one he had occupied hitherto.

Pragmatic as ever, Rossini pointed out that the composer would then have to be his own librettist, which for him would be an almost unattainable goal. For Wagner, of course, it was not. He pointed to the Oath-swearing scene in *Guillaume Tell*, and got Rossini to acknowledge that he had considerably modified the libretto at that point to conform to his own – and by implication better – artistic sense. Again, Rossini's practical approach intruded. How would the singers, and the public, take to this music of the future? In Wagner's vision, all would be caught up in the higher realm, and all would aspire to better things. That was too much for Rossini; as far as he was concerned, it sounded the death-knell for melody. Yet again Wagner cited Rossini's own music – 'Sois immobile' from *Guillaume Tell* – where, in the former's opinion, Rossini was using an extremely free vocal line, accentuating each word against a sobbing accompaniment on the cellos, and so reaching 'the highest peaks of lyric expression'. To this Rossini retorted: 'So I was writing the music of the future without realising it?' The reply was worthy of

Rossini himself: 'You composed music of all times, maestro, and that is the best.'

Still the pragmatic Rossini made one more point. If one followed Wagner's ideas to the limit, then one would only use solo voices, no choruses, not even ensembles. Wagner replied, and this time yet again cited Rossini's music, his use of chorus in *Moïse*, and again Rossini found himself having written 'music of the future'. He no longer composed, he said; rather, he was at the age where one decomposed. He was too old to look towards new horizons, but what Wagner had said – in spite of his detractors – would give young people food for thought. Rossini managed to bring the interview to a happy conclusion: 'As far as I am concerned, I was of my time. It behoves others – you in particular . . . to create something new and to succeed – which I wish for you with all my heart.'

According to Michotte, Wagner had not thought for one moment that he would ever 'convert' Rossini to his point of view, and in the circumstances he was pleasantly surprised that Rossini was so urbane and seemed so anxious to hear Wagner explain his position. Rossini's cry from the heart about the death-knell of melody was a spontaneous reaction. There was nothing controlled or contrived about it. Wagner's chief aim, however – again, according to Michotte – had been to study Rossini, to find out why, at the age of thirty-seven, he renounced everything he had achieved with *Guillaume Tell*. It was almost inconceivable to Wagner that a man could have shrugged off his genius as one might discard a cumbersome burden, and show no more interest in it whatsoever. Of course, the two men never became friends, and further mischief was caused between them, despite the continuing efforts of individuals such as Michotte, and even Liszt, to prevent any ill feeling.

What must have been hard for Wagner to bear was the enormous public esteem Rossini continued to enjoy in Paris; and his reputation was further enhanced when a French version of *Semiramide* – expanded to four acts, with ballet music composed by Carafa – was given a lavish staging at the Opéra on 9 July 1860 and ran for some thirty performances by mid-December. The success of this version was due in no small part to the singing of the Marchisio sisters from Turin, Barbara and Carlotta. Rossini inscribed a copy of the published French version of *Semiramide* to them: 'To my beloved friends and incomparable interpreters, Carlotta and Barbara Marchisio, possessors of that song which is sensed in the soul.' For a moment the vocal style that Rossini thought gone for ever had suddenly been recovered. Carlotta died in 1872, but Barbara lived until 1919 and sang in the performance of the *Stabat Mater* given in the Palazzo Vecchio, Florence, when Rossini was reburied in Santa Croce in May 1887. In an act of generosity to Carafa, now aged seventy-two (though he would outlive Rossini), the composer made over his rights in the French version of his opera to his friend. It is estimated that Carafa received some 15,000 francs by the end of the year.

In the autumn of 1860, the Viennese critic Eduard Hanslick visited Rossini at his villa in Passy. Naturally, in view of Hanslick's well-known implacable hostility to Wagner, the interview between Rossini and Wagner some six months earlier was mentioned, though they did not go into great detail; or, if they did, Hanslick omitted it from his account of the visit.[10] According to him, Rossini said that Wagner did not look at all like a revolutionary. Hanslick noticed that Rossini's table was covered with pieces of music, which were almost all new arrangements from *Semiramide*, sent to him by publishers making hay while the sun continued to shine – pot-pourris, impromptus, quadrilles and the like. It is interesting that the reason Rossini gave to Hanslick for not going to the theatre, certainly to the opera, was the 'urlo francese'. No one knew how to sing any longer – except, of course, the Marchisio sisters. For Hanslick it had been a day of sunlight, admiring the decoration of the villa and the flowerbeds in the shape of musical instruments, and the golden lyre over the gate which indicated that Rossini was now in residence.

The composer and pianist Ignaz Moscheles and his wife were also visitors to Passy this summer. Their son, Felix, was in Paris, and had visited Rossini several times, following his initial introduction by his father. It is interesting that during this visit, which took place between those of Wagner and Hanslick, Rossini also mentioned the screaming and shouting that had become current. 'All I want', he said, 'is a resonant, full tone. . . . I don't care whether it is for speaking or for singing; everything ought to sound melodious.'[11]

It was not until the next year, 1861, that the Rossinis began their annual removal from Chaussée d'Antin to Passy on a regular basis. That year, instead of a *samedi soir* on Easter Saturday, on Good Friday, 29 March, the *Stabat Mater* was performed with Barbara and Carlotta Marchisio as soloists, with Cesare Badiali and the tenor

Soleri, accompanied by a double quartet. Two years later a similar programme was devised for Good Friday, when sections of both the Rossini and the Pergolesi *Stabat* settings were given, with some of Rossini's piano pieces, too. It was his practice to include, alongside his own music, that of contemporaries such as Gounod or Verdi, and then add something from Mozart, Cimarosa or, as in this case, Pergolesi.

In June 1861 the commission organising the London Exhibition of 1862 asked Auber, Meyerbeer and Rossini to compose pieces for the opening of the exhibition. Not surprisingly, perhaps, Rossini declined, though Verdi contributed his *Inno delle nazioni*. However, Rossini did agree to provide something for the Société des Concerts du Conservatoire later that year, in order to raise funds for a monument to Cherubini. Rossini completed the original version of *Le Chant des Titans* at Passy on 15 September 1861. It was for four bass voices in unison, with piano and harmonium accompaniment. Rossini now expanded the work to include, in addition to the original four voices, chorus and orchestra, and in this form it was first heard at the Opéra on 22 December 1861. The original scoring for piano and harmonium is an interesting pointer to the *Petite Messe solennelle*.

La Revue et gazette musicale reported a week later that the new composition, *Le Chant des Titans*, had somewhat taken its listeners by surprise. It was not the Rossini they were used to, by any means. Far from being melodious, and easy on the ear, it had a rather savage quality. Even so, it had to be repeated by almost unanimous appeal from the audience. In writing to Alphonse Royer, Director of the Opéra, about the work in advance of its performance (during the course of October) Rossini said: 'There is not the smallest *roulade*, chromatic scale, trill or arpeggio; it is a simple chant, in a Titanic rhythm, and a very little bit angry.'[12] The piece was repeated in Vienna on 15 April 1866, this time to raise funds for a monument to Mozart, along with a pastorale, *La notte del santo natale* for bass and eight-part chorus, composed in 1863 and sung at one of the *samedi soirs*. Both pieces were included in *Les Péchés de vieillesse*, which we shall now consider.

Virtually all the music that Rossini wrote in the last decade of his life, apart from the *Petite Messe solennelle*, consists of small pieces (for the most part) contained in thirteen volumes known collectively as *Les Péchés de vieillesse* – 'The Sins of Old Age'. At least one of them, however, is much earlier, namely the cantata *Giovanna d'Arco*, in

Volume 11, which dates from 1832 in its original form and was revised in 1852. Some others are either arrangements of works composed previously or variants of works appearing elsewhere in the volumes. Some were composed with the *samedi soirs* in view, others were occasional pieces and some, presumably, were simply the product of Rossini's intermittent urge to compose: for, despite having said to Fétis that he had never had the desire to compose, there must have been occasions when ideas came to Rossini in spite of himself, out of sheer habit.

Volume 1 of the *Péchés* is entitled *Album italiano* and is a group of vocal pieces, mostly for solo voice, with one duet and two quartets, all with piano accompaniment. We know that number 3 from this volume, the bolero 'Tirana alla spagnola', was sung by Marie Battu at a *samedi soir* on 17 April 1866, and on 18 April 1868 the tenor Italo Gardoni sang number 11, 'Il fanciullo smarrito', as he had done on 1 March 1867. Also in that programme he sang a duet from *La traviata* with Patti; she sang the *cavatina* from *Semiramide*, and the programme ended with the quartet from *Rigoletto*, in which Patti and Gardoni were joined by an otherwise unknown Mlle Lliannes, and Enrico delle Sedie. From a strictly musical point of view, however, it is the song 'L'ultimo ricordo' ('The last souvenir'), number 4 from this volume, for baritone, which is notable because it achieves considerable power of expression and has been unjustly ignored. The last souvenir of the title is a flower which a dying man presses into his wife's hand. She carried the flower on their wedding day, and by introducing his own wife's name, Olympe, Rossini made it a highly personal composition.

After the Italian volume, Volume 2 is *Album français*, and complements the first in so far as it is primarily a group of songs with piano accompaniment. One of them, 'Adieux à la vie', number 9, for mezzo-soprano, is worthy of more attention. It is one of Rossini's single-note songs, but from the accompaniment comes a rich and varied texture which throws the words into focus. There are three choral items in this volume which are of interest. Number 1 is the eight-part 'Toast pour le nouvel an' with plenty of contrast and a good deal of tra-la-la. Number 6 is 'La nuit de Noël' heard in its Italian version in Vienna in 1866, as we saw earlier. The contrast between the solo baritone and the restrained, even remote, eight-part chorus enhances the pastoral effect suitable to Christmas. Number 12 is a hunting chorus, 'Chœur de chasseurs démocrates', which was written at the request of baronne James de Rothschild in 1862 to celebrate the visit of Napoléon III to their new country home, the Château de Ferrières. The male chorus, provided by singers from the Opéra, was accompanied by tam-tam and two drums. Rossini was present on that occasion, since his name appears beneath that of the emperor in the visitors-book. The existence of such a work indicates not only how some of the *Péchés de vieillesse* came into being, but also the nature of Rossini's social life – and, indeed, the very fabric of his existence at this time. Not all the events were so happy or enjoyable, however.

The death of Meyerbeer in 1864 was the occasion for the composition of the first item in Volume 3, collectively entitled *Morceaux réservés*. The words of the first piece are by Émilien Pacini – as, indeed, are many of the texts set in these volumes – and the full title indicates precisely what it is: 'A few bars of funeral chant: to my poor friend Meyerbeer.' It is for male voices and drum, and achieves a stark and dignified effect with its crescendos and pianos. In addition to Rossini's musical tribute, however, the death of Meyerbeer is said to have provoked some wry comment from Rossini. According to Verdi, a nephew of Meyerbeer composed a funeral march for his late uncle and took it to Rossini for his approval. After hearing it played through, Rossini said: 'Very good, very good! But, really, wouldn't it have been better if you had died and your poor uncle had written the march?' Also in this volume of 'Reserved pieces' are *Le Chant des Titans*, number 6, already referred to, and two choral works, an *Ave Maria* for chorus and organ, number 4, and *Cantemus Domino*, an unaccompanied eight-part setting at the end of which Rossini wrote: 'That was a waste of time!'

One of the more unusual pieces of the volume is number 5, 'L'amour à Pékin', which is based on a whole-tone scale of C, D, E, F sharp, A sharp, C (though Rossini notated it C, D, E, F sharp, A flat, B flat, C). As *Le Ménestral* reported after its performance by Marietta Alboni on 18 April 1868:

> Mme Alboni sang a song on the Chinese scale, which is both a true masterpiece and a compositional *tour de force*: it is a scale consisting of six tones without semitones. . . . This daring and curious way of singing the scale creates very strange harmonic combinations; and yet one would think them quite natural. In

short, it is a discovery by the Maestro (and he is perfectly capable of them).

To contemporary ears, of course, the effect is nothing like as piquant as it was in 1868. Alboni sang 'L'amour à Pékin' at what turned out to be the very last *samedi soir*, on 26 September 1868.

Volumes 4–8 inclusive are all piano pieces, and the titles alone show the wry Rossinian humour at work. Volume 4 consists of 'Four beggars' – the French dessert of dried figs, almonds, raisins and hazelnuts – and four *hors d'œuvres* – radishes, anchovies, gherkins and butter. Volume 5 is *Album for Adolescent Children*, and Volume 6 *Album for Adroit Children*. Volume 7 is *Cottage Album*, whereas Volume 8 is *Castle Album*. Rossini always denigrated his pianistic ability by referring to himself as a pianist of the fourth class, whereas in reality he was clearly a highly accomplished performer. Within these volumes are some apt parodies of earlier music, such as Clementi and Bach, as well as contemporaries such as Chopin, Mendelssohn, Offenbach and Liszt. His knowledge of the keyboard repertoire was patently extensive. There are also some very original Rossini pieces, too, such as 'Une Caresse à ma femme', number 7 of Volume 6, which has an almost Fauréesque harmonic touch in the outer sections, and number 9, which records the train derailment in Belgium that Rossini experienced many years earlier and never forgot. It ends with the comment: 'All this is more than naïf, but it is true!'

Another journey features in Volume 9, which contains pieces for piano, violin, cello, harmonium and horn, though nine out of the twelve are in fact for piano. The journey in question is entitled 'Marche et reminiscences pour mon dernier voyage', number 7, and in it Rossini portrays himself arriving at the Gates of Heaven, knocking, and then offering extracts from his works in order to gain admittance. There are extracts from *Tancredi*, *La cenerentola*, *La donna del lago*, *Semiramide*, *Le Comte Ory*, *Guillaume Tell*, *Otello*, *Il barbiere di Siviglia* and then the composer's portrait in music. Eventually he is admitted, and the piece ends with the word 'Requiem'.

It is difficult to know precisely how seriously we are meant to take a piece such as this. There is a similar one in Volume 6, number 3, 'Memento homo' in C minor, which opens with three low Cs, marked 'bell'. When the Roman painter Guglielmo de Sanctis was in Paris in 1862 he visited Rossini several times, first at Chaussée d'Antin and then in Passy. By 14 May he had plucked up enough

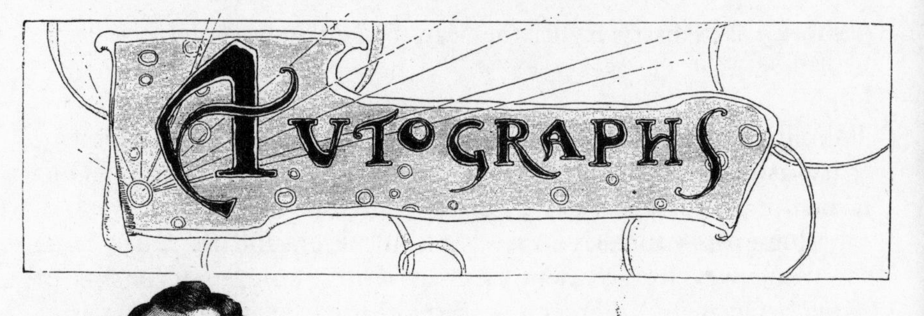

FACSIMILE OF A CURIOUS AUTOGRAPH OF ROSSINI, THE GREAT COMPOSER, WHO HAS HERE ALSO SET HIS NAME AND SURNAME TO MUSIC.

A mon ami et Professeur
Dont la bonté touchante,
L'esprit charmant,
sont les élémens de bonheur pour Tous, Presti-
digitateur par Philanthropie, je joins ici mes
Benédictions à celles des malheureux de Trélazé
elles sont aussi sincères que la realité du Bien-
fait comme restera pour lui Inaltérable l'affection de son élève

Passy ce 8 Juillet
1863

A setting of Rossini's signature to music, dating from 1863.

courage to ask Rossini to play for him. The composer did so, telling De Sanctis that the pieces he would hear were among his recent compositions – 'Une caresse à ma femme' and 'Memento homo'. Thoughts of death were now never far away from Rossini, especially as friends and acquaintances began to die. In a letter to Angelo Catelani dated 26 June 1862, Rossini complained that all his biographies – without exception – were full of absurdities and things that were pure imagination, and nauseating to greater or lesser degree.[13] He would, if he were less philosophical, deny them, but he knew that the present generation would not have the time to read what he had written. He went on to mention his health and raise the question of how long he had to live. Of course there is no reason why Rossini should only have been serious in these pieces when he was considering death. The tender 'Une caresse à ma femme' surely represents a genuine expression of affection for the person who had become so crucial to his existence.

Volume 10 contains only six piano pieces, whereas Volume 11 is a collection of ten vocal pieces, including the cantata *Giovanna d'Arco*. Volume 12 is entitled *Quelques Riens pour album* ('Some bagatelles for albums') and is a group of twenty-four piano pieces, and Volume 13 is the *Musique anodine* that he dedicated to his wife, as we saw earlier, on 15 April 1857, and consists of a prelude and six settings of the Metastasio text beginning 'Mi lagnerò tacendo. . .'.

In many ways *Les Péchés de vieillesse* holds up a mirror to Rossini's world in the last decade of his life. It was a richly varied life; and, although he let many things pass by, he continued to be positive and active in his attitude to music-making, both through the *samedi soirs* and through all who came to visit him. It was as if he had sifted through the many pages of music he had written, read or played, and added some responses to his current life; parodies of, or reactions to, other composers' music; but almost all of them miniatures, if not in actual length, then in scale and scope. Some are pure gems, whereas others remain little better than the *morceaux de salon* they lampoon. Sometimes they have an appealing freshness; at others they may be banal or even in dubious taste. The whimsicality of many of the titles makes one suspect that Rossini was deliberately concealing what might well have been a genuine sentiment, or a serious essay in a particular genre. That was Rossini, however; and in these late pieces he was certainly not going to worry about such niceties.

CHAPTER ELEVEN

The Last Mortal Sin

During the summer of 1863, Rossini was hard at work on the first extended composition that he had undertaken since the *Stabat Mater*, and which was to be the last major work of his career. At the age of seventy-one, he was composing a large-scale Mass, which he himself would entitle, with conscious irony, *Petite Messe solennelle*. Between the *Stabat Mater* and the new work there had been precious little religious music, apart from the *Trois Chœurs Religieux* (1844), a *Tantum ergo* for two tenors, bass and orchestra for Bologna (1847), *O salutaris hostia* for soprano, alto, tenor and bass late in 1857, and a *Laus Deo* for mezzo-soprano in 1861. Certainly nothing here pointed to an extended mass, though 'La Nuit de Noël' from *Les Péchés de vieillesse*, with its piano and harmonium accompaniment, does foreshadow the unusual scoring of the *Petite Messe*.

The original forces Rossini envisaged for the Mass were soprano, alto, tenor and bass soloists, a chorus of eight voices, two pianos and harmonium. On the second page of the autograph score of the original version, now in the library of the conservatoire in Pesaro, Rossini wrote: 'Twelve singers of three sexes, men, women and *castrati*, will be sufficient for its performance: that is to say eight for the chorus, four for the solos, a total of twelve cherubim . . . this little composition . . . is, alas, the last mortal sin of my old age.' Rossini also noted that there was a parallel between twelve singers and twelve apostles in Leonardo's fresco of 'The Last Supper' in Milan. He begged forgiveness from God, but at least there would be no Judas at his supper – all the singers would sing in tune and with devotion. There is also a 'letter to God' as part of the composer's dedication, including a pun on the difference between *musique sacrée* (sacred music) and *sacrée musique* (damned music). 'Is it really sacred music that I have just composed, or is it simply damned music? I was born for *opera buffa*, as Thou well knowest. Little skill, a little bit of heart, and that is all. So be Thou blessed, and admit me to Paradise.'

The Mass had its first performance at 2 o'clock on the afternoon of Sunday, 14 March 1864, on the occasion of the dedication of the private chapel of the comte and comtesse Pillet-Will, in their home in rue Moncey. The work was dedicated to the comtesse. Auber had selected the chorus from students at the conservatoire, and Jules Cohen had rehearsed them. The soloists, from the Théâtre-Italien, were the Marchisio sisters, Italo Gardoni, and the Belgian bass Louis Agniez, known as Agnesi. The two pianists were George Mathias and Andrea Peruzzi, whilst Albert Lavignac played the harmonium. Rossini gave the tempo for each section, standing near the accompanists and turning the pages for Mathias. There was a small group of guests which included Auber, Carafa, Meyerbeer and Ambroise Thomas. There was a second performance the following day, attended by the papal nuncio, government officials and many other distinguished people, though it seems that Rossini himself was not present. Meyerbeer was, however, and when it was over wrote an almost ecstatic letter to Rossini:

> To Jupiter Rossini. Divine Master! I cannot permit the day to close without thanking you again for the enormous pleasure given me by the experience of hearing twice your latest sublime creation; may Heaven preserve you to a hundred, so that you may procreate again some other, similar masterpiece, and may God grant me a similar age so as to hear and admire those new aspects of your immortal genius. Your constant admirer and old friend. . . .

When told of Meyerbeer's reactions, Rossini asked – only half-jokingly, as it turned out – 'Will his health allow these emotions?'

The 'Kyrie' of the Mass begins with an open A (marked *pppp*) in the accompaniment, sounding over the space of three octaves in the bass, and then initiates an *andante maestoso* figure in the piano, in octaves, against sustained suspensions from the harmonium. From the outset, then, Rossini uses the assorted keyboard accompanying instruments in a way that exploits their innate characteristics. The distinctive timbres of the *Petite Messe* are clearly imagined from the outset; and one appreciates why it was that subsequently, when it was felt that public demand would induce someone to orchestrate the work, Rossini decided that he would do it himself, in a way that ensured as little distortion of the work's textures and timbres as possible. Tonally the first movement oscillates from A minor to C minor – an example of Rossini's recurring predilection for keys a minor third apart. The voices enter quietly, with the parts laid out close together, before the horizons expand and the melodic line emerges in the major. The central 'Christe' is a chaste unaccompanied section in C minor, rather in the style of Palestrina, though with Rossini's own harmonic touches. The 'Kyrie' returns in C minor, then moves strikingly to A major; and the ending is on the open A from which the movement grew.

Energetic chords from the accompaniment open the 'Gloria', the soprano solo introduces the vocal section, followed by the full choir. After a long pause, alternating bass piano chords in $\frac{2}{4}$ time, again marked *pppp*, prepare for the lyrical bass solo entry with the words 'et in terra pax'. The soprano then enters with 'Laudamus te', and with the bass chorus entry the harmonium lends its support to the texture. The far-ranging modulations at this point must have been one of the factors which made the work so fresh for its first listeners. The 'Gratias agimus' is a tenderly lyrical *terzetto* for contralto, tenor and bass, and the 'Domine Deus' a martial tenor solo of ferocious difficulty.

A duet for soprano and contralto at the 'Qui tollis' reminds one of the vocal quality with which the Marchisio sisters had delighted Rossini, and which he in turn was only too happy to celebrate at this point. The 'Quoniam' is a long and elaborate bass solo written, like the 'Domine Deus', against a march background. The final section of the 'Gloria' – 'Cum Sancto Spiritu' – is for soloists and chorus, which takes up the opening material and then rounds off with a deliciously airy fugue.

The 'Credo' is marked 'allegro cristiano', the sort of ironic Rossini wit that is so evident in the music of his last years. It is, after all, a devotional work, and although it could just as easily have been marked 'allegro moderato' Rossini is giving a gentle reminder to all concerned that the creed is a fundamental assertion of Christian belief. The 'Crucifixus' for soprano solo, with its syncopated piano part, is one of the most individual and deeply felt sections of the whole Mass. Like Bach, Rossini uses intense chromaticism to increase the pain and suffering implied by the word itself. Soloists and chorus combine for the vigorous 'Et resurrexit', and the final section, 'Et vitam venturi saeculi, amen', is a fugue, as demanded by classical tradition.

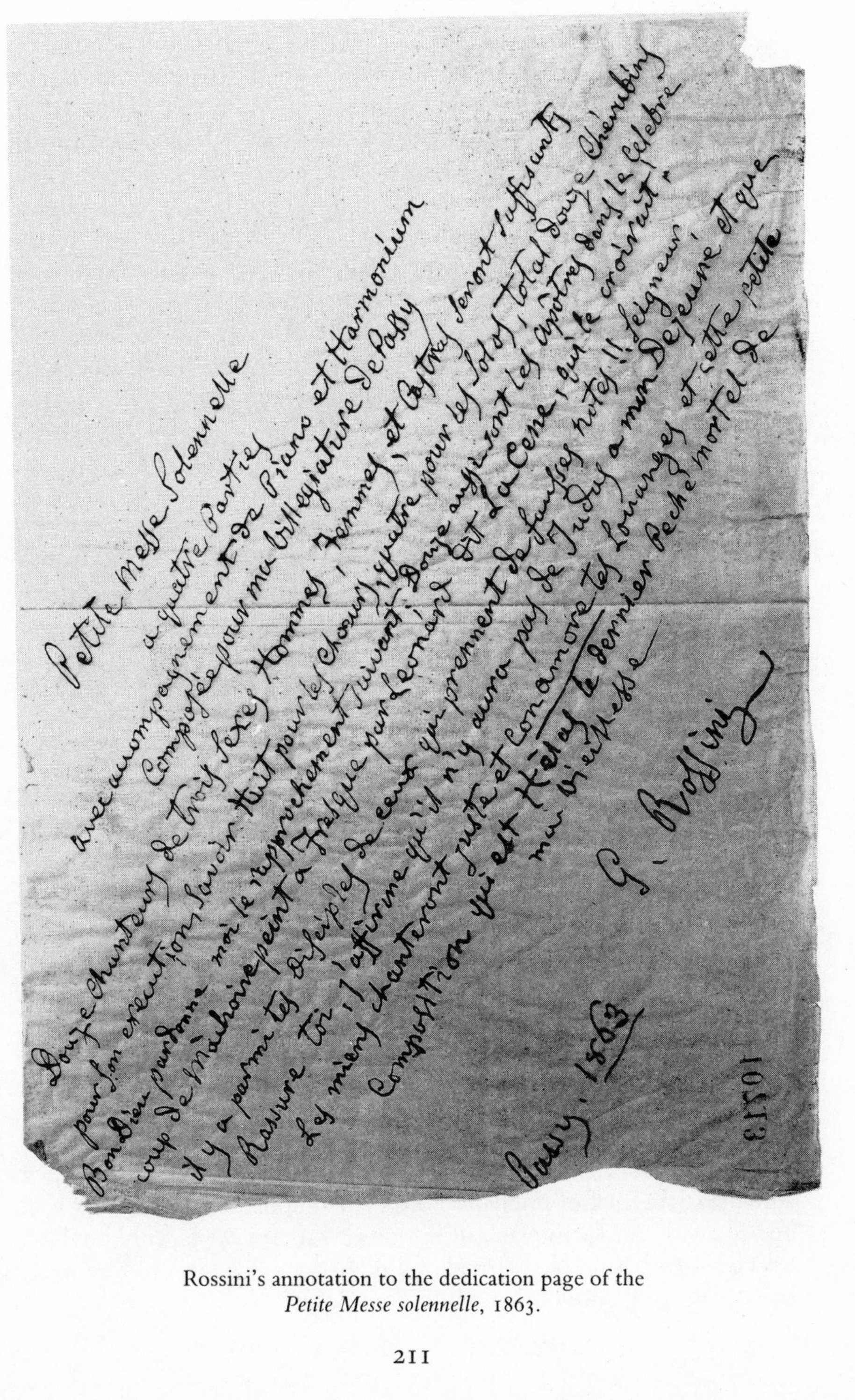

Petite Messe Solennelle
a quatre Parties
avec accompagnement de Pianos et Harmonium
Composée pour ma villegiature de Passy
Douze chanteurs de trois sexes Hommes, Femmes et Castrés seront suffisants
pour son execution, savoir Huit pour les Choeurs, quatre pour les Solos, total douze Chérubins
Bon Dieu pardonne moi le rapprochement suivant. Douze aussi sont les Apôtres dans le célèbre
coup de Machoire peint a Fresque par Leonard dit La Cene, qui le croirait.
il y a parmi tes Disciples de ceux qui prennent de fausses notes!! Seigneur
Rassure toi, j'affirme qu'il n'y aura pas de Judas a mon Dejeuner et que
Les miens chanteront juste et con amore tes Louanges et cette petite
Composition qui est Hélas le dernier Peché mortel de
ma vieillesse

Passy, 1863

G. Rossini

Rossini's annotation to the dedication page of the *Petite Messe solenelle*, 1863.

Rossini wrote a 'religious prelude' for the Offertory, and as long ago as 1872, when August Ambros published his observations on the Mass, it was pointed out how much this section owes to Bach in spirit, though Roncaglia also suggested that it looks forward to Franck, too.[1] The 'Sanctus' for unaccompanied chorus is succeeded by a 'Benedictus' in barcarolle rhythm. There is another soprano solo, 'O salutaris hostia', which is an extra-liturgical piece with a certain tension between the elegant vocal line and the harmonic dissonances in the accompaniment; but it is surpassed by far in lyricism and intensity by the contralto solo in the closing 'Agnus Dei'. The section is in E minor, but goes into the major at the climax with telling effect, and the prayer for pity and mercy contained in the word 'miserere' is passionately conveyed by Rossini. Very possibly it was his last musical offering to Barbara Marchisio and, through her, to the contralto voice which he loved so much and favoured in so many of his works.

Almost inevitably, Rossini was asked to orchestrate the Mass, but its composition had so exhausted him that at first he refused. He also refused a request in early April 1864 from a very old friend, Giovanni Pacini, to write a small instrumental composition for the Società del Quartetto of Florence. In his reply of 8 April, Rossini wrote that his long silence since giving up his musical career in 1829 had made him lose the ability to compose, as well as his knowledge of the possibilities of the various instruments, which had evolved considerably over the last twenty-five years. He then referred to his rank as a fourth-class pianist, and said that no matter how modestly he rated himself:

> The pianists of every nation (who assassinate me in my own home) wage an underhand and bitter war against me (behind my back), so that I am unable to find any pupils, in spite of the modest charge of twenty *soldi* for my lessons; nor do I have any opportunity to appear [in public], because I am not asked; and so I live (as far as a pianist is concerned) under the public scourge. . . . My Giovanni! . . . If you do not weep [at this], what does make you weep?[2]

It is a curious letter to have been written so soon after the success of the Mass, and it seems extraordinary that Rossini should have been lamenting the lack of pupils, whom he had done nothing to seek that one is aware of, or the lack of invitations to appear in public which he would certainly have turned down. As for the question of money, he was more than comfortably off by now.

Left: A rather informal study of Rossini in his declining years, his slightly quizzical expression showing a more sympathetic side to his personality than the imperturbably urbane figure projected by the familiar 'official' portraits from his later years.

Right: The title page of the Ricordi edition of the *Petite Messe solennelle* (1863), with a facsimile of the composer's signature underneath his photograph in which he wears one of the several wigs that he sported in later years.

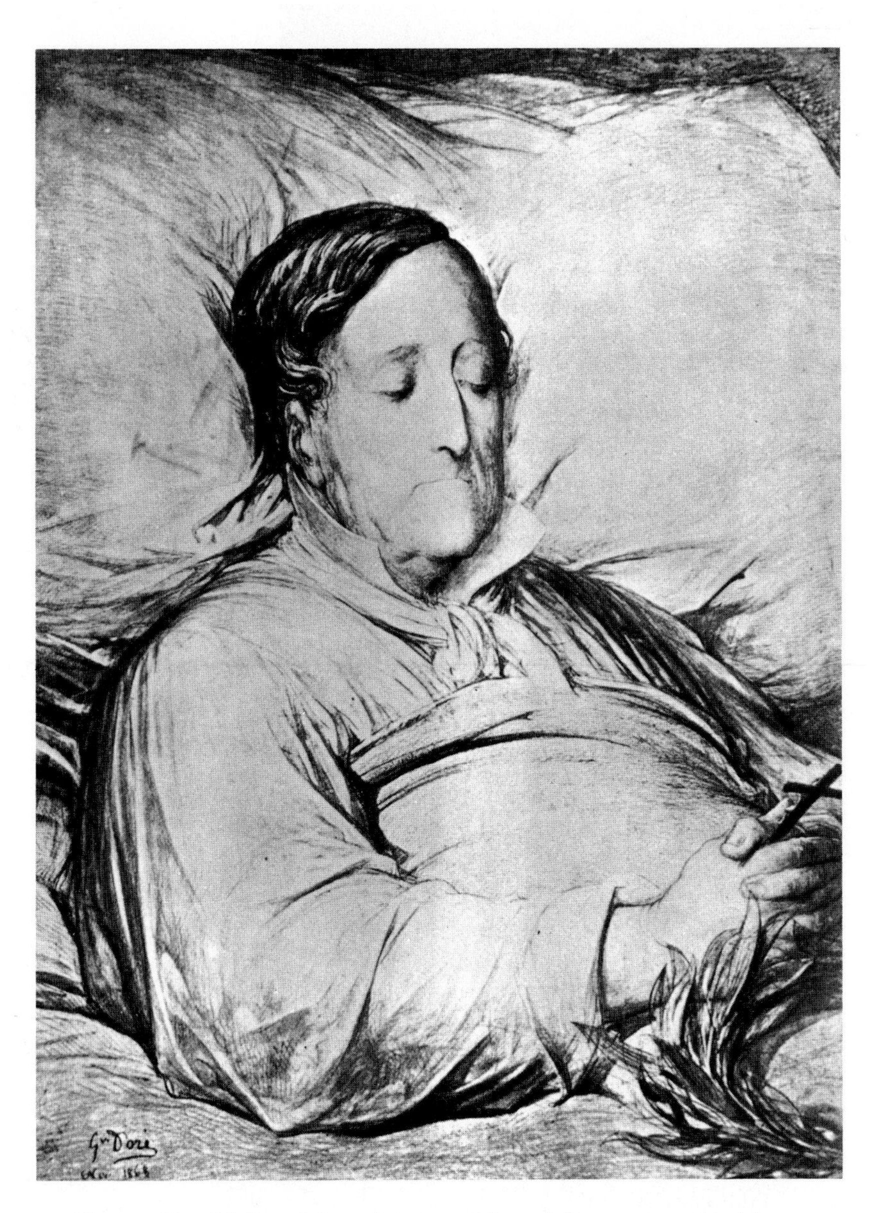

Gustave Doré (1832–83) made two studies of the composer on his deathbed in November 1868, which he used for a subsequent painting and this engraving. Doré had been a frequent guest at, and contributor to, the Rossini *samedi soirs*, where Giulio Ricordi heard him sing in 1867, and commented on Doré's beautiful baritone voice, and the great taste and expression he displayed in his singing. Rossini himself referred to Doré as 'a great singer'.

Having had his outburst, Rossini then thanked Pacini for his cantata, *Rossini e la patria*, that was to be performed in Pesaro in August that year, to a text by Luigi Mercantini, to celebrate his name-day.

Despite Rossini's repeated assertions that he had lost the ability to compose – which on the evidence of the *Petite Messe* he clearly had not – it was nevertheless true that its composition had exhausted him, at least temporarily. For this work, however, he was determined that no one else should undertake the orchestration, so over the course of 1866–7 he produced the full score, running to almost five hundred pages. Although a performance of the orchestrated version was announced for the Birmingham Festival of 1867, Rossini did not in fact authorise any performance during his lifetime; and it was not heard for the first time until three months after his death, on 24 February 1869, at the Théâtre-Italien.

Meyerbeer's pious wish, expressed in the letter of 15 March 1864 (quoted above), that Rossini might live to be a hundred and produce another masterpiece similar to the *Petite Messe*, and that Meyerbeer himself might live to hear it, was to remain no more than a hope. Towards the end of April 1864, whilst still working on the score of *L'Africaine*, which was by then in rehearsal at the Opéra, Meyerbeer fell ill, and died on 2 May. Rossini and he had known each other for almost fifty years, and Meyerbeer's death affected him profoundly. As we saw previously, Rossini composed his 'Chant funèbre' in memory of his friend.

He was constantly asked to give his opinion of other people's music, and on 2 May, the very day that Meyerbeer died, he had written to a composer in Orvieto, Vincenzo Ferrari-Stella, who had sent him various of his compositions, both sacred and profane.[3] Rossini managed to say something polite in the most general terms, but especially singled out for praise the way in which Ferrari-Stella treated the vocal lines: 'In the calamitous times in which we find ourselves, it is good that there should exist *maestri* who do not allow *bel canto*, which is one of the most beautiful Italian endowments, to become too attenuated.'

Another such letter had to be written the following month (by now from Passy), on 19 June 1864, to Angelo Catelani in Modena.[4] Catelani (1811–66) was a composer, conductor and musicologist whose correspondence with Rossini went back more than twenty years. Since 1859 he had been librarian of the Biblioteca Estense in

Modena. Now, in 1864, he had sent Rossini his *Messa Pisa pastorale* for his judgement. Reading between the lines, it was a fairly poor effort, but Rossini's letter is a masterpiece of tact. As he points out at the start of the letter, if one sets out to compose a Mass of very short duration, with very modest vocal and instrumental forces, in a pastoral convention – $\frac{6}{8}$ time, which Catelani seems to have stuck to doggedly throughout the whole of the work – then one has denied oneself all that is 'greatest and seductive in musical composition, which is variety in the rhythm, breadth and development in the thoughts, and luxurious colouring in the instrumentation'. Without such effects, what is a composer to do? Rossini might well have pointed to his *Petite Messe*, where he managed to achieve much of this with minimal resources. Of course he is blaming the church authorities, and saying that if a composer of sacred music obeys the rules, or sticks to the directives, then the result is bound to be dull. Even so, Rossini makes it clear that Catelani's music does little to make the situation any better – he even refers to 'monotony' in the rhythm. It is an occasion for Rossini to voice his own views on what church music ought to be, which is every bit as exciting and colourful as secular music. Rossini was to return to the question of church music, especially the matter of the prohibition of women from singing in churches, and even approached the Pope himself on the subject.

On Rossini's name-day in 1864 there were celebrations not only at the villa in Passy, but also in Pesaro, and on 13 August he was made a *grand officier* of the Légion d'honneur by Napoléon III. Vittorio Emanuele II also honoured him, a week later, by making him a commander of the Order of Saints Maurice and Lazarus. In Pesaro there was a ceremonial unveiling of a seated bronze statue, donated by the directors of the railway company, Ferrovie Romane, which was hardly suitable for such a determined non-railway-user as Rossini. After the playing of the overture to *La gazza ladra*, the Italian Minister of the Interior, Ubaldino Peruzzi, unveiled the statue and consigned to the Mayor of Pesaro the document appointing Rossini to the Order of Saints Maurice and Lazarus. It was estimated that some 20,000 people attended, and listened to a special *Inno* set by Mercadante, using Rossini melodies, which was followed by the overture to *Semiramide*. The orchestra numbered 205 and the choir 255.

That evening, in the Teatro Rossini, a second *Inno* was performed, this one by Giovanni Pacini, and the one referred to by Rossini in the letter of 8 April quoted above, followed by a performance of *Guillaume Tell*. That evening, the streets were illuminated, especially the former via del Duomo, henceforth via Rossini, and a band played in the piazza. Ironically, the Bologna municipal band had made its way to Pesaro to take part in the festivities there, so that a military band had to play in Bologna instead on this day. In Bologna a commemorative tablet was placed near the entrance to the Liceo Musicale, and the adjacent piazza was renamed Piazza Rossini. Lugo sent Rossini a patent of nobility, and Arezzo named him honorary president of the commission set up to honour Guido d'Arezzo, the monk whose musical method became the basis of all medieval teaching. In a ceremony in Rome that would have appealed especially to Rossini, the Accademia dei Quiriti celebrated his eighteenth birthday, since there had only been that number of leap years since 1792.

However, none of the Italian celebrations and honours gave Rossini any desire to return to his homeland, despite a glowing account sent him on 21 August by Vincenzo Alberti.[5] Rossini's reply, dated 2 September 1864, makes it abundantly clear that nothing that Bologna chose to do would ever make him change his mind about the city: 'You have painted with the brushes of a Salvator Rosa all the details of the ceremony held that same day [21 August] in the Piazza del Liceo in my honour. . . . If they [i.e., the Bolognesi] had been different, I was sufficiently well disposed not to have left Bologna. . . . I have read the inscription, and now I can boast of having been stoned' – thus making a pun on the stone tablet placed in his memory. As if to underline the point, he signed himself 'Rossini of Pesaro'.[6] He certainly had not the slightest intention of returning to Pesaro, Bologna, or anywhere else in Italy, for that matter. Indeed, on 17 November he completed the sale of his property in Florence, thus closing yet another chapter.

Certain bonds with Italy were indissoluble, however, and one of them was his association with the Ricordi family and its publishing house. He now received a gift of the Ricordi edition of twenty-one piano scores of his operas, the first batch of what was intended as a complete collection of Rossini's operatic output. As the composer wrote to thank Tito Ricordi on 14 December 1864, however, he felt obliged to issue a caveat:

> The edition you have undertaken will give rise (with reason) to many criticisms because the same piece of music will be found in

> different operas; the time and money granted me for composing were so homeopathic [meaning very little] that I hardly had time to read the so-called poetry to be set to music: only the maintenance of my most beloved parents and poor relatives was in my heart.

Historically the tradition had never been for operas to be regarded as finished individual creations, let alone suitable for preservation in a collected edition, if only because conditions tended to vary so much from city to city, or even on different occasions in the same city where opera might be presented. Moreover, Rossini knew that in some of his *fiaschi* there lay good music that was worthy of being salvaged.

Times were changing, however, and Rossini became increasingly aware of what those changes implied for him. Ricordi had mooted the idea of a collected edition as early as 1852, and Rossini wrote to Giovanni Ricordi on 24 February that year from Florence, pointing out that such publication would show up his inadequacies. He had an outburst to the architect Doussault about it in June 1854, expressing his anger. It had seemed perfectly reasonable to him to 'save from shipwreck' sections from operas that had failed, and include them elsewhere: 'An opera that had been whistled at seemed to me to be totally dead – and lo, everything has been brought back to life.'[7] Operas were now seen as immutable sacrosanct works of art, whereas Rossini had been born into a tradition where the concept of art had a much wider application.

Nevertheless life went on. The Ricordi incident did not help his health that winter of 1864–5, however, for in these last years he was plagued by bronchial trouble at this season. Early in the new year, on 3 January, Rossini wrote to thank Michele Costa in London for having sent him some Stilton cheese, which he had been unable to enjoy until now because of uncertain health. Having tasted some of the cheese that very day, however, he now felt much better. He imagined that regular consumption of Stilton would induce one to compose classical oratorios and descend to posterity, one's head crowned with laurels. He was keen for Costa to discover whether there was a hospital for cancerous diseases in London, because a friend of his in Bologna had invented a medicine for the disease, compounded of vegetables, which Rossini swore by. It was to be cancer that finally carried Rossini off, though he seems to have had no idea at this stage that he suffered from it. He had, however, recommended the medicine to others, and seen its effects. Nevertheless the image of Rossini as the *bon viveur* was kept alive by such letters. On 28 May the following year (1866) Rossini wrote to thank Costa again for cheese, this time Cheddar, whose spelling gave him some problems. From Carafa came a story of a Russian princess who wished to make Rossini's acquaintance and had waited for two hours in the street merely to encounter him. Rossini's comment was that all she needed to do was to buy the finest bunch of asparagus available, and she might come and see him at any time.

One of the very few accounts to give the impression that the Rossinis did actually keep a good table was that of Weber's son, Max Maria, who visited the Chaussée d'Antin apartment first on 21 March 1865, and at the end of his time with Rossini was invited to dinner the following Saturday. He said that Rossini and his guests were totally absorbed in appreciating the excellent dinner. Rossini flirted with some of the young women present, though it seems to have been entirely in good part. Hanslick told the story of a beautiful lady who was so overcome the first time that she met Rossini that she had no idea how to address him. 'Great *maestro*? Prince of Music? Divine Genius?'

'I'd prefer it if you would call me *mon petit lapin* [a term of endearment which means literally "my little rabbit"],' the composer is said to have replied.[8]

During the course of their private conversation, which, as recorded by Weber, yielded few revelations, Rossini said complimentary things about his guest's father. Weber noticed that there were works by Mozart and Gluck on Rossini's desk, but no Wagner. After dinner on the Saturday evening Weber heard what he called some new Spanish Romances by Rossini. It is not clear precisely what these might have been, though a piece such as the duet 'Les amants de Séville' from Volume 3 of *Les Péchés de vieillesse* has the flavour of what Bizet was to capture in *Carmen* (1873–4), and of course there was a strong Spanish influence on French composers lasting well into the present century. Rossini also composed two late songs for soprano and piano – 'A Grenade' and 'La Veuve andalouse' – which are not in any of the volumes of *Les Péchés de vieillesse*.

Weber remarked how Rossini became irritated if the performers took liberties with his music, which reminded him of his father. He seems to have missed by only a week a visit from Liszt – now Abbé Liszt – who played some of Rossini's pieces. He, however, took considerable liberties with the music, but they were so close to Rossini's intentions that the latter turned to the other guests and said: 'This man is a devil.' Weber paid a return visit in the summer of 1867, when Rossini had gone to Passy for the summer. He commented on the whistle of a train nearby, which Weber expected would upset the older man. Not at all, was the reply, for the whistle reminded him of those he had heard at some of his operas in his youth.[9]

On 24 April 1865 the *Petite Messe solennelle* was given once again at the Pillet-Will home, though Rossini was not present. He took some pleasure, however, from the fact that the work had now been 'received', as he told Francesco Florimo in a letter of 10 June.[10] He found it somewhat ironic that he was now regarded as a classic, a learned composer. No doubt Padre Mattei, if he were still alive, would alter his opinion of his wayward pupil now. What was also true was that, as well as being regarded as something of a classic as far as his own music was concerned, he was regarded as a repository of information about certain long-dead composers. From appeals made to him by correspondents, it is clear that he had something of a reputation beyond his immediate circle. In 1862 he had been asked to support the erection of a statue to Rameau, and in the course of his reply indicated that he had what was for those days an unusually wide knowledge of Rameau's output, and was in the habit of having his music performed.[11] In July 1865 he became involved in quite detailed research with Angelo Catelani in Modena into the career of Alessandro Stradella.[12] He did not miss the opportunity, however, to ask Catelani in a letter of 8 December 1865 to order some pigs' trotters and other local specialities from a butcher in Modena, Bellentani, who had supplied him for a number of years.

Despite the good food, however, illness struck again that winter, and on 27 January 1866, when he wrote to Giovanni Pacini, he said that he had had catarrh for the last two months, which was why he had taken so long to answer his letter.[13] As we have seen, Rossini was punctilious in his response to letters, no matter from whom they came, and it was most unusual for him to delay writing to virtually anyone, let alone an old friend. He had also omitted to write and thank Pietro, Barbaia's son, for his letter of 8 November 1865, which had accompanied a portrait of Rossini's mother. Most unusually for Rossini, he did not reply until 27 April 1866.[14]

Rossini's letter to Pacini on 27 January, referred to above, became an important statement of his philosophy, though of course by now it was very much that of an old man who feels himself increasingly out of sympathy with his times:

> This art [music], which has alone as its base 'idealism' and 'sentiment', is unable to avoid the influence of the time in which we live. Idealism and sentiment have today turned entirely to steam, rapine and barricades. . . .
>
> Dear Giovanni, be at peace; bear in mind my philosophical intention to abandon my Italian career in 1822, the French one in 1829; such foresight is not given to all; God accorded it to me and I bless Him always.

Rossini went on to say how he had taken consolation from being a pianist (of the fourth class), and recommended Pacini to do the same. He also expressed his hope that he would see Bellini's ashes returned to his homeland, and be able to embrace Pacini before he (Rossini) died, since he had such fond memories of his father, Luigi, who had created the role of Don Geronio in *Il turco in Italia* and sung the role of Taddeo many times in *L'italiana in Algeri*. Rossini's association with the family therefore spread over three generations, since Giovanni's son, Emilien, provided Rossini with many of the texts he set in the last years of his life.

This valedictory atmosphere was dispelled in the months that followed as Rossini threw himself with great vigour into a campaign to get the Pope to change the rules governing the prohibition against women singing in church. In a letter of 23 March 1866, he enlisted the help of Luigi Crisostomo Ferrucci, Librarian of the Biblioteca Laurenziana in Florence, to prepare a suitable text in Latin to send to Pius IX.[15] Ferrucci obliged, and on 26 April Rossini wrote to thank him and tell him that he had sent the letter to the papal nuncio in Paris, Monsignor Chigi. Rossini had to wait three months before receiving a reply, full of blessings, praise and affection, but containing no reference to his request. He wrote to Ferrucci again on 14 October, therefore, to say that he was going to write again, this time in Italian, and try to solicit a reply to his specific request.[16]

Since Rossini had again been asked to look at the religious compositions of others, this time Padre Placido Abela, Prior of Montecassino, he used the occasion of his reply, dated 17 October 1866, to inform Abela of the Pope's reply and announce his intention of pursuing the matter in Italian when the political situation was calmer. As he had pointed out in his very first letter to Ferrucci, it was not just a question of having his own *Petite Messe solennelle* performed in a church with female singers. Since the papacy had forbidden the practice of castration, there were fewer and fewer male sopranos and contraltos. He did not find boys' voices an adequate substitute. How, then, could the Church expect its music to improve unless women were allowed to sing? He was still ruminating on the matter the following June (1867) in another long letter to Ferrucci.[17]

It is possible that, in December 1866, Rossini suffered a mild stroke or thrombosis, because he was unable to move about for some weeks, let alone go outside. Winters had now become increasingly difficult for him, but he recovered and celebrated his seventy-fifth birthday on 28 February 1867, and continued to receive the seemingly endless stream of visitors. In March it was Tito Ricordi and his son Giulio, then twenty-six, who had come to Paris for the first performance of *Don Carlos* at the Opéra on 11 March. They called on Rossini at nine o'clock in the morning, as he had suggested. Tito Ricordi presented Rossini with the first of his author's rights, since it was he who had advised the composer, following the passing of the Italian law relating to rights in June 1865, to take the steps necessary to safeguard his interests. He handed over the sum of forty-five gold napoleons whilst Olympe was out of the room, but hearing her coming back Rossini slipped the money into a drawer, saying that he would keep it for his pocket money and send Ricordi the receipt the following day. Giulio Ricordi remembered that they were present for the *samedi soir* of 1 March when Patti, Alboni, Gardoni and Delle Sedie ended the evening with the quartet from *Rigoletto*. Only Verdi, the young man maintained, could compete with Rossini as an accompanist. One wonders whether Alboni did in fact sing on this occasion, since the printed programme bears the name of Mademoiselle Lliannes.

The following month the German composer and writer Emil Naumann recorded his visit to Rossini, at a time when he was working on the orchestration of the *Petite Messe*.[18] He explained that he did not want Sax or Berlioz to be given the task, since that would swamp the singers: 'That is why I am now in the process of adding a string quartet and a few modest wind instruments to my choruses and arias. That is what one always used to do, and it will give my poor singers an opportunity to be heard.' It is to Naumann that Rossini is supposed to have made his notorious remark that Wagner had some good moments, but some bad quarters of an hour.

In July, Eduard Hanslick, who had been convinced that his previous visit in 1860 would be his only chance to see Rossini before he died, was pleasantly surprised to find both him and Auber (aged seventy-five and eighty-five respectively) still alive.[19] Hanslick, in common with Wagner for once, found it hard to come to terms with Rossini's self-deprecation: 'He is only comfortable with light humour and gentle mockery, and when he derides his compositions, one is never entirely sure whether it is at his own expense or that of others.' As Hanslick noted, Rossini received so much adulation by now that if he actually took it seriously he would become unbearable. So, since serious disapproval, let alone anger, was foreign to Rossini's nature, he had devised this way of – as Hanslick put it – 'knocking the censer out of the admirer's hand by playful self-ridicule'.

Also referred to in the conversation was the recently heard *Hymne à Napoléon III et à son vaillant peuple*, which Rossini termed 'drinking music'. It had been commissioned for the awards ceremony on 1 July 1867 of the Exposition Universelle which Rossini said had turned Paris into a Babylon.[20] The text was by Émilien Pacini, and the score was inscribed by Rossini: 'Hymne (accompanied by large orchestra and military band) for baritone (solo), a pontiff; chorus of high priests, chorus of victuallers, of soldiers, and of people. Dances, bells, side drums and cannon.' When Gaetano Fabi wrote from Bologna to congratulate Rossini, the latter replied on 17 July: '. . . my poor composition, which I wrote out to be sung in my garden at Passy, *en famille*, and definitely not in such solemn circumstances. What could I do! I was asked, and I couldn't refuse.' The enormous forces assembled – 600 members of the orchestra, 200 members of the military band, and 400 members of the chorus, under the direction of Jules Cohen – were far too much for the slight musical substance, and *La Revue et gazette musicale* did not hesitate to say so. This provoked Olympe to take up her pen once again in her husband's defence; though he, of course, had determined never to become involved in such controversy, and on this occasion he was all too aware of the weakness of his own position. The *Hymne* was heard again – at the Opéra this time – on 15 August that year, and at the Palais de l'Industrie three days later, after which it was forgotten in France.

The winter of 1867–8 was again a hard one for Rossini. When the Opéra celebrated the official five hundredth performance of *Guillaume Tell* on 10 February 1868, soloists, chorus and orchestra went to Chaussée d'Antin afterwards to serenade the composer and present a wreath. Since 1868 was a leap year, Rossini was able to celebrate his seventy-sixth birthday on the proper day – 29 February – this year. In addition to Rossini and Olympe, ten people sat down to dinner that evening: Marietta Alboni, Antoine Berryer, the son of the ballerina, Emilia Bigottini, Gustave Doré, Jean-Baptiste Faure and his wife Caroline Faure-Lefébure, Edmond Michotte, Moïnna, comte Pillet-Will and Jean-Frédéric Possoz, Mayor of Passy. Baronne de Rothschild had sent a cake with the inscription 'Bonheur et santé – 1868'. Another confection consisted of a swan (Rossini was long known as the Swan of Pesaro) with outstretched wings, holding up garlands on which were the names of Rossini's major works. At the end of the meal Antoine Berryer made a short speech which, he said, had moved him more than any other speech he had made of a similar nature; then, after dinner, more guests arrived, and as a souvenir of the occasion Doré gave Olympe a fan that he had painted.

It was exactly a month later that Rossini was addressed from Florence in a very gracious letter from Emilio Broglio, Minister for Public Education, the intent of which only became apparent in the last paragraph. Broglio intended setting up a Società Rossiniana, of which the composer should naturally be president, and through its subscriptions and concerts make money sufficient for the Government to be able to transfer its control of and responsibility for Italy's conservatoires to the society, thus freeing the State of the obligation to provide an annual budget of 400,000 lire.

The publication of Broglio's letter in Italy caused a furore. Amongst various unfortunate turns of phrase, two at least backfired on him. He admitted that he was 'ignorant' as far as music was concerned, and he said that there had been no opera in Italy for forty years, apart from four operas by Meyerbeer. Verdi had just received from Broglio a diploma nominating him *commendatore* of the Order of the Crown of Italy. Verdi returned it with the following letter:

> This order was instituted to honour those who benefit Italy, either in the forces, literature, sciences or the arts. A letter to Rossini from Your Excellency, though you are ignorant of music (as you yourself say and believe), maintains that no opera has been composed in Italy for forty years. Why, then, has this decoration been sent to me? The address is certainly wrong, and I return it.

As he explained to friends, it was not only for himself but for the memory of Bellini and Donizetti that he made his gesture. Boito, too, joined in, and published an open letter to the minister on 2 May 1868.[21] Lauro Rossi, Director of the Conservatoire in Milan, wrote to Rossini in dismay; and, in his reply on 21 June, Rossini admitted that it had not occurred to him what Broglio was actually proposing.[22] Rossi published this reply, which went some way towards soothing some of the anger felt in the musical establishment.

There is no doubt that Broglio was inept in the way he handled the affair, whatever the merits of the idea that he was proposing. A similar arrangement had worked in Russia, where the formation of the Russian Musical Society in 1859 soon led to the founding of the conservatoires in St Petersburg and Moscow, and ultimately in other Russian cities. However, having said that, there was a considerable difference between the situation in Russia, where previously there had been no conservatoires at all, and Italy, where there were well-established conservatoires in several cities, with traditions going back centuries. It was something which the unification of Italy threw into focus, because expenditure on musical foundations had previously been funded from individual and independent sources, even when this meant the treasuries of the kingdoms, republics, and so on. Put together as a national sum, however, it suddenly appeared quite a large amount as part of the country's budget. Furthermore, as the example of France was to demonstrate as the nineteenth century progressed, rigid state control and virtual centralisation of higher musical education in one institution had ultimately a deadening effect. France continued to produce musicians who were technically brilliant, but fewer and fewer composers as time went by, and the effects continued into the twentieth century. Italy has produced even fewer, and the standard in many of the Italian conservatoires leaves much to be desired. One might say that Broglio had identified the problem, but for totally the wrong reasons.

Then there was the extraordinarily insulting implication that Bellini, Donizetti and Verdi had composed nothing of value. Broglio might well have been ignorant in musical matters, and the identification of genuine talent among contemporary composers at any one time is a notoriously hazardous undertaking. The history of music is strewn with examples of inflated nonentities on the one hand and barely recognised geniuses on the other. Even so, the very fact that all three composers had developed international careers must surely have counted for something, even to Broglio. If nothing else, however, the whole affair demonstrated yet again the extent to which Rossini had become a living monument.

In early August 1868, Rossini received a letter from the young Constantino Dall'Argine (1842–77), who had already had a certain amount of success with his opera *I due orsi* in Milan the previous year, and was now intending setting *Il barbiere di Siviglia*, so wrote to Rossini, with much the same aim in mind as Rossini himself when deciding to follow the path already trodden by Paisiello.[23] Dall'Argine wanted to dedicate his new opera, which was to be given in Bologna at the Teatro Comunale, to Rossini. Its first performance, on 11 November 1868, caused intense friction between the pro- and anti-Rossini and Dall'Argine factions.[24] Two days later, however, Rossini was dead.

One of the last honours that Rossini received was that of Grand Knight of the Order of the Crown of Italy, and on 10 September he sent what was probably his last completed composition, *La corona d'Italia*, for military band, to Broglio on behalf of Vittorio Emanuele II. In his covering letter Rossini pointed out that he had included saxophones in the scoring, but that if Italian bands did not yet have them, then Broglio might commission some recognised composer of military band music to adjust it accordingly.[25] However, Broglio was to be most careful to protect the rights, and not allow the work to be pirated. Italian bands had not yet taken up the saxophone, so Broglio ordered them from Paris. However, there is no record that the music was performed at this time, the Government fell shortly afterwards, and Broglio was turned out of office. The music was eventually performed on 25 November 1878, however, outside Palazzo Quirinale, in celebration of the safe return of King Umberto I and Queen Margherita from Naples, where an attempted assassination had occurred.

In Paris the *samedi soirs* were resumed in the autumn, but the one on 26 September turned out to be the last. Rossini was not well. When he wrote to Luigi Ferrucci on 18 October, he was suffering from an irritation of the mucous membrane, and he complained of weak legs.[26] Ferrucci had told him that one of his cousins, who was a Malerbi, still had the spinet that Rossini had played on in Lugo in 1802. Rossini said that he had practised daily on it, but that it was a barbarous instrument, especially by comparison with the modern piano. Even so, that spinet would be preferable as an accompanying instrument for use by singing teachers to some of the strident pianofortes which did not, in Rossini's opinion, encourage sensitive singing.

When Rossini's final illness began it was nothing bronchial; but what appeared at first to be a rectal fistula was undoubtedly cancer. It was decided that an operation was necessary, but Rossini was too weak and ill to undergo surgery there and then. By 3 November, however, Rossini's bronchial condition had improved to the point where it was felt that he could now undergo surgery. At the composer's request, Dr Auguste Nélaton, Napoléon III's doctor, was called in. He had developed a porcelain-tipped probe to locate bullets in the body, which had been used on Garibaldi at the battle of Aspromonte in 1862, as well as a rubber catheter. Dr Nélaton was anxious that Rossini should not remain under chloroform for any longer than was necessary, because of his heart condition. He therefore performed the operation in five minutes, during the course of which he discovered a cancer and removed as much of it as possible. For the next two days Olympe dressed her husband's wound, for he would not have anyone else approach him. On 5 November, however, Dr Nélaton was worried by the appearance of the wound, and decided to operate again. For the following three days it seemed that a normal healing process was taking place, and the doctor felt optimistic about the chances of saving Rossini's life. This gave the composer a new sense of purpose, and he responded to treatment. It took four men to lift Rossini out of his bed each morning, transfer him to a second bed while clean linen was being put on the first, and then return him to it. Despite the extreme care with which they carried out their task – made all the more difficult because of Rossini's extreme weight – he was often in great pain. He continued in this way until he was finally released from his suffering at 11.15 on the evening of 13 November.

Epilogue

In the morning of Saturday, 14 November 1868, Gustave Doré came and made two sketches of Rossini on his deathbed, from which he made a painting and an engraving. A wig is in place, and beneath it Rossini's relaxed face reveals nothing of the intense suffering he had experienced prior to his death. It is as if he were in an almost beatific sleep, though the folds of skin beneath his jaw and the generally elongated aspect of the face indicate how much weight he had lost latterly. His body was embalmed on 16 November by a process with which he had apparently been much impressed at the Exposition Universelle the year before, whereby a liquid was injected into the blood vessels with the aim of preventing decomposition. That same evening the coffin was taken to the église de la Madeleine, where it was intended the funeral service should take place. But since the church only held 2,000 people, and some 5,000 had asked for invitations, it was decided to hold the ceremony in the église de la Trinité, the church which fills the vista at the top of Chausée d'Antin as one looks north from outside Rossini's apartment building. It was decided to wait until noon on Saturday, 21 November, so as to allow a delegation from Pesaro time to reach Paris. The Mayor of Pesaro had sent a telegram to Olympe, addressed to 'Contessa Pélissier-Rossini', expressing condolences and announcing the decision to send a deputation.[1]

In Rossini's original will, dated 5 July 1858, in Paris, he directed that no more than 2,000 lire (francs) at the most were to be spent on his funeral; but ten years later the ceremony had assumed an international significance, and was therefore tantamount to a state funeral. Even so, an attempt was made to respect Rossini's wishes, and funeral trappings were kept to a minimum, though a music committee was appointed, under the presidency of Auber, and Jules Cohen was chosen to conduct. There was no orchestra, apart from a saxophone ensemble which played independently. The bulk of the music was for voices and organ.

As the coffin was carried into the church, the organ played the Scene of the Shadows music from *Mosè*; then the assembled voices – the whole of the student body from the Conservatoire – and many of the singers from the Opéra, the Opéra-Comique and the Théâtre-Italien sang the 'Introibo' from Jomelli's *Messa dei morti*, a work which Rossini had always admired. Next came parts of the 'Dies irae' – the opening verse was adapted to the 'Mater dolorosa' from Rossini's *Stabat Mater* and was sung by Christine Nilsson, Rosine Bloch, Tamburini and Nicolini, with chorus. Then Alboni and Patti sang 'Liber scriptus' to the music of 'Quis est homo' from the *Stabat Mater*, and another verse from 'Dies irae' – 'Quid sum miser' – was sung by the baritone Faure to the music of 'Pro peccatis suae gentis', again from the *Stabat Mater*.

The choir followed this with the 'Lacrymosa' from Mozart's *Requiem*, and Christine Nilsson sang 'Vidit suum dulcem natum' from Pergolesi's *Stabat Mater*. For the Elevation 'Pie Jesu' was sung to 'Quando corpus morietur' from Rossini's *Stabat Mater* by Gabrielle Krauss, Eleonora Grossi, Nicolini and Agnesi. Finally, for the 'Agnus Dei', the prayer from *Mosè* was adapted, sung by Patti, Alboni and three male singers. At the end of the service the wind ensemble played Beethoven's Funeral March, arranged by Gevaert. Beethoven himself had made an orchestral arrangement of the march from the Opus 26 piano sonata, as part of the incidental music for Duncker's play *Leonora Prohaska* (1815). The manuscript found its way into the library of the Paris Conservatoire, and in the time at his disposal it would seem likely that Gevaert simply reworked Beethoven's own version.

It was not until about two o'clock that the procession began to emerge from the church, on a cold dull afternoon. The emperor was represented by vicomte de la Ferrière, Grand Chamberlain of the Court, princesse Mathilde attended in person, as did Prince Metternich, Maréchal Vaillant, comte Nieuwerkerke and representatives of the Académie Française, the Académie des Beaux-Arts and the Conservatoire. The eighty-six-year-old Auber had insisted on standing near the coffin throughout the ceremony, and now, as one of the pallbearers, insisted on walking to the Père-Lachaise cemetery.

Among other pallbearers were the Italian ambassador, Prince Poniatowski, Ambroise Thomas and the Italian consul. There was a guard

Rossini's funeral cortège in front of L'église de la Trinité, Paris, 1868.

of honour outside the church, and bands played. Despite the cold north wind, crowds filled the windows and lined the route to the cemetery, which took nearly two hours to reach, and where all the various representatives then made their speeches over the grave.

That evening there were special performances of Rossini works at the Théâtre-Italien and the Théâtre-Lyrique, though *Guillaume Tell*, planned for the Opéra, had to be held over until 28 November because certain singers were indisposed. At that performance, the deputation from Pesaro was present in Madame Rossini's box. Olympe's role in the subsequent history of Rossini's mortal remains was to cause considerable problems.

Even before the funeral, on 17 November, Verdi had written to Tito Ricordi, proposing that on the anniversary of Rossini's death a new Requiem Mass should be performed, and that the Mass should be composed by Italy's leading composers, headed by Mercadante.[2] Since he had been blind since 1862, only a few bars would be expected of him. Verdi then began to propose certain restrictions. Composers and eventual performers were not only to give their services free, but would also be expected to make a contribution towards expenses. There was to be no foreign participation or extra-musical assistance; if that happened, Verdi would resign at once. The performance was to take place in the Basilica of San Petronio in Bologna, which Verdi declared was Rossini's real musical homeland. Knowing how much Rossini had grown to hate Bologna, and had clearly left a handsome sum under the terms of his will for a Liceo Musicale to be set up in Pesaro, this was somewhat perverse of Verdi, to say the least. He then proposed that after the first performance the Mass should be shut away, inalienably, in the archives of the Liceo Musicale in Bologna, except for performances on Rossini anniversaries 'when posterity might think of celebrating him'. Verdi also suggested that an approach should be made to the Pope so that women might be permitted, exceptionally, to sing in the first performance, but since Verdi was not in the papal good graces it had better be someone other than himself. Then a committee would have to be set up to decide which composer should take each section of the Mass and make the necessary arrangements. Verdi was quite aware that such a Mass, by its very nature, would lack cohesion, no matter how good the individual sections might be. Nevertheless it would serve to demonstrate how greatly Rossini had been venerated. One wonders, even so, about Verdi's motivation in proposing this scheme. His own attitude to Rossini was scarcely one of veneration.

With hindsight one might have predicted that the project would never succeed, even if only one or two of Verdi's proposals had been enforced. The commission was duly set up, however, and by May 1869 had selected composers to take the thirteen sections of the Mass. In an effort to overcome the problem of musical homogeneity, specific prescriptions had been made as to length, form, tonality and tempo, and some of the sections had been completed. Mercadante had been unable to contribute even his few token bars, but Angelo Mariani had agreed to conduct, even though he had expected to be asked to compose one of the sections. Verdi had been assigned the closing 'Libera me', which he later used in his own *Requiem* dedicated to Manzoni.

The committee had hoped to use the chorus and orchestra of the Teatro Comunale in Bologna, whose impresario was L. Scalaberni. It was at this point that the whole venture foundered. Alessandro Luzio attributed its failure to the rather unenthusiastic attitude of Angelo Mariani, the proposed conductor, the lack of interest shown by the civic authorities in Bologna, and the refusal of Scalaberni to allow his singers and orchestra to participate. In his defence, Scalaberni published a letter on 6 October in *Il monitore di Bologna*, in which he set out his position in detail. First, he said that he had never given any undertaking to allow the artists under contract to him to participate in the Mass. Second, he felt that private individuals ought not to be expected to contribute to the expenses of what was essentially a national and, by extension, state occasion, especially when the younger generation of composers such as Boito, Dall'Argine, Faccio and Marchetti had been excluded. Third, despite assurances from the committee to the contrary, the preparation of such a significant work would certainly have disrupted the season of opera performances at the Teatro Comunale which had opened on 1 October. Fourth, when Scalaberni's contract with the City of Bologna had been drawn up three years previously, no one had foreseen Rossini's death. Finally, on a somewhat sour note, the impresario said that the committee ought to have approached some rich businessman to fund their project, rather than himself, who had six children to provide for and was, by implication, poor. The planned performance did not, therefore, take place; and, on 17 June 1878, Verdi wrote that its failure was not the fault of the composers, but of the indifference, or even ill-will, of others.

On 18 November 1868, the day after his initial letter to Tito Ricordi about the *Requiem*, Verdi had written to Giuseppe Piroli, mentioning the departure of the Pesarese delegation for Paris, and predicting that they would have great difficulty in persuading Olympe to agree to the removal of her late husband's remains. It had been decided that there would be a funeral ceremony, and a monument to Rossini in Santa Croce in Florence, which by now had become the national pantheon. On 12 December, Verdi again wrote to Piroli, accusing Olympe of holding out against the Italian authorities in the hopes that she, too, would find a resting-place in Santa Croce. Olympe survived until 1878, when she died on 22 March, after an illness that had lasted some six months.

It was now possible to carry out the intentions of Rossini as specified in his will and its various codicils. The Liceo Musicale was set up in Pesaro, and the first Rossini Prizes were instituted. The Maison de Retraite Rossini was begun in 1883, and opened for retired singers in January 1889. The problem now arose over Olympe's remains. She had always wanted to be united with Rossini symbolically after her death, and realising that the Italian authorities would be unlikely to accord the same honours to her as they wished to bestow on her late husband she resisted approaches from both Florence and Pesaro. For her, then, their final resting-place would be Père-Lachaise. However, after Rossini's death she hoped that she might be able to persuade the Italian authorities that if she agreed to let Rossini's remains go to Florence they might accept that she, too, would rest there. This is what had caused Verdi's anger in his letter to Giulio Ricordi of 12 December 1868. He wrote that if she succeeded he would become a Turk. In due course, however, Olympe changed her mind, and wrote into her will that she should remain in Père-Lachaise, but that her husband's remains should go to Italy. As she expressed it: 'I make this sacrifice in all humility; I have been sufficiently glorified by the name that I bear. My faith, my religious feelings, give me the hope of a reunion that transcends the earthly.'

So it came about that, three months after Olympe's death, a committee was set up in Florence to arrange for the reception of Rossini's remains. Verdi was invited to be honorary president, but virtually said that he had done his share over the Mass and declined. The central government had agreed to defray the cost of transportation of the coffin from Paris to Florence, but there was a change of administration, and it was not until 4 December 1886 that a new proposal was put to the Italian parliament and was adopted unanimously. A new committee was formed by the Florence Conservatoire, under the presidency of Marchese Filippo Torrigiani, to organise the ceremony, which was fixed for 3 May 1887. As the coffin was taken into the church, a chorus some five hundred strong sang 'Dal tuo stellato soglio' from *Mosè in Egitto*. The following afternoon the *Stabat Mater* was sung in the Palazzo Vecchio with Marie-Louise Durand, Barbara Marchisio, Giovanni Sani and Romano Mannetti as soloists, followed by the overture to *Guillaume Tell*.

Florence observed the centenary of Rossini's birth on 29 February 1892, but there was still no monument marking his final resting-place. A competition was held in 1897, but no entry was deemed suitable, and so a second competition was held the following year. Eventually a modified design in neo-Renaissance style by the sculptor Giuseppe Cassioli was erected, and dedicated on 23 June 1902. In the cartouches on the base appear the names of Pesaro, Florence and Paris. There is no reference to Naples or Venice, let alone Bologna, which thus remained excluded to the very end.

In the immediate aftermath of Rossini's death in 1868, as one might expect, many grandiloquent words were spoken and written. In Italy, however, only certain operas were standing the test of time. Scalaberni's opera season that had opened on 1 October 1869 had put *Otello* alongside Meyerbeer's *Le Prophète* and *Les Huguenots* with Verdi's *Un ballo in maschera*. In Milan *Otello* was mounted in the summer of 1870 at La Scala, and again in the autumn of 1873 at Teatro dal Verme, and continued to be played until displaced by Verdi's *Otello* in 1887. *Il barbiere di Siviglia* enjoyed even greater popularity, and became known as the impresarios' standby, playing during no fewer than eighty seasons in Milan between 1817 and 1873, and in some years appearing on as many as four different occasions. In 1865, for example, it ran in both the spring and autumn seasons at the Carcano, autumn at La Scala, and Advent at Santa Radegonda.[3]

Not everyone shared this enthusiasm for Rossini's music, by any means. In 1871, Conte Opprandino Arrivabene sent Verdi some verses in praise of Rossini and asked the composer to set them to music. Verdi's reply was complimentary about the verses, but pointed out that he was no good at occasional pieces, and preferred not to compose them if he could help it. What he then went on to say, however, indicates his real feelings about Rossini and his music. If he had made a trill and a rising scale, imitating a nightingale, would that constitute a melody? Melodies, he went on, do not consist of scales, trills or clusters of notes. He then drew a contrast between the melodies of the Chorus of the Bards and the prayer in *Mosè*, and those of the *cavatinas* in *Il barbiere di Siviglia*, *La gazza ladra* and *Semiramide*. What are they, then? Whatever you like, but not melodies, and not even good music. 'Don't get angry if I treat Rossini somewhat badly in your eyes, but Rossini is not afraid of being treated badly, and the art [of music] will gain a great deal when the critics can say, and will have the courage to say, the entire truth about him.'

Verdi gave the impression that until then the 'truth' about Rossini had been concealed, as if by tacit agreement, by musicians and critics alike. This was far from the truth. Of course there was, on the one hand, the most idolatrous praise lavished by officialdom, which the sort of language used on such occasions in French and Italian only seems to make more hollow than it is. Rossini himself found it all rather too much, and one suspects that, had he been in a position to comment on his funeral, he would have been very dry about all the official speeches at the graveside, and most concerned about Auber's state of health. On the other hand, commentators such as Wagner, Berlioz, and many others taking their cue from them, had been highly critical of the Rossini phenomenon as a whole, and abusively rude about the man himself. As early as December 1829, the *New Monthly Magazine* published a long article spread over three issues – 108, 109 and 110 – and continued in the issues for January and February 1830, which is a very carefully considered appraisal of his style, but refers to his 'indolence' in the latter part of the article, and asks how long the Rossinomania [sic] will last. It is perhaps not difficult to see, therefore, why Rossini was eventually dismissed by the critics, the composers (for the most part) and the self-righteous, who all too easily made him into a caricature – both as man and musician – that he himself had had a hand in creating.

As Rossini left Bologna in 1848 when anarchy seemed about to take over, so he had withdrawn from the world of opera as he became aware of the changes in voices, orchestras and staging that were taking place. His facility might possibly have taken him forward, as he said to Wagner in 1860 – 'So I too had some disposition for the music of the future?' – but his instinct told him that in reality he had not the stomach for it. As his subsequent physical and mental or – as we would say today, no doubt – psychosomatic state indicated, it was a decision that brought heavy personal consequences in its wake.

On occasion he clearly did have the desire to compose; and when, for example, he came into contact with the Marchisio sisters in 1860, he suddenly found that the sort of voice he had known and loved in his younger days might still exist, and the desire was all the more stimulated. It was too late by then, certainly as far as opera was concerned. The time was out of joint. Nor did he help his cause by allowing *pasticcios* of his works, and even assisting in their creation, as with *Robert Bruce* in 1846. The whole artistic climate had begun to be against him. Moreover, by the time that Ricordi began publication of the complete edition of his operas in 1852, Rossini knew that critics would pounce on the fact that some of the music had been salvaged from failures and recycled. Once Wagner had begun to spin his long, unbroken threads, every note that a composer wrote had to be heavy with significance. But by then Rossini was too tired, too old, too near the next world to worry about this one.

So his reputation gradually sank, through a combination of condemnatory high-mindedness and a dearth of artists capable of performing his music properly. Except for a very few operas, overtures and individual arias, little of his output was available or accessible to the public at large. It became all too easy to mock the Rossini 'idiom', since it had been copied and debased so in the process; and it is still much more difficult to approach his work with sensitivity and a stylistic awareness, so as to create at least a point of departure from which to appraise the music.

It is no good simply regarding Rossini as the first in a succession of nineteenth-century Italian composers of opera that progresses through Bellini and Donizetti to Verdi, and which then, with Mascagni and Puccini, leads us neatly into the twentieth century – as if Rossini were the founder of a school which perpetuated his ideals. If we consider Verdi's criticisms of Rossini's melodic construction, it is apparent that Verdi, for one, was no follower of Rossini, let alone an emulator. On the other hand, it would be hard to imagine how Italian opera on its home ground – as opposed to its manifestation as Parisian *grand opéra* – would have survived without Rossini. Here, then, is a fundamental aspect of Rossini's achievement; he kept Italian opera alive at a time when it was all but extinct, and in so doing he made possible the flowering that took place during the rest of the century.

Rossini took the tradition as he found it, divided sharply into serious opera and comic opera, with a third genre, *semiseria*, somewhere between the two, and deployed his talents with equal facility in all three genres. He was remembered by posterity, however, chiefly as a composer of comic opera, with *Il barbiere di Siviglia*, though he was also known to have composed at least one *grand opéra*, *Guillaume Tell*, which was rarely performed. Very few people knew that he had composed any serious Italian operas, though there were two relatively familiar religious pieces, the *Stabat Mater* and the *Petite Messe solennelle*. The fact that Rossini was chiefly known as a composer of comic opera meant that it was well-nigh impossible to treat these last two works with any degree of seriousness. Where overtures to such operas as *La gazza ladra* or *La scala di seta* were known and performed, very few people knew anything about those operas at all, whether they were serious, comic, or semi-serious. This was not wilful ignorance, for with the best intention in the world it was almost impossible to gain access to scores, let alone hear the works in performance.

Why was it, then, that Rossini was thought of so highly in his own day, but progressively fell into oblivion? The basic answer is that styles and fashions change. The style of singing that Rossini had been accustomed to in his younger days, as well as the technique of singing itself, changed. He declined to write for the new style, even though it gave a new lease of life to *Guillaume Tell* at the Paris Opéra from 1837 onwards. And revivals of works such as *Moïse et Pharaon* and *Semiramide* (in French) took place there as late as 1852 for the former, and 1860 for the latter, with some less successful productions at the Italien in between. By and large, however, it meant that Rossini's serious Italian operas were consigned to oblivion *en bloc*, apart from *Otello*, which survived in Italy until dislodged by Verdi's opera on the same subject in 1887.

The example of Verdi offers an illustration as to why Rossini's serious operas did not survive. Musically Verdi was more readily accessible to the audience at large than Rossini was in all but a few of his operas. Verdi's melodies were more expansive – as, indeed, were Bellini's – more grateful for the voice, more easily memorable at first or second hearing, and generally the vocal line was much less elaborate than Rossini's. There is more than a grain of truth in what

Verdi said about Rossini's melodies being composed of snatches, of nuclei strung together, charming no doubt in themselves, but not constituting anything like the great lyrical sweep of a Verdi tune. As well as making the music more direct and popular in its appeal, Verdi also brought the dramatic content down to more popular themes and concepts (with some exceptions for his Paris operas). The chorus and orchestra, too, featured more prominently in Verdi's scheme of things, whereby opera was generally 'democratised'.

This is not to say that Rossini had anticipated none of Verdi's developments. On the contrary, he began to break down the rigid divisions between serious and comic opera, and the ways in which aria and recitative were usually deployed. He introduced much greater flexibility in his approach to the component parts and combined them in ways which had rarely been used in Italian opera hitherto. In addition to his finales, far more complex and tightly organised than in any previous native Italian operas, Rossini began to create unbroken scenes consisting of a succession of arias, duets and ensembles – anticipating the methods of the mature Verdi. He also gave the chorus much more to do than had been dreamed possible hitherto, and he used the orchestra with sensitivity and flair. Chorus and orchestra thus became integral parts of the music-drama, contributing to the overall expressiveness, whereas before they had simply fulfilled a subsidiary role as far as the main drama was concerned.

Rossini's particular and individual contribution was his dynamism and exuberance; his music often burns and crackles with vitality. At no time, however, did he think of himself as a conscious reformer of opera as Gluck, for example, had been; nor was he a child of the Romantic movement, which saw the artist as an inspired prophetic genius. He was, first and foremost, a practical working musician, and as such he was an early victim of Romanticism; for, having shown the way that Romantic Italian opera might develop, he drew back and left others to carry out the task. From a historical standpoint, then, this was one of his chief failures. Another was his failure to take up the possibility offered by his own *semiseria* opera *La gazza ladra* to 'democratise' the medium much sooner than Verdi did. At the same time, however, as *grand opéra* became bigger and grander, and usually tragic, Rossini's own personality became a crucial factor. He was not by temperament attracted to composing the sort of operas in the style that was now becoming fashionable. It has been suggested that he was afraid of losing the success and adulation he had enjoyed previously, and that to some extent that success had spoilt him, because it had come too soon and too easily.

But the real reasons are surely more complex. It cost him enormous physical and mental distress not to compose in the years after his retirement from the operatic stage. The act of composition would have been a release for Rossini, and it might well have been easier to compose than not to do so. Of course he was well enough off not to need to compose, whereas the need to earn his living might well have kept his faculties engaged. The compositional process was one for which, as he himself was well aware, he had considerable facility. This combination of factors, however, seems to indicate that he did not renounce operatic composition easily or lightly, on the spur of the moment. It was a consciously planned step, with devastating personal consequences in the mid-term.

Rossini therefore paid a considerable personal price for this act of renunciation, though in the eyes of some it may well have seemed an act of cowardice. He had already done at least one good deed in revitalising Italian opera, and that at a time when the opera composer was still very much an artisan, far from the Romantic hero of a later age. Rossini had no contract with his public – which was in any case notoriously fickle – whereby he was to effect his own immolation. He had already driven himself extremely hard in his younger days, and now in his late thirties began to feel the effects. He was tired, and he was ill. He saw that changes were taking place on both the political and artistic fronts with which he had little sympathy. More specifically, vocal and compositional techniques had altered to the point where Rossini had no interest in following their development. Indeed, he was in a sense clairvoyant when he made his decision to abandon operatic composition; for, although Meyerbeerian *grand opéra* took over many of the techniques of *Guillaume Tell*, it destroyed that opera's inherent classicism. Rossini's sweeping, carefully constructed design was fragmented into a mosaic of smaller, self-contained sections, crafted to make the maximum immediate effect. Too often the result was merely meretricious. After contemplating his past, present and possible future, Rossini decided that once *Guillaume Tell* was achieved he would take his leave, making the opera truly the swansong of the Swan of Pesaro.

Once he had put himself outside the mainstream of opera, however, then his works began to fall out of the repertoire; and in something of a vicious circle, since there were fewer performances, there were fewer performers able to cope with the vocal lines. The advent of the Marchisio sisters for the 1860 revival of *Semiramide* was something of a final tribute to the *bel canto* style which had already long since had its day. Public taste, too, altered, and Rossini began to seem tame by comparison with the popular composers of *grand opéra*. Even so, one ought not to forget that, in their day, his serious Parisian operas – *Le Siège de Corinthe*, *Moïse et Pharaon* and *Guillaume Tell* – were thought powerful in their effect, and during the 1830 Revolution the staff of the Opéra became so excited by the expression given to the theme of freedom in *Guillaume Tell* that the administration became somewhat alarmed. In Bologna, in 1848, *Guillaume Tell* was cited by Padre Ugo Bassi as proof of Rossini's credentials as a partisan of freedom – though admittedly after Bassi contributed to precipitating Rossini's departure from the city.

Of course, the problem of vocal style was one that also affected Bellini and Donizetti, too, in due course, so that they eventually suffered a fate similar to Rossini's. With a few exceptions, their operas fell out of the repertoire as *bel canto* went out of fashion. There were, of course, other factors, such as the advent of *verismo* late in the century, which made the plots and stylised dramatic and musical gestures of *bel canto* opera even less acceptable to current taste.

The fact that these *bel canto* operas have once again come back into the repertoire at all has been due largely to singers and conductors in this century who have been prepared to devote time and energy, and precious vocal resources, to reviving them. Inevitably, though regrettably, this initially tended to make the operas simply vehicles for a particular singer to demonstrate his or (usually) her vocal ability, and whilst the performers are naturally of paramount importance, since without them the works would not be revived, this is but one strand contributing to the revaluation of the operas as a whole. Another strand is sympathetic production. All too often productions are entrusted to producers who put their faith in sensationalism or cheap gimmicks. Of course, this is by no means confined to Rossini productions; but, at a time when one might hope for a just and fair reappraisal, it does the cause of the Rossini revival little good.

All opera production must grow out of the music, and must serve the music, as opposed to the plot or theme. This requires understanding of the music itself, the vocal style – crucial for Rossini – and the traditions and influences that contributed to the work's emergence and genesis. All too often, however, one sees productions where the producer seems to have virtually no conception of what the music is about, or even what it is for. It is perhaps easier to condemn, but at a time when 'authenticity' in performance, instrumentation, accuracy of editions, and vocal style, has been made such an important issue, and each year sees the boundaries of 'authentic' style pushed closer to the present day, it seems extraordinary that where opera production is concerned 'authenticity' remains a closed book. If, on the one hand, a relatively straightforward production of *Guillaume Tell* is mounted which allows the music to be heard in a setting and with action that is sympathetic to it, the critics will complain that the cause of opera production has been set back thirty years. On the other hand, when a production is overlaid with a jejune 'interpretation' of the substance of the opera that positively obliterates the music and whatever sensitivity the singers may bring to it, then the critics will hail the boldness of the producer. We should remember that there were no producers in Rossini's day.

It is unfortunate that singers and conductors do not seem to wield the necessary authority or influence to curb some of the wilder excesses of producers. All too often, alas, the singers at least, but apparently conductors, too, seem to think that a particular slant to a production will in some way enhance the opera's appeal. Sadly this is true as far as some critics and *habitués* of the opera house are concerned, but it has nothing to do with the music. *Le Comte Ory* remains the same whether the producer chooses to present it as mock-medieval fantasy or psycho-sexual drama, though in the latter instance the delicacy of the music may well be destroyed or at the very least submerged.

There is no doubt that Rossini's operas present considerable difficulties as far as casting and staging are concerned. But with sympathetic and intelligent – as opposed to merely slick – production, and sensitive and accurate treatment of the scores, it is possible to reveal the good things in them. Constructive criticism has its part to play, too, and at last we seem to have moved away from the attitude that it was not quite the done thing for serious people to find anything to appreciate in Rossini. Max Maria von Weber told the story that his father left *La cenerentola* halfway through a performance saying: 'I'm going. Now I'm beginning to like the stuff myself.' George Bernard Shaw, who pronounced Rossini to be 'the greatest master of claptrap who ever lived', also admitted that he was so taken by a concert of Rossini music at the Crystal Palace that: 'After a careful look round to see that none of my brother-critics were watching I wore away about an eighth of an inch from the ferrule of my umbrella in abetting an encore.'

Shaw's somewhat grudging admission nevertheless puts a finger on what is unique in Rossini's music: his spontaneity, his *joie de vivre*, and his seemingly inexhaustible rhythmic impulse, which makes the world a brighter – if not necessarily a better – place. Without writing the emotionally charged tunes of a Verdi, he nevertheless underpinned his deft, shapely melodies with catchy rhythmic patterns that make them both arresting in the opera house and memorable well beyond their immediate context. There is, at best, a kind of innocence in his music – an innocence touched by wit and elegance – that is rare in our over-sophisticated soul-searching cultural environment. This is one reason for Rossini's unique appeal, but also helps to explain why some people will always remain unresponsive to his art.

Rossini never lost sight of the human, and humane, dimension to our existence, which is what made him a reluctant hero. One tends to associate such values with the very essence of Italian culture and society, developed over the centuries, values which manage to survive, despite the obsessive material and cultural acquisitiveness of our age. What indeed does it profit a man if he gain the whole world, but loses his soul in the process? Rossini surely came to feel the same about his own age, and there are certain parallels to be drawn between our society and the one in which he lived in his later years. Just as his operas came to seem tame to audiences thrilled by Meyerbeer's grandiose concoctions, so we today find that Rossini has to be approached with uncommon care and sensitivity if we are not to respond similarly. Those delicious touches of orchestration, those sly unexpected modulations can so easily pass us by if we do not remain constantly alert and involved – an exigent requirement in an age when so much of our energy is directed towards obviating such a need.

Fortunately the operas are being given regularly nowadays by major companies and enterprising festivals, and some of the greatest opera singers of the century have chosen to perform the often taxing vocal parts. Rossini's birthplace holds annual festivals, during which two operas are usually given, and a critical edition of the operas is gradually being published. What, one wonders, would Rossini say to that?

Catalogue of Rossini's Works

OPERAS

Demetrio e Polibio, dramma serio in 2 acts. Libretto by V. Viganò-Mombelli after Metastasio's *Demetrio*. Composed prior to 1808. Teatro Valle, Rome, 18 May 1812.

La cambiale di matrimonio, farsa comica in 1 act. Libretto by G. Rossi after C. Federici's play (1790). Teatro San Moisè, Venice, 3 November 1810.

L'equivoco stravagante, dramma giocoso in 2 acts. Libretto by G. Gasparri. Teatro del Corso, Bologna, 26 October 1811.

L'inganno felice, farsa in 1 act. Libretto by G. Foppa after G. Palomba's libretto for Paisiello's opera of the same name (Naples, 1798). Teatro San Moisè, Venice, 8 January 1812.

Ciro in Babilonia ossia La caduta di Baldassare, dramma con cori in 2 acts. Libretto by F. Aventi. Teatro Comunale (Municipale), Ferrara, ?14 March 1812.

La scala di seta, farsa comica in 1 act. Libretto by G. Foppa after Planard's libretto for Gaveaux's *L'Échelle de soie* (Paris, 1808). Teatro San Moisè, Venice, 9 May 1812.

La pietra del paragone, melodramma giocoso in 2 acts. Libretto by L. Romanelli. Teatro alla Scala, Milan, 26 September 1812.

L'occasione fa il ladro (*Il cambio della valigia*), *burletta* in 1 act. Libretto by L. Prividali. Teatro San Moisè, Venice, 24 November 1812.

Il signor Bruschino ossia Il figlio per azzardo, farsa giocosa in 1 act. Libretto by G. Foppa after A. de Chazet and E.-T. Maurice Ourry's *Le Fils par hazard* (1809). Teatro San Moisè, Venice, late January 1813.

Tancredi, melodramma eroico in 2 acts. Libretto by G. Rossi after Voltaire's *Tancrède* (1760). Teatro La Fenice, Venice, 6 February 1813.

L'italiana in Algeri, dramma giocoso in 2 acts. Libretto by A. Anelli (revised) for Mosca's opera of the same name (Milan, 1808). Teatro San Benedetto, Venice, 22 May 1813.

Aureliano in Palmira, dramma serio in 2 acts. Libretto by G.-F. Romanelli. Teatro alla Scala, Milan, 26 December 1813.

Il turco in Italia, dramma buffo in 2 acts. Libretto by F. Romani from C.

Mazzolà's libretto of the same name. Teatro alla Scala, Milan, 14 August 1814.

Sigismondo, dramma in 2 acts. Libretto by G. Foppa. Teatro La Fenice, Venice, 26 December 1814.

Elisabetta, regina d'Inghilterra, dramma in 2 acts. Libretto by G. Schmidt from C. Federici's play of 1814, which was based on S. Lee's *The Recess* (1783–5). Teatro San Carlo, Naples, 4 October 1815.

Torvaldo e Dorliska, dramma semiserio in 2 acts. Libretto by C. Sterbini. Teatro Valle, Rome, 26 December 1815.

Il barbiere di Siviglia, commedia in 2 acts (original title *Almaviva, ossia L'inutile precauzione*). Libretto by C. Sterbini from Beaumarchais' *Le Barbier de Séville* (1775) and also from G. Petrosellini's libretto for Paisiello's *Il barbiere di Siviglia* (St Petersburg, 1782). Teatro Argentina, Rome, 20 February 1816.

La gazzetta, dramma/opera buffa in 2 acts. Libretto by G. Palomba from Goldoni's *Il matrimonio per concorso* (1763). Teatro dei Fiorentini, Naples, 26 September 1816.

Otello ossia Il moro di Venezia, dramma in 3 acts. Libretto by F. Berio di Salsa after Shakespeare's *Othello* (1602–4). Teatro del Fondo, Naples, 4 December 1816.

La cenerentola ossia La bontà in trionfo, dramma giocoso in 2 acts. Libretto by J. Ferretti from Perrault's *Cendrillon* (1697) and other libretti – C. G. Étienne for Isouard's *Cendrillon* (Paris, 1810) and F. Romani for Pavesi's *Agatina, o La virtù premiata* (Milan, 1814). Teatro Valle, Rome, 25 January 1817.

La gazza ladra, melodramma in 2 acts. Libretto by G. Gherardini after D'Aubigny and Caigniez' *La Pie voleuse* (1815). Teatro alla Scala, Milan, 31 May 1817.

Armida, dramma in 3 acts. Libretto by G. Schmidt from Tasso's *Gerusalemme liberata*. Teatro San Carlo, Naples, 11 November 1817.

Adelaide di Borgogna, dramma in 2 acts. Libretto by G. Schmidt. Teatro Argentina, Rome, 27 December 1817.

Mosè in Egitto, azione tragico-sacra in 3 acts. Libretto by A. L. Tottola, after F. Ringhieri's *L'Osiride* (1760). Teatro San Carlo, Naples, 5 March 1818.

Adina, farsa in 1 act. Libretto by G. Bevilacqua-Aldobrandini. Composed 1818. Teatro São Carlos, Lisbon, 22 June 1826.

Ricciardo e Zoraide, dramma in 2 acts. Libretto by F. Berio di Salsa. Teatro San Carlo, Naples, 3 December 1818.

Ermione, azione tragica in 2 acts. Libretto by A. L. Tottola from Racine's *Andromaque*. Teatro San Carlo, Naples, 27 March 1819.

Edoardo e Cristina, dramma in 2 acts. Libretto by G. Schmidt, revised by G. Bevilacqua-Aldobrandini and A. L. Tottola from the libretto for

Pavesi's *Odoardo e Cristina* (1810). Teatro San Benedetto, Venice, 24 April 1819.

La donna del lago, melodramma in 2 acts. Libretto by A. L. Tottola after Scott's *The Lady of the Lake* (1810). Teatro San Carlo, Naples, 24 September 1819.

Bianca e Faliero ossia Il consiglio dei tre, melodramma in 2 acts. Libretto by F. Romani after A. V. Arnault's *Blanche et Montcassin* (1798). Teatro alla Scala, Milan, 26 December 1819.

Maometto II, dramma in 2 acts. Libretto by C. della Valle after his *Anna Erizo* (1820). Teatro San Carlo, Naples, 3 December 1820.

Matilde (di) Shabran ossia Bellezza e cuor di ferro, melodramma giocoso in 2 acts. Libretto by G. Ferretti after F.-B. Hoffmann's libretto for Méhul's *Euphrosine* (Paris, 1790) and J. M. Boutet de Monvel's *Mathilde* (1799). Teatro Apollo, Rome, 24 February 1821.

Zelmira, dramma in 2 acts. Libretto by A. L. Tottola after Dormont de Belloy's *Zelmire* (1762). Teatro San Carlo, Naples, 16 February 1822.

Semiramide, melodramma tragico in 2 acts. Libretto by G. Rossi after Voltaire's *Sémiramis* (1748). Teatro La Fenice, Venice, 3 February 1823.

Il viaggio a Reims ossia L'albergo del giglio d'oro, dramma giocoso in 1 act. Libretto by L. Balocchi based partly on De Staël's *Corinne, ou L'Italie* (1807). Théâtre-Italien, Paris, 19 June 1825.

Le Siège de Corinthe (revision of *Maometto II*), *tragédie lyrique* in 3 acts. Libretto by L. Balocchi and A. Soumet from libretto of *Maometto II*. Opéra, Paris, 9 October 1826.

Moïse et Pharaon ou Le Passage de la Mer Rouge (revision of *Mosè in Egitto*), *opéra* in 4 acts. Libretto by L. Balocchi and E. de Jouy from libretto of *Mosè in Egitto*. Opéra, Paris, 26 March 1827.

Le Comte Ory, opéra/opéra comique in 2 acts. Libretto by E. Scribe and C. G. Delestre-Poirson from their own play (1817). Opéra, Paris, 20 August 1828.

Guillaume Tell, opéra in 4 acts. Libretto by E. de Jouy, H.-L.-F. Bis and others after Schiller's *William Tell* (1804). Opéra, Paris, 3 August 1829.

Adaptations with Rossini's participation:

Ivanhoé, opéra in 3 acts. Libretto by E. Deschamps and G.-G. de Wailly from Scott's *Ivanhoe* (1819), the music adapted by A. Pacini from various Rossini operas. Théâtre de l'Odéon, Paris, 15 September 1826.

Robert Bruce, opéra in 3 acts. Libretto by A. Reyer and G. Vaëz, the music adapted by A.-L. Niedermayer from *La donna del lago* and various other Rossini operas. Opéra, Paris, 30 December 1846.

Adaptations without Rossini's participation, of which the more notable are:

La Fausse Agnès, opéra bouffon in 3 acts. Libretto by Castil-Blaze. Théâtre de l'Odéon, Paris, 13 June 1826.

Le Neveu de monseigneur, opéra bouffe in 2 acts. Libretto by J.-F.-A. Bayard, Romieu and T.-M. F. Sauvage. Théâtre de l'Odéon, Paris, 7 August 1826.

Le Testament, opéra in 2 acts. Libretto by J.-H. de Saur and L. de Saint-Géniès. Théâtre de l'Odéon, Paris, 22 January 1827.

Monsieur de Pourceaugnac, opéra bouffon in 3 acts. Libretto by Castil-Blaze (?). Théâtre de l'Odéon, Paris, 24 February 1827.

Cinderella, or The Fairy and the Little Glass Slipper, comic opera in 2 acts. Libretto adapted by M. R. Lacy from the libretto of *La cenerentola*. Covent Garden, London, 13 April 1830.

Andremo a Parigi?, opera comica in 2 acts. Libretto by L. Balocchi and H. Dupin adapted from *Il viaggio a Reims* (as was the music). Théâtre-Italien, Paris, 26 October 1848.

Un curioso accidente, opera buffa in 2 acts. Libretto by G. Berettoni. Théâtre-Italien, Paris, 27 November 1859.

SACRED COMPOSITIONS

Rossini wrote several early sacred compositions, mostly settings of liturgical texts, and the majority for male voice soloists and orchestra, with or without male voice chorus. Most remain in manuscript, some have been lost, and some remain still to be located. The earliest work to be dated accurately at present is the *Messa* for Bologna (1808), a composite work by students at the Liceo Musicale, for which Rossini provided three sections: 'Christe eleison', TTB, orch.; *Gradual* 'Benedicta et venerabilis', TTB, orch., and 'Qui tollis'; 'Qui sedes', S, horn and orch.

Messa (Ravenna), solo male voices, male voice chorus and orch., 1808. Kyrie, Gloria and Credo only.

Messa (Rimini) SATB and orch., 1809.

Quoniam, B and orch., 1813.

Messa di gloria, SATTB, chorus and orch., Naples, 24 March 1820.

Preghiera 'Deh tu pietoso cielo', S and piano, *c.*1820.

Tantum ergo, STB and orch., 1824.

Stabat Mater, SSTB, chorus and orch. First version (six numbers by Rossini and six by Tadolini), 1832, first performed Good Friday, 1833, Madrid. Second version (10 numbers, all by Rossini), 1841, first performed Théâtre-Italien, Paris, 7 January 1842.

Trois chœurs religieux, female voices and piano. (1) 'La Foi' (P. Goubaux); (2) 'L'Espérance' (H. Lucas); (3) 'La Charité' (L. Colet). First performed Salle Troupenas, Paris, 20 November 1844.

Tantum ergo, TTB and orch., Bologna, 28 November 1847.

O salutaris hostia, SATB, Paris, 29 November 1857.

Laus Deo, mezzo and piano, Paris, 1861.

Petite Messe solennelle, SATB, eight-part chorus; first version with two pianos and harmonium, performed Paris, 14 March 1864. Second version with orchestral accompaniment first performed Théâtre-Italien, Paris, 24 February 1869.

CANTATAS, INCIDENTAL MUSIC, HYMNS AND CHORUSES

Il pianto d'Armonia sulla morte di Orfeo (G. Ruggia), cantata, T, chorus and orch., Liceo Musicale, Bologna, 11 August 1808.

La morte di Didone, cantata, S, chorus and orch., 1811. First performed Teatro San Benedetto, Venice, 2 May 1818.

Dalle quete e pallid'ombre (P. Venanzio), cantata, SB and piano, Venice, 1812.

Egle ed Irene, cantata, SA and piano, Milan, 1814.

Inno dell'Indipendenza ('Sorgi, Italia, venuta è già l'ora') (G. Giusti), hymn, Teatro Contavalli, Bologna, 15 April 1815.

L'Aurora, cantata, ATB and piano, Rome, November 1815.

Le nozze di Teti e di Peleo (A. M. Ricci), cantata, SSSTT, chorus and orch., Teatro del Fondo, Naples, 24 April 1816.

Edipo a Colonno, incidental music to Sophocles' *Oedipus at Colonus*, trans. G. Giusti, B, chorus and orch., pre-1817.

Omaggio umiliato (A. Niccolini), cantata, S, chorus and orch., Teatro San Carlo, Naples, 20 February 1819.

Cantata (G. Genoino) for visit of Francis I, STT, chorus and orch., Teatro San Carlo, Naples, 9 May 1819.

La riconoscenza (G. Genoino), cantata, SATB, chorus and orch., Teatro San Carlo, Naples, 27 December 1821.

La Santa Alleanza (G. Rossi), cantata, BB, chorus and orch., Verona Arena, 24 November 1822.

Il vero omaggio (G. Rossi), cantata, Sopranista, STTB, chorus and orch., Teatro Filarmonico, Verona, 3 December 1822.

Omaggio pastorale, cantata, 3 female voices and orch., Treviso, (?)1 April 1823.

Il pianto delle muse in morte di Lord Byron, canzone, T, chorus and orch., London, 9 June 1824.

De l'Italie et de la France, hymn, SB, chorus and orch., Paris, 1825.

Cantata per il battesimo del figlio del banchiere Aguado, 6 solo voices and piano, Paris, 16 July 1827.

L'armonica cetra del nume, solo voices, chorus and piano, Bologna, 2 April 1830.

Giovanna d'Arco, cantata, S and piano, Paris, 1832, revised 1852.

Santo Genio dell'Italia terra (G. Marchetti), chorus and orch., Turin, 11 March 1844.

Su fratelli, letizia si canti (Canonico Golfieri), chorus and orch., Bologna, 23 July 1846.

Cantata in onore del Sommo Pontefice Pio Nono (G. Marchetti), 4 solo voices, chorus and orch., Rome, 1 January 1847.

Segna Iddio ne'suoi confini (F. Martinelli), chorus with band accompaniment arranged by D. Liverani, Bologna, 21 June 1848.

E foriera la Pace ai mortali (G. Arcangeli after Bacchilde), hymn, Bar., male voices and piano, Florence, 26 June 1850.

Hymne à Napoléon III et à son vaillant peuple: 'Dieu tout puissant' (E. Pacini), hymn, Bar., chorus, orch., and military band, Paris, 1 July 1867.

MISCELLANEOUS VOCAL MUSIC (see also *Péchés de vieillesse*)

Se il vuol la molinara, S and piano, ?1801.

Dolce aurette che spirate, T and orch., 1810.

La mia pace io già perdei, T and orch., 1812.

Qual voce, quai note, S and piano, 1813.

Alla voce della gloria, B and orch., 1813.

Amore me assisti, ST and piano, *c.*1814.

Three numbers for G. Nicolini's *Quinto Fabio* (1817):

Coro e cavatina 'Cara Patria, invitta Roma', S, chorus and orch.

Aria 'Guida Marte i nostri passi', T, chorus and orch.

Duet 'Ah! per pietà t'arresta', SS and orch. (possibly not by Rossini).

Il trovatore ('Chi m'ascolta il canto usato'), T and piano, Naples, 1818.

Il Carneval di Venezia ('Siamo ciechi, siamo nati') (Rossini, Paganini, M. d'Azeglio and Lipparini), TTBB and piano, Rome, 1821.

Beltà crudele ('Amori scendete') (N. di Santo-Magno), S and piano, Naples, 1821.

La pastorella ('Odia la pastorella') (N. di Santo-Magno), S and piano, Naples, *c.*1821.

Canzonetta spagnuola 'En medio a mis dolores' ('Piangea un di pensando'), S and piano, Naples, 1821.

Infelice ch'io son, S and piano, Naples, 1821.

Addio ai Viennesi ('Da voi parto, amate sponde'), T and piano, Vienna, 1822.

Dall'Oriente l'astro del giorno, STTB and piano, London, 1824.

Ridiamo, cantiamo, che tutto sen va, STTB and piano, London, 1824.

In giorno si bello, SST and piano, London, 1824.

Tre quartetti da camera, Paris, 1827:

(1) Unidentified.

(2) 'In giorno si bello', SSTB and piano.

(3) 'Oh giorno sereno', SATB and piano.

Les Adieux à Rome ('Rome pour la dernière fois') (C. Delavigne), T and piano/harp, Paris, 1827.

Orage et beau temps ('Sur les flots inconstants') (A. Betourne), TB and piano, Paris, *c.*1830.

La passeggiata ('Or che di fiori adorna'), S and piano, Madrid, 1831.

La dichiarazione ('Ch'io mai vi possa lasciar d'amare') (Metastasio), S and piano, Paris, *c.*1834.

Les Soirées musicales, Paris, *c.*1830–5.

(1) *La promessa* ('Chi'io mai vi possa lasciar d'amare') (Metastasio), S and piano.
(2) *Il rimprovero* ('Mi lagnerò tacendo') (Metastasio), S and piano.
(3) *La partenza* ('Ecco quel fiero istante') (Metastasio), S and piano.
(4) *L'orgia* ('Amiamo, cantiamo') (C. Pepoli), S and piano.
(5) *L'invito* ('Vieni o Ruggiero') (C. Pepoli), S and piano.
(6) *La pastorella dell'Alpi* ('Son bella pastorella') (C. Pepoli), S and piano.
(7) *La gita in gondola* ('Voli l'agile barchetta') (C. Pepoli), S and piano.
(8) *La danza* ('Già la luna è in mezzo al mare') (C. Pepoli), T and piano.
(9) *La regata veneziana* ('Voga o Tonio benedetto') (C. Pepoli), SS and piano.
(10) *La pesca* ('Già la notte s'avvicina') (Metastasio), SS and piano.
(11) *La serenata* ('Mira, la bianca luna') (C. Pepoli), ST and piano.
(12) *Li marinari* ('Marinaro in guardia stà') (C. Pepoli), TB and piano.

Deux Nocturnes (Crével de Charlemagne), ST and piano, Paris, *c.*1836.

(1) *Adieu à l'Italie* ('Je te quitte, belle Italie').
(2) *Le Départ* ('Il faut partir').

Nizza ('Nizza, je puis sans peine', 'Mi lagnerò tacendo') (E. Deschamps, Metastasio), S and piano, Paris, *c.*1836.

L'Ame délaissée ('Mon bien aimé') (C. Delavigne), S and piano, Paris, *c.* 1844.

Recitativo ritmato also *Francesca da Rimini* ('Farò come colui che piange e dice') (Dante), S and piano, Florence, 1848.

La separazione ('Muto rimase il labbro') (F. Ucelli), S and piano, *c.*1858. Originally composed to the text 'Mi lagnerò tacendo' (Metastasio), a text which Rossini set many times, especially as album leaves.

Deux Nouvelles Compositions (E. Pacini), S and piano, Paris, *c.*1860.

(1) *A Grenade* ('La nuit règne à Grenade').
(2) *La Veuve andalouse* ('Toi pour jamais').

INSTRUMENTAL WORKS (see also *Péchés de vieillesse*)

Six *Sonate a quattro* in G, A, C, B flat, E flat, D for 2 violins, cello and double bass, Ravenna, *c.*1804.

Overture *al conventello* in D for orchestra, *c.*1806.

Five duets in E flat, E flat, B flat, E flat, E flat for 2 horns, *c.*1806.

Sinfonia/Overture in D for orchestra, 1808.

Sinfonia/Overture in E flat for orchestra, 1809.

Overture *obbligata a contrabasso* in D for orchestra, *c.*1807–10.

Variazioni a più istrumenti obbligati in F for 2 violins, viola, cello, clarinet in B flat and orchestra, 1809.

Variazioni di clarinetto in C for clarinet and orchestra, 1809.

Andante e tema con variazioni in F for flute, clarinet, horn and bassoon, 1812.

Andante e tema con variazioni in F for harp and violin, Naples, *c.*1820.

Passo doppio for military band, 1822. Lost.

Waltz in E flat for piano, Venice, ?1823.

Serenata in E flat for 2 violins, viola, cello, flute, oboe and cor anglais, Paris, 1823.

Duetto in D for cello and double bass, London, 1824.

Rendez-vous de chasse in D for 4 hunting horns and orchestra, Paris, 1828.

Fantasie in E flat for clarinet and piano, Paris, 1829.

Three military marches in G, E flat, E flat, for the marriage of the duc d'Orléans, Fontainebleau, 1837.

Scherzo in A minor for piano, 1843, revised in 1850.

Tema originale di Rossini variato per violino da Giovacchino Giovacchini in A for violin and piano, 1845.

March ('Pas-redoublé') in C for military band, 1852.

Thème de Rossini suivi de deux variations et coda par Moscheles Père in E for horn and piano, Paris, 1860.

La corona d'Italia in E flat for military band, Paris, 1868.

PÉCHÉS DE VIEILLESSE (1857–68)

Volume 1. *Album italiano*

(1) *I gondolieri*, SATB and piano.
(2) *La lontananza* (G. Torre), T and piano.
(3) *Bolero* ('Tirana alla spagnola'), S and piano.
(4) *Elegia* ('L'ultimo ricordo') (G. Redaelli), Bar. and piano.
(5) *Arietta* ('La fioraia fiorentina'), S and piano.
(6) *Duetto* ('Le gittane') (G. Torre), SA and piano.
(7) *Ave Maria* ('A te, che benedetta'), on two notes, A and piano.
(8)–(10) *La regata veneziana*, 3 canzonettas for Mezzo and piano:
Anzoleta avanti la regata ('La su la machina'). In French version *Barcarolle* ('Plus de vent perfide').
Anzoleta co passa la regata ('Ixe qua vardeli povereti').
Anzoleta dopo la regata ('Ciapa un baso').

(11) *Il fanciullo smarrito* ('Oh! chi avesse trovato un fanciulletto') (A. Castellani), T and piano.
(12) *La passeggiata*, SATB and piano.

Volume 2. *Album français*

(1) *Toast pour le nouvel an* ('En ce jour si doux') (E. Pacini?), SSAATTBB.
(2) *Roméo* ('Juliette chère idole') (E. Pacini), T and piano.
(3) *Pompadour la grande coquette* ('La perle des coquettes') (E. Pacini), S and piano.
(4) *Un Sou* ('Pitié pour la misère') (E. Pacini?), TBar. and piano.
(5) *Chanson de Zora; La petite bohémienne* ('Gens de la plaine') (E. Deschamps), Mezzo and piano.
(6) *La Nuit de Noël* ('Calme et sans voile') (E. Pacini), B solo, SSAATTBar.Bar., piano and harmonium.
(7) *Le Dodo des enfants* ('Mon fils, rose ephémère') (E. Pacini), Mezzo and piano.
(8) *Le lazzarone* ('Au bord des flots d'Azur') (E. Pacini), Bar. and piano.
(9) *Adieux à la vie* ('Salut! dernière aurore') (E. Pacini), elegy on one note for Mezzo and piano.
(10) *Soupirs et sourires* ('Dans le sentier des roses'), nocturne for ST and piano. Also with Italian text as 'Il cipresso e la rosa' (G. Torre).
(11) *L'Orphéline du Tyrol* ('Seule, une pauvre enfant') (E. Pacini), Mezzo and piano.
(12) *Chœur de chasseurs démocrates* ('En chasse amis, en chasse') (E. Pacini), male voice chorus, tam-tam and 2 drums.

Volume 3. *Morceaux réservés*

(1) *Quelques mesures de chant funèbre: à mon pauvre ami Meyerbeer* ('Pleure, pleure, muse sublime') (E. Pacini), male voice chorus and drum.
(2) *L'Esule* ('Qui sempre ride in cielo') (G. Torre), T and piano.
(3) *Les Amants de Séville* ('Loin de votre Séville') (E. Pacini), AT and piano.
(4) *Ave Maria* ('Ave Maria, gratia plena'), chorus and organ.
(5) *L'Amour à Pékin* ('Mon cœur blessé') (E. Pacini), 'on the Chinese scale', A and piano.
(6) *Le Chant des Titans* ('Guerre! Massacre! Carnage!') (E. Pacini), 4 basses and orchestra (original version 4 basses in unison, piano and harmonium).
(7) *Preghiera* ('Tu che di verde il prato'), 4T2Bar.2B. Also with French text as 'Dieu créateur du monde'.
(8) *Au chevet d'un mourant* ('De la douleur naît l'espérance') (E. Pacini), elegy for S and piano.
(9) *Le Sylvain* ('Belles nymphes blondes') (E. Pacini), romance for T and piano.

(10) *Cantemus Domino, imitazione ad otto voci reali*, SSAATTBB.
(11) *Ariette à l'ancienne* ('Que le jour me dure') (J.-J. Rousseau), Mezzo and piano.
(12) *Le Départ des promis* ('L'honneur appelle') (E. Pacini), SSAA and piano.

Volume 4. *Quatre Mendiants et quatre hors d'œuvres*

Rossini described volumes 4 to 8 as 'A little of everything: a collection of fifty-six semi-comical pieces for the piano'.

Quatre mendiants

(1) *Les Figues sèches* in D.
(2) *Les Amandes* in G.
(3) *Les Raisins* in C.
(4) *Les Noisettes* in B minor, B major.

Quatre hors d'œuvres

(1) *Les Radis* in A minor.
(2) *Les Anchois* in D.
(3) *Les Cornichons* in E.
(4) *Le Beurre* in B flat.

Volume 5. *Album pour les enfants adolescents*

(1) *Première communion* in E flat.
(2) *Thème naïf et variations idem* in G.
(3) *Saltarello à l'italienne* in A flat.
(4) *Prélude moresque* in E minor.
(5) *Valse lugubre* in C.
(6) *Impromptu anodin* in E flat.
(7) *L'Innocence italienne*; *La Candeur française* in A minor, A major.
(8) *Prélude convulsif* in C.
(9) *La Lagune de Venise à l'expiration de l'année* 1861!!! in G flat.
(10) *Ouf! les petits pois* in B.
(11) *Un Sauté* in D.
(12) *Hachis romantique* in A minor.

Volume 6. *Album pour les enfants dégourdis*

(1) *Mon Prélude hygiénique du matin* in C.
(2) *Prélude baroque* in A minor.
(3) *Memento homo* in C minor.
(4) *Assez de memento: dansons* in F.
(5) *La Pesarese* in B flat.
(6) *Valse torturée* in D.
(7) *Une Caresse à ma femme* in G.
(8) *Barcarole* in E flat.
(9) *Un Petit Train de plaisir comico-imitatif* in C.
(10) *Fausse Couche de polka-mazurka* in A flat.

(11) *Étude asthmatique* in E.
(12) *Un Enterrement en Carnaval* in D.

Volume 7. *Album de chaumière*

(1) *Gymnastique d'écartement* in A flat.
(2) *Prélude fugassé* in E.
(3) *Petite Polka chinoise* in B minor.
(4) *Petite Valse de boudoir* in A flat.
(5) *Prélude Inoffensif* in C.
(6) *Petite Valse* ('L'huile de Ricin') in E.
(7) *Un Profond Sommeil*; *Un Réveil en sursaut* in B minor and D major.
(8) *Plein-Chant Chinois*, scherzo in A minor.
(9) *Un Cauchemar* in E.
(10) *Valse boiteuse* in D flat.
(11) *Une Pensée à Florence* in A minor.
(12) *Marche* in C.

Volume 8. *Album de château*

(1) *Spécimen de l'ancien régime* in E flat.
(2) *Prélude pétulant-rococo* in G.
(3) *Un Regret*; *Un Espoir* in E.
(4) *Boléro tartare* in A minor.
(5) *Prélude prétentieux* in C minor and C major.
(6) *Spécimen de mon temps* in A flat.
(7) *Valse anti-dansante* in F.
(8) *Prélude semipastorale* in A.
(9) *Tarantelle pur sang* (*avec traversée de la procession*) in B minor (also for chorus, harmonium and handbell *ad libitum*).
(10) *Un Rêve* in B minor.
(11) *Prélude soi-disant dramatique* in F sharp.
(12) *Spécimen de l'avenir* in E flat.

Volume 9. *Album pour piano, violin, harmonium et cor*

(1) *Mélodie candide* in A for piano.
(2) *Chansonette* in E flat for piano.
(3) *La Savoie aimante* in A minor for piano.
(4) *Un Mot à Paganini*, elegy in D for violin and piano.
(5) *Impromptu Tarantellisé* in F for piano.
(6) *Échantillon du chant de Noël à l'italienne* in E flat for piano.
(7) *Marche et réminiscences pour mon dernier voyage* in A flat for piano.
(8) *Prélude, thème et variations* in E for horn and piano.
(9) *Prélude italien* in A flat for piano.
(10) *Une Larme: thème et variations* in A minor for cello and piano.
(11) *Échantillon de blague mélodique sur les noires de la main droite* in G flat for piano.
(12) *Petite Fanfare à quatre mains* in E flat for piano (2 or 4 hands).

Volume 10. *Miscellanée pour piano*

(1) *Prélude blageur* in A minor.

(2) *Des tritons s'il vous plaît* (*montée-descente*) in C.

(3) *Petite Pensée* in E flat.

(4) *Une Bagatelle* in E flat.

(5) *Mélodie italienne: une bagatelle* ('In nomine Patris') in A flat.

(6) *Petite Caprice* (*style Offenbach*) in C.

Volume 11. *Miscellanée de musique vocale*

(1) *Ariette villageoise* ('Que le jour me dure') (J.-J. Rousseau), S and piano.

(2) *La Chanson du bébé* ('Maman, le gros bébé t'appelle') (E. Pacini), Mezzo and piano.

(3) *Amour sans espoir, Tirana à l'espagnole rossinizé* ('Fault-il gémir d'amour sans retour') (E. Pacini), S and piano.

(4) *A ma belle mère, Requiem aeternam*, A and piano.

(5) *O salutaris, de campagne*, A and piano.

(6) *Aragonese* ('Mi lagnerò tacendo') (Metastasio), S and piano.

(7) *Arietta all'antica dedotta dal O salutaris ostia* ('Mi lagnerò tacendo') (Metastasio), S and piano, based on *O salutaris hostia*, 29 November 1857.

(8) *Il candore in fuga*, SSATB.

(9) *Salve amabilis Maria*, motet SATB (also as *Hymne à la musique* ('Chantons! Toi par qui règne le Génie')).

(10) *Giovanna d'Arco*, cantata, S, piano and strings.

Volume 12. *Quelques Riens pour album*

Twenty-four pieces for piano.

Volume 13. *Musique anodine*

Prélude for piano and 6 *petites mélodies*, all settings of 'Mi lagnerò tacendo' (Metastasio):

(1) A and piano.

(2) Bar. and piano.

(3–4) S and piano.

(5) Mezzo and piano.

(6) Bar. and piano.

OTHER LATE WORKS

Canone scherzosa a quattro soprani democratici, or *Canone perpetuo per quattro soprani*, for 4 sopranos and piano.

Canone antisavant (G. Rossini), for 3 voices.

La Vénitienne, canzonetta in C for piano.

Petite Promenade de Passy à Courbevoie in C for piano.

Une Réjouissance in A minor for piano.

Encore un peu de blague in C for piano.
Tourniquet sur la gamme chromatique, ascendante et descendante in C for piano.
Ritournelle gothique in C for piano.
Un Rien (pour album) ('Ave Maria'), S and piano.
Sogna il guerrier (pour album) (Metastasio), Bar. and piano.
Brindisi ('Del fanciullo il primo canto'), B and chorus.
Solo for cello (with added piano accompaniment) in A minor.
Questo palpito soave, S and piano.
L'ultimo pensiero ('Patria, consorti, figli') (L. F. Cerutti), Bar. and piano.
Thème in E flat for piano.

VOCAL EXERCISES AND CADENZAS

Gorgheggi e solfeggi for solo voice and piano, Paris, *c.*1827.
15 petits exercises pour égaliser les sons . . . , for solo voice, Paris 1858.
Petit gargouillement, for solo voice, Paris, 1867.

Vocal variants and cadenzas for Rossini's operas exist in various locations, most notably Brussels (Fonds Michotte), Chicago (University Library), Paris (Opéra), Milan (Conservatorio) and New York (Pierpont Morgan Library).

Notes

Introduction

1 E. Michotte, *Souvenirs personnels: la visite de R. Wagner à Rossini, Paris 1860* (Paris, 1906).
2 Letter of Rossini to Verdi, 27 December 1865.
3 F. Toye, *Rossini: A Study in Tragi-Comedy* (London, 1934), p. xi.

Chapter 1. The Genius Takes Wing

1 Stendhal, *Vie de Rossini* (Paris, 1824), ch. 1.
2 F. Hiller, *Plaudereien mit Rossini*, Vol. 2 of *Aus dem Tonleben unserer Zeit*, 2 vols (Leipzig, 1868).
3 E. Michotte, 'Rossini e sua madre: ricordi della sua infanza', *La cronaca musicale* (Pesaro, 1913), p. 5.
4 A.-J. Azevedo, *G. Rossini: sa vie et ses œuvres* (Paris, 1864), p. 21.
5 Facsimile in A. Casella, *Rossiniana* (Bologna, 1942), pp. 37–9.
6 C. Burney, *Music, Men and Manners in France and Italy, 1770* (London, 1974), p. 89.
7 Stendhal, *Rossini*, ch. 12.
8 Hiller, *Plaudereien*.
9 Even as late as 1845 and 1846, Verdi wrote arias specially for Rossini's protégé, the tenor Ivanoff.
10 Leopold Mozart to his wife, 14 April 1770, in *The Letters of Mozart and His Family*, trans. and ed. E. Anderson, 3rd edn (London, 1985), p. 127.
11 P. Gossett, 'The overtures of Rossini', *Nineteenth-Century Music*, Vol. 3 (1979–80), p. 16.

Chapter 2. Failures and Successes

1 Report on Rossini's health by Bologna physician, sent by Olympe (Rossini's second wife) to Hector Couvert in Paris in 1842. The text is given

in H. Weinstock, *Rossini: A Biography* (New York, 1968), pp. 379–81.
2 F. Hiller, *Plaudereien mit Rossini*, Vol. 2 of *Aus dem Tonleben unserer Zeit*, 2 vols (Leipzig, 1868), p. 41.

Chapter 3. Triumph in Venice

1 *Byron's Letters and Journals*, ed. L. A. Marchand, Vol. 4 (London, 1975), p. 172.
2 Stendhal, *Vie de Rossini* (Paris, 1824), ch. 2.
3 J. Budden, *The Operas of Verdi*, Vol. 1 (London, 1973), p. 8.
4 Byron, *Don Juan*, canto XVI, stanza 45.
5 G. Carpani, *Le Rossiniane ossia Lettere musico-teatrale* (Padua, 1824).
6 L. and M. Escudier, *Rossini: sa vie et ses œuvres* (Paris, 1854), p. 15.
7 A. Zanolini in *L'ape italiana rediviva* (Paris, 1836).
8 G. Radiciotti, *Gioacchino Rossini: vita documentata, opere, ed influenza su l'arte*, 3 vols (Tivoli, 1927–9).
9 The lady in question was probably Anna Ricciarda d'Este, wife of Alberico Barbiano di Belgiojoso, and not the more famous Cristina Belgiojoso-Trivulzio (1808–71), who only became Rossini's patroness later.

Chapter 4. The Lure of the South: Naples and Rome

1 H. Acton, *The Bourbons of Naples* (London, 1956), pp. 641–2.
2 Isabella Colbran had sung in the first of the operas in 1813, and very probably in the second in 1815.
3 Stendhal, *Vie de Rossini* (Paris, 1824), chs 12 and 13.
4 L. Spohr, *Selbstbiographie*, Vol. 2 (Kassel, 1960–1).
5 The libretto was printed in Rome by Crispino Puccinelli, *presso* San Andrea in Valle (n.d., but 1816).
6 Verdi was writing to thank Bellaigue for a copy of the latter's *Les Musiciens*, which he had sent to the composer.
7 G. Righetti-Giorgi, *Cenni di una donna già cantante sopra il maestro Rossini* (Bologna, 1823).
8 A.-J. Azevedo, *G. Rossini: sa vie et ses œuvres* (Paris, 1864).
9 E. Michotte, *Souvenirs: une soirée chez Rossini à Beau-séjour (Passy) 1858* (Brussels, *c.*1910).

Chapter 5. Years of Industry

1 G. Radiciotti, *Gioacchino Rossini: vita documentata, opere, ed influenza su l'arte*, 3 vols (Tivoli, 1927–9), Vol. 1, p. 317 n.

2 L. S. Silvestri, *Della vita e delle opere di Gioachino Rossini* (Milan, 1874), p. 126.
3 H. Acton, *The Bourbons of Naples* (London, 1956), p. 655.
4 *Moscheles' Leben nach Briefen und Tagebücher herausgegeben von seiner Frau* (Leipzig, 1872).
5 A. de Musset, *Poésies complètes* (Paris, 1933), p. 342.
6 *Giacomo Meyerbeer: Briefwechsel und Tagebücher*, ed. H. Becker, Vol. 1 (Berlin, 1960), p. 359.
7 A. Cametti, *Un poeta melodrammatico romano . . .* (Milan, n.d. [1898]).
8 *La cenerentola . . . dramma giocoso. Poesia di Giacomo Ferretti romano . . .* (Rome, 1817).
9 Silvestri, *Rossini*, p. 147.
10 Stendhal, *Vie de Rossini* (Paris, 1824), ch. 37.
11 Letter of Rossini to Conte Gordiano Perticari, 15 January 1864.
12 *Meyerbeer*, p. 360.
13 Stendhal, *Rossini*, ch. 14.
14 *Byron's Letters and Journals*, ed. L. A. Marchand, Vol. 6 (London, 1975), p. 132.
15 *Bollettino del primo centenario Rossiniano*, Pesaro, 17 March 1892, p. 19.
16 G. Leopardi, *Lettere*, ed. F. Flora (Milan, 1949), p. 393.
17 G. Pacini, *Le mie memorie artistiche* (Florence, 1875), p. 17.

Chapter 6. THE GOD OF HARMONY

1 H. Acton, *The Bourbons of Naples* (London, 1956), p. 681.
2 ibid., p. 683.
3 Letter of Paganini to L. Germi, 20 August 1818.
4 M. d'Azeglio, *I miei ricordi*, Vol. 2 (Florence, 1867), p. 146.
5 G. Zavadini, *Donizetti: vita, musiche, epistolario* (Bergamo, 1948), p. 231.
6 *Journal des débats*, 11 March 1822.
7 Stendhal, *Correspondance*, Vol. 2, p. 164.
8 F. Walker, 'Rossiniana in the Piancastelli Collection', *Monthly Musical Record,* Vol. 90 (1960), pp. 141–2.
9 E. Michotte, *Souvenirs personnels: la visite de R. Wagner à Rossini, Paris 1860* (Paris, 1906).
10 *Thayer's Life of Beethoven*, revised edn by E. Forbes, Vol. 2 (Princeton, NJ, 1967), p. 805.
11 ibid., p. 804.
12 ibid.
13 Byron, *The Age of Bronze*, canto XVI.
14 F. Hiller, *Plaudereien mit Rossini*, Vol. 2 of *Aus dem Tonleben unserer Zeit*, 2 vols (Leipzig, 1868), pp. 68–70.

Chapter 7. Triumph and Farewell

1 A. Porter, 'A lost opera by Rossini', *Music and Letters*, Vol. 45 (1964), p. 39; and J. Johnson, 'A lost Rossini opera recovered: *Il viaggio a Reims*', *Bollettino del Centro Rossiniano di Studi* (1983), pp. 55–7 and 110–12, which links de Staël's *Corinne* with Gozzi's *La Fille de l'air ou Sémiramis dans sa jeunesse.*
2 Comtesse Merlin (née Mercedes Jaruco) was born in Havana and studied singing with Manuel Garcia.
3 G. Favre, *Boïeldieu: sa vie – son œuvre* (Paris, 1944–5), Vol. 1, p. 227.
4 *Letters of Harriet, Countess Granville*, ed. F. Leveson Gower, 3rd edn (London, 1894), Vol. 1, p. 240.
5 ibid., p. 243.
6 R. H. Gronow, *The Reminiscences and Recollections of Captain Gronow* (London, 1892), Vol. 2, p. 108; and H. S. Edwards, *The Life of Rossini* (London, 1869), p. 262.
7 *The Quarterly Musical Magazine and Review*, Vol. 6 (1824), p. 50.
8 *Edizione critica delle opere di Gioachino Rossini*; see Johnson, 'A lost Rossini opera'.
9 G. Radiciotti, *Gioacchino Rossini: vita documentata, opere, ed influenza su l'arte*, 3 vols (Tivoli, 1927–9), pp. 64–5, 68.
10 H. Berlioz, *Memoirs*, trans. and ed. D. Cairns, revised edn (London, 1990), pp. 413–14.
11 J. Ebers, *Seven Years of the King's Theatre* (London, 1828), p. 310.
12 L. S. Silvestri, *Della vita e delle opere di Gioachino Rossini* (Milan, 1874), p. 126.
13 F. Walker, 'Rossiniana in the Piancastelli Collection', *Monthly Musical Record*, Vol. 90 (1960), pp. 142–3.
14 H. Berlioz, '*Guillaume Tell* de Rossini', *Gazette musicale de Paris,* Vol. 1 (1834), pp. 326–51.

Chapter 8. The Return to Italy

1 Letter of Rossini to La Rochefoucauld in Bibliothèque Nationale, Paris.
2 Tadolini (1793–1872) had been a fellow-student with Rossini in Bologna. He composed operas, staged between 1815 and 1827, then became conductor and *maître de chant* at the Théâtre-Italien by 1831. He married the soprano Eugenia Savorini.
3 Robert was trying to engage Malibran for the Théâtre-Italien.
4 Letter of Rossini to Mme de la Tour de St-Ygest in Bibliothèque Nationale, Paris, and Piancastelli Collection, Forlì.
5 F. Hiller, *Felix Mendelssohn-Bartholdy: Briefe und Erinnerungen* (Cologne, 1874), trans. M. E. von Glahn (London, 1874), p. 56.

6 F. Walker, 'Rossiniana in the Piancastelli Collection', *Monthly Musical Record*, Vol. 90 (1960), p. 145.
7 A. Walker, *Franz Liszt, the Virtuoso Years, 1801–1847* (London, 1983), p. 250.
8 Piancastelli Collection, Forlì: undated letter from Rossini to Robert, but dated by reference in a letter from Robert to Rossini in A. Soubies, *Le Théâtre-Italien, de 1801 à 1913* (Paris, 1913), p. 100.

Chapter 9. Bologna and the End of an Era

1 F. Walker, 'Rossiniana in the Piancastelli Collection', *Monthly Musical Record*, Vol. 90 (1960), p. 145.
2 ibid.
3 *La Revue et gazette musicale*, no. 61 (Paris, 1841).
4 Maurice Schlésinger (1797–1871) was a son of Martin Adolf Schlésinger, who had founded his business in Berlin in 1810, and became one of Beethoven's publishers.
5 *Selected Letters of Richard Wagner*, trans. and ed. S. Spencer and B. Millington (London, 1987), p. 89.
6 *Lettere di G. Rossini*, ed. G. Mazzatinti and F. and G. Mario (Florence, 1902), p. 127.
7 Walker, 'Rossiniana', p. 146.
8 The complete report is published in translation in H. Weinstock, *Rossini: A Biography* (New York, 1968), pp. 379–81.
9 Walker, 'Rossiniana', p. 147.
10 L. Rognoni, *Rossini* (Parma, 1956), p. 246.

Chapter 10. Paris and the Sins of Old Age

1 F. Hiller, *Plaudereien mit Rossini*, Vol. 2 of *Aus dem Tonleben unserer Zeit*, 2 vols (Leipzig, 1868).
2 Piancastelli Collection, Forlì.
3 Published in *Le Ménéstral*, Paris, 30 July 1920.
4 C. Saint-Saëns, *École buissonière* (Paris, 1913), p. 265.
5 L. Engel, *From Mozart to Mario* (London, 1886), Vol. 2, p. 79.
6 E. Michotte, *Souvenirs: une soirée chez Rossini à Beau-séjour (Passy) 1858* (Brussels, *c.*1910).
7 H. Berlioz, *Memoirs*, trans. and ed. D. Cairns, revised edn (London 1990), p. 488.
8 *Selected Letters of Richard Wagner*, trans. and ed. S. Spencer and B. Millington (London, 1987), p. 89.
9 L. Rognoni, *Rossini* (Parma, 1956), pp. 333 ff.
10 The original article appeared in the Vienna *Neue freie Presse*, and was

then reprinted in Hanslick's *Aus dem Concertsaal* (Vienna/Leipzig, 1870).

11 *Aus Moscheles' Leben* (Leipzig, 1872), adapted from the German by A. D. Coleridge as *Life of Moscheles* (London, 1873), Vol. 2, p. 270.

12 Rognoni, *Rossini*, pp. 247–8.

13 ibid., p. 248.

Chapter 11. The Last Mortal Sin

1 A. A. Ambros, *Bunte Blatter*, 2 vols (Leipzig, 1872–4), Vol. 1, ch. 6 passim; G. Roncaglia, *Rossini, l'olimpico*, 2nd edn (Milan, 1953), p. 512.

2 L. Rognoni, *Rossini* (Parma, 1956), pp. 249–50.

3 ibid., pp. 250–1.

4 ibid., p. 253.

5 Rossini credited Alberti with the composition of the inscription, though it has also been attributed to Conte Carlo Pepoli, then mayor of Bologna.

6 C. Sartori, 'Una lettera inedita di Rossini', *Rivista musicale Italiana*, Vol. 46 (1942), p. 4.

7 Doussault's account was published in *La Revue de Paris*, March 1856.

8 'Letter from Paris', dated 18 July 1867, in *Neue freie Presse*, Vienna.

9 K. M. von Weber, 'Ein Name besser als eine Hausnummer . . .', *Deutsche Rundschau*, Vol. 5 (1875) p. 257.

10 Florimo is of course best-known as the biographer of Bellini.

11 Rognoni, *Rossini*, p. 249.

12 ibid., pp. 254–5.

13 ibid., pp. 256–7.

14 ibid., pp. 260–1.

15 ibid., pp. 257–60.

16 ibid.

17 Quoted in 'Di giorno in giorno', *La Nazione*, Florence, 12 April 1893.

18 *Italienische Tondichter*, Vol. 4 (Berlin, 1883), p. 541.

19 *Neue freie Presse*, Vienna, 18 July 1867.

20 See note 17 above.

21 In *Il Pungolo*, 2 May 1868; also R. de Rensis (ed.), *Critiche e cronache musicali di Arrigo Boito*, p. 52.

22 Rognoni, *Rossini*, pp. 265–6.

23 ibid., pp. 267–8.

24 Dall'Argine's music had previously fulfilled a similar role in Milan earlier in the year, this time in opposition to Boito.

25 Letter of 10 September 1868, quoted in G. Radiciotti, *Gioacchino Rossini:*

vita documentata, opere, ed influenza su l'arte, 3 vols (Tivoli, 1927–9), Vol. 2, p. 488, n. 2.

26 Rognoni, *Rossini*, p. 272.

Epilogue

1 L. S. Silvestri, *Della vita e delle opere di Gioachino Rossini* (Milan, 1874), p. 73.

2 *La gazzetta musicale di Milano*, supplemento straordinario, Milan, 29 February 1892, pp. 22–3.

3 Silvestri, *Rossini*, p. 126.

Select Bibliography

Specific references to works consulted have been given in the notes to the text as and when appropriate, and there are extensive bibliographies in Herbert Weinstock's *Rossini: A Biography* (New York, 1968; reprinted 1987); at the end of Philip Gossett's article on Rossini in *The New Grove Dictionary of Music and Musicians* (London, 1980), Vol. 16, reprinted in *The New Grove Masters of Italian Opera* (London, 1983); and in Richard Osborne's *Rossini* (London, 1986).

The Fondazione Rossini in Pesaro is preparing a new edition of Rossini's correspondence, which numbers thousands of letters, but most recent literature on Rossini is confined to learned journals not readily accessible to the general reader. The choice of biographical works available in the English language is still lamentably small: namely Weinstock, Gossett and Osborne mentioned above, to which may be added:

Lord Derwent, *Rossini and Some Forgotten Nightingales* (London, 1934).

H. S. Edwards, *The Life of Rossini* (London, 1869), revised as *Rossini and His School* (London, 1881).

N. Till, *Rossini, His Life and Times* (London, 1983).

F. Toye, *Rossini: A Study in Tragi-Comedy* (London, 1934; paperback reprint New York, 1963).

To which one may add:

W. Ashbrook, *Donizetti* (London, 1968).

W. Dean, 'Rossini's French operas' and 'Rossini's Italian operas', in *The New Oxford History of Music*, Vol. 8, ed. G. Abraham (Oxford, 1982), pp. 103 ff. and pp. 403 ff.; see also pp. 377 ff.

A. Heriot, *The Castrati in Opera* (London, 1956; reissued in paperback 1960).

J. Rosselli, *The Opera Industry from Cimarosa to Verdi: The Role of the Impresario* (London, 1984).

W. Weaver, *The Golden Century of Italian Opera from Rossini to Puccini* (London, 1980; reissued in paperback 1988).

Index of Persons and Places

Page references in italic refer to illustrations within the text.

Index of Rossini's Compositions

Page references in italic refer to illustrations within the text.